OHIO STATE FOOTBALL
The Great
TRADITION

BY JACK PARK

LEXINGTON PRESS

Production direction and interior design: Gary Hoffman
Editor: Dave Stephenson
Foreword: Archie Griffin
Illustrations: Tom Hayes
Cover design: Gary Hoffman
Front cover photo: Warren Motts
Back cover photo: Mike Greer

Library of Congress Catalog Card Number: 92-90355
ISBN: 1-881462-45-5
SAN: 297-6730

LEXINGTON
PRESS

1601 West Fifth Avenue, Suite 208 • Columbus, Ohio 43212
Printed in the United States of America

To my wonderful wife, Sue, who has brought immense happiness to my life and direction to our family. Without her encouragement and assistance, this book would never have been possible.

Woody Hayes was upset with his squad's practice and refused to allow the Big Ten Skywriters to watch drills when they arrived in Columbus to preview the 1958 Ohio State team. Visibly upset, most of the writers and broadcasters moved on to the next city. The following season, Hayes showed his true hospitality, serving lemonade and cookies to the group.

OHIO STATE FOOTBALL
The Great TRADITION
BY JACK PARK

CONTENTS

FOREWORD

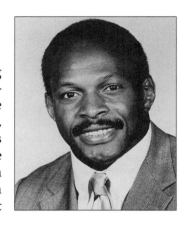

*I*t's been 17 years since I hung up my Ohio State helmet and jersey-number 45 following the 1976 Rose Bowl, and I still find myself reliving, almost daily, four spectacular years playing football at The Ohio State University. Treasured memories both on and off the field made my stay on campus in the 1970s one of the finest times in my life.

When one chooses to attend school and play for one of the most prestigious programs in the history of college football, not to mention for coach Woody Hayes, some of the more distant memories get dusted off and revived with a book on Buckeye football.

OHIO STATE FOOTBALL . . . THE GREAT TRADITION should be the latest addition to your scarlet and gray memorabilia room. It will treat Ohio State fans as well as followers of college football to an unusual look at one of the premier programs in the country.

In addition to reliving many of the great games and championship seasons, OHIO STATE FOOTBALL . . . THE GREAT TRADITION presents little-known facts from the past 102 years and delves into fascinating events and stories which many of the coaches and players, like myself, are still reminiscing today.

While the legendary Paul Brown will long be recognized as one of the great innovators of football as well as the coach of Ohio State's first national championship squad in 1942, OHIO STATE FOOTBALL . . . THE GREAT TRADITION shares the memories of Brown's first game at Ohio State in 1941, when gatekeepers at Ohio Stadium wouldn't allow him entrance into the Horseshoe without a ticket or proper identification. I bet they learned their lesson when Coach Hayes arrived in '51.

In addition to countless other anecdotes, you'll find chapters devoted to the longtime series between Ohio State and the rest of the Big Ten, including Penn State, which becomes the newest conference member in 1993. These chapters culminate with a special look at the Ohio State-Michigan series — these are some of my favorite pages.

And who to author a unique historical look at Ohio State football but Jack Park.

One of the most respected authorities on Buckeye football, Jack became an instant fan when he saw his first game in Ohio Stadium at age nine. Since then he's witnessed nearly 300 games, home and away. His daily radio commentaries on Ohio State football have been aired in Columbus for the past 15 seasons.

Jack is also a Certified Public Accountant and is a member of the Football Writers Association of America. He and I have crossed paths on the speaking circuit numerous times, and I know without question his efforts in the pages to follow will only complement the many entertaining speeches he's presented to alumni groups, associations, corporations and charity organizations over the years.

Enjoy OHIO STATE FOOTBALL . . . THE GREAT TRADITION, and Go Buckeyes!

Archie Griffin
Two-Time Heisman Trophy Winner
Ohio State Class of '76

PREFACE

*T*he great tradition of Ohio State football means different things to different people. For me, being a loyal fan through many championship seasons has been great fun. But more importantly, college football continues to be one of the most positive influences in my life.

Championship football teams are built around strong leadership, desire, effort, sacrifice and teamwork. Understanding and developing these qualities and applying them to other parts of our lives helps us become better at whatever we choose to do.

This book recalls many of the great moments as well as a few disappointing ones in the long and glorious history of Ohio State football. It also emphasizes the many humorous and unusual incidents which are so much a part of the Buckeye football tradition.

A special thank you goes to Archie Griffin for his time, encouragement and assistance with the book's development.

I am deeply indebted to my good friends, Gary Hoffman and Dave Stephenson, for their day-to-day guidance and help. Gary designed the chapters and cover while Dave edited the manuscript and kept me focused on subjects which are of greatest interest to our readers. Working very closely with them has been extremely pleasant and rewarding. Rusty Miller, Randy Ford and Jerry Lima also spent considerable time helping us develop the book's format.

Artist Tom Hayes, one of Ohio State's most devoted fans, furnished excellent illustrations to complement 12 of the more than 100 humorous stories throughout the book.

Sports Information Director Steve Snapp and his staff have provided valuable information and assistance for many years. Mike Lawler, an avid Buckeye fan now living in Atlanta, generously made programs and memorabilia from his vast collection available for our use.

The majority of the pictures came from the outstanding collection of Chance and Sonny Brockway, and from The Ohio State University photo archives. The Brockways, who have photographed Ohio State games for many seasons, spent considerable time with us and suggested many photos to complement our script. Archivist Jana Drvoto was likewise very helpful with our photo selection.

A sincere thanks goes to Tom Stewart, Ed Douglas and the other fine people at WBNS Radio (AM 1460) for having me as part of their football broadcast crew each fall. Many of the stories which follow originated from material I developed over the seasons for our WBNS broadcasts.

The opportunity to provide the weekly "OSU Time Capsule" columns each season for Jim Toms, Marty Rozenman and Brian Rapp at *Suburban News Publications* has been very valuable experience for arranging much of this book's materials.

Finally, I will forever be grateful to my parents, Mr. and Mrs. E. N. Park, for being such great parents and for providing me the opportunity to attend Ohio State games at an early age. Some of my fondest childhood memories are of Saturday afternoons at Ohio Stadium with my friends and family.

I hope you find this book as enjoyable to read as it has been to prepare.

Jack Park

Buckeye Football
1890 – 1991

DECADE	W	L	T	PCT.	POINTS SCORED		
					OSU	OPP.	DIFF.
1890-1899	40	38	5	.512	1,138	1,076	62
1900-1909	69	26	7	.711	1,812	722	1,090
1910-1919	55	16	8	.747	1,701	398	1,303
1920-1929	44	27	7	.609	1,079	547	532
1930-1939	57	19	5	.735	1,681	453	1,228
1940-1949	57	27	6	.667	1,850	1,224	626
1950-1959	63	24	5	.712	1,916	1,089	827
1960-1969	68	21	2	.758	2,006	1,053	953
1970-1979	91	20	3	.811	3,405	1,317	2,088
1980-1989	82	35	2	.697	3,387	2,200	1,187
1990-	15	8	1	.646	626	407	219
TOTALS	**641**	**261**	**51**	**.699**	**20,601**	**10,486**	**10,115**

1. The Building of The Great Tradition

HARLEY, HAYES, HEISMANS AND MORE

*T*he Great Spectacle of Ohio State Football, modern-day style, contrasts sharply with the early years. While an Ohio Stadium crowd of approximately 94,000 fans watch the Buckeyes each home Saturday, a more informal gathering of about 700 witnessed Ohio State's very first game of "Foot Ball" against Ohio Wesleyan on Friday, May 3, 1890. The game was played in Delaware, Ohio, with Ohio State winning 20-14. OSU's first touchdown, then counting just four points, was scored by Joseph H. Large.

A very informal "intramural" type of football was contest-

1890: The Tradition begins

ed on campus in the late 1880s. George N. Cole, an 1891 graduate of Ohio State, helped organize the 1890 team by taking up a collection to purchase a "real" football, and by sending to the Spaulding Athletic Supply Company for a rules book. Cole also persuaded his friend, Alexander S. Lilley, to serve as the team's volunteer coach. Lilley lived on East Main Street in Columbus and rode a horse to get to the campus. From a very humble beginning was born one of today's "elite of college football." A plaque honoring Lilley hangs above the archway leading to the Ohio State dressing room in Ohio Stadium.

By 1890, football was already going strong in the East and portions of the Midwest. The first Harvard-Yale encounter took place in 1875, Michigan fielded its first squad in 1879 and the Lafayette-Lehigh rivalry began in 1894.

OSU's early opponents were mainly Ohio teams including Kenyon, Western Reserve, Denison, Wooster and Wittenberg. Otterbein was the opening game opponent on 15 different occassions. There were 11 head coaches during the first 23 years from 1890-1912. In contrast, John Cooper became just the 10th head coach since John Richardson resigned following the 1912 season.

The year 1913 was extremely significant in the development of Ohio State football as the Buckeyes became the newest member of the Western Conference (now the Big Ten) and John W. Wilce began a 16-year regime as coach. The Western Conference originated in 1896 with seven charter members: Chicago, Illinois, Michigan, Minnesota, Northwestern, Purdue and Wis-

Buckeye fans file into old Ohio Field

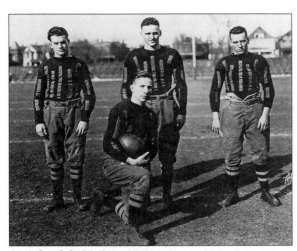

1917 backfield (kneeling) Howard Yergis, (left to right) Chic Harley, Richard Boesel and Pete Stinchcomb

consin. Indiana and Iowa both entered in 1900 while Chicago withdrew after the 1939 season and was replaced by Michigan State in 1953.

THE "CHIC" HARLEY ERA

Ohio State registered its first perfect season (7-0) and captured its initial Big Ten title in 1916. The Buckeyes were led by the legendary Charles W. "Chic" Harley, a sophomore halfback from Columbus East High School whose impact on Ohio State football was beyond imagination. Harley was truly a natural at every sport and his very modest and warm manner made him extremely popular with teammates and fans alike. Ohio State also produced its first All-American lineman in 1916, tackle Bob Karch from Columbus South High School.

Before Harley, Columbus high schools regularly played before larger crowds than did Ohio State. With Harley — Ohio State's first three-time All-American in 1916-17-19 — that all changed. During that span, Ohio State gained a national reputation by winning two conference championships and compiling a three-year record of 21-1-1. Interest in the Buckeyes swelled and suddenly old Ohio Field along High Street was too small to handle the crowds. This public enthusiasm sparked the fund drive to build Ohio Stadium, which was dedicated in 1922.

The 1920 season featured another fine halfback in Gaylord "Pete" Stinchcomb who, like Harley, was later inducted into the College Football Hall of Fame. This squad became the first Ohio State team to play in the Rose Bowl after capturing another Big Ten crown with a regular season record of 7-0. Even though Ohio State lost to California 28-0 during its initial trip to Pasadena, football had taken a strong hold on the Ohio State campus. The outcome would be different when these two foes would again meet some 29 seasons later, also in the Rose Bowl.

Ohio State suffered a major embarrassment in 1921 when Oberlin College upset the Buckeye 7-6, at old Ohio Field. Just five years earlier, Ohio State had defeated Oberlin 128-0. Wilce was so aggravated after the humiliating upset that he ordered his team back onto the field for a hard practice immediately after the game. Search lights were brought in so the team could continue their scrimmage past sunset. The hard practices continued into the next week and apparently had some effect — Ohio State won its next four games, all by shutouts.

THE MOVE TO OHIO STADIUM

After great success in the closing seasons at Old Ohio Field, the Buckeyes incurred losing records the first few years at Ohio Stadium from 1922-24. Amid fan criticism, Wilce announced his resignation following the 1928 campaign to devote full time to the practice of medicine. During his 16 seasons, Wilce won three

Ohio Stadium under construction

Big Ten titles and finished second three times. His overall record was a very impressive 78-33-9. He later became director of The Ohio State University's Health Services.

WILLAMAN AND SCHMIDT: CONTRASTING STYLES

Wilce was replaced by Sam Willaman, a Wilce assistant, who had been a fine fullback for the Buckeyes from 1911-13. Willaman was a strong fundamentalist who paid great attention to detail. He inherited one of Ohio State's finest athletes ever in Wes Fesler, who was equally as talented on the basketball court or baseball diamond. Fesler was extremely graceful and well-coordinated and was a three-time All-American end from 1928-30.

Although Willaman compiled a five-year record of 26-10-5, his teams finished no higher than second in the conference. Fans were growing disgruntled with his style of play which they considered too conservative and lacking imagination. While Ohio State lost only two games his last two seasons, both losses were to Michigan. Under pressure from both the fans and administration, Willaman resigned following the '33 season.

If Willaman's offense did indeed lack diversification, his successsor, Francis Schmidt, more than compensated for it. Schmidt, a tall, outspoken, likeable Texan, had compiled a sparkling five-year record of 46-6-5 at Texas Christian. He was a master of the "razzle-dazzle" offense, with each play designed to go the distance. Two or three laterals behind the line of scrimmage were very common. Schmidt was truly an offensive genius, years ahead of his time.

Schmidt's first squad in 1934 went 7-1 with only a one-point loss to Illinois preventing a conference championship. OSU went 7-1 again the next season, tying Minnesota for the Big Ten crown with a 5-0 league mark. It was Ohio State's first title in 15 years. The lone loss to Notre Dame, however, is one of the most famous games in college football history.

Both schools were undefeated and aiming for the national championship as they clashed November 2 at Ohio Stadium. Ohio State led 13-0 after three quarters but the Irish rallied for three fourth-quarter touchdowns (the final score with just 30 seconds remaining) to win, 18-13. During football's 100th anniversary in 1969, this game was selected the most exciting contest during the first century of college football.

Schmidt's 1939 team captured another Big Ten title even with a season-ending loss at Michigan 21-14. This is the only year Ohio State has been able to win the conference title outright while losing to Michigan. A 23-20 win over powerful Minnesota at Minneapolis was significant as All-American quarterback Don Scott led the way with three touchdown passes.

Three-time All-American Wes Fesler

After Ohio State fell to 4-4 in 1940 including a 40-0 drubbing at home to Michigan, Schmidt submitted his resignation when he learned he would not be rehired for another season. Dissension had been growing all season among the players and his teams had now lost three in a row to the Wolverines.

In seven years, Schmidt gave Ohio State one of its most colorful eras in Big Ten history. But there was too much concern about his use of talent and the lack of organization in his coaching staff. It was time for another change and Ohio State was becoming the "Graveyard of Coaches."

BROWN AND THE FIRST NATIONAL TITLE

Ohio State's new coach in 1941 was Paul Brown, 32, the youngest coach in the Western Conference. In nine seasons as coach at Massillon High School, Brown transformed his alma mater into a national prep power. Massillon amassed a 58-1-1 record from 1935-40, and his last team outscored its opponents 477-6.

Groundskeeping legend Tony Aquilla and his sweeping crew

Brown was a popular choice to succeed Schmidt. He was strongly endorsed by the sportswriters from around the state and by the Ohio High School Football Coaches Association. Brown was a strong disciplinarian who stressed fundamentals, execution and organization. He made an immediate impact on Ohio State football. His first team went 6-1-1 tying with Michigan for second place in the conference behind Minnesota.

But a great deal happened following the close of the '41 season. After Japan's December 7 attack on Pearl Harbor, the nation became totally involved in the war effort in both Europe and the South Pacific. With most major universities immediately taking an active part in the training of young men to serve as military officers, the status of college football was very much in question.

Many military bases fielded football teams in 1942 to help promote morale. The Big Ten made two rule changes: first, allowing member schools to schedule ten games rather than the previous limit of eight; and second, allowing the scheduling of

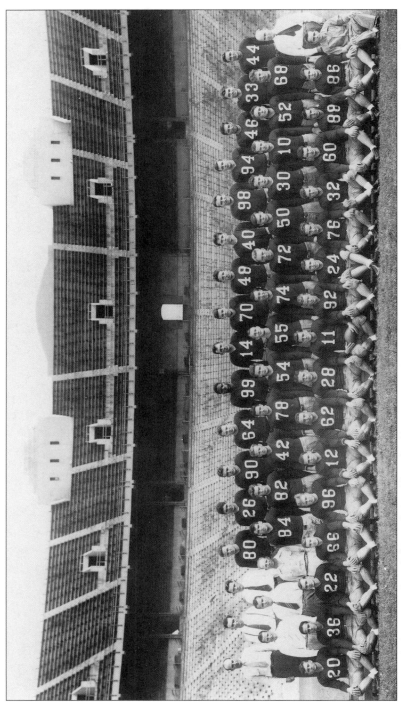

1942: Paul Brown (top left) and the school's first national champions

games with the service teams. Ohio State added Fort Knox and the Iowa Seahawks to its '42 schedule.

Brown's 43-man roster of '42 included 24 sophomores, 16 juniors and only three seniors. The 34-year-old coach had lost 18 lettermen from '41, including the entire starting backfield of quarterback John Hallabrin, halfbacks Dick Fisher and Tom Kinkade, and fullback Jack Graf, who had been selected the Big Nine's most valuable player. The Buckeyes were pre-season picks for about third or fourth place in the '42 conference race.

Ohio State operated primarily from the single-wing formation. The Buckeyes' starting line had the veteran Bob Shaw and Don Steinberg at the ends and Bill Willis and Chuck Csuri at the tackle. Lin Houston and Hal Dean occupied the guard spots and Bill Vickroy returned at center. A reserve tackle was Don McCafferty of Cleveland, later head coach of the Baltimore Colts and Detroit Lions.

Captain George Lynn was the starting quarterback. The halfback posts went to Paul Sarringhaus and Les Horvath, while sophomore Gene Fekete, a swift and powerful runner, was the starter at fullback.

Paul Brown and his 1942 backfield (left to right) Les Horvath, Gene Fekete, George Lynn and Paul Sarringhaus

Ohio State opened September 26 with a surprisingly easy 59-0 rout of the Fort Knox Army Base service team. The following week was much tougher as Indiana invaded Ohio Stadium with one of its finest teams of all time. In one of the season's toughest games, the Buckeyes came from behind twice to defeat the Hoosiers 32-21. Next came a home contest with Southern California on October 10. The Trojans were still smarting from a 33-0 pasting from Ohio State the year before on the West Coast. Ohio State spotted Southern California a first-quarter score, then stormed back to win 28-12.

BUCKEYES RANKED NUMBER ONE

Following the win over Southern Cal, the unbeaten Buckeyes topped the weekly *Associated Press* poll. The Big Ten dominated the top 20 with Michigan third, Illinois fifth, and Wisconsin seventh. Minnesota was rated 14th and Iowa 19th.

The next week, Ohio State scored in each quarter to shut out Purdue 26-0 before a home crowd of 45,943. While the attendance may seem low by today's standards, it was extremely high for the war period when civilian travel was very limited. The Ohio Stadium crowd was the largest in the country for the third consecutive week. Brown's forces traveled to Evanston on October 24 for a hard fought 20-6 win over Northwestern, the only team to defeat Ohio State in 1941.

A TASTE OF BAD WATER

Undefeated Ohio State next headed for Madison for the biggest test of the season, a showdown with sixth-ranked Wisconsin. The 5-0-1 Badgers had been pointing for Ohio State all season. They were coached by Harry Stuhldreher, former quarterback of Notre Dame's "Four Horsemen" backfield in 1924. Stuhldreher, like Brown, was from Massillon. It was the Badgers' homecoming game with a record crowd of nearly 45,000 in attendance.

For Ohio State, the weekend could hardly have been any worse. The Bucks suffered their first and only loss of the season, 17-7. For starters, the Badgers were extremely talented and Ohio State simply could not contain the open field running of Elroy Hirsch (later nicknamed "Crazylegs").

After spotting Wisconsin a 10-0 halftime lead, the Buckeyes cut the deficit to 10-7 with a 96-yard march early in the final

The '42 Ohio State-Wisconsin game was broadcast to what was believed to be, at the time, the largest audience ever to hear a football game. More than 200 stations carried NBC's broadcast throughout the United States and to the many servicemen around the world. Bill Stern did the play-by-play for NBC, while Bill Corley of WBNS and Wib Pettigrew of WOSU provided game coverage for central Ohio.

quarter. But the Badgers put together a final drive, culminating with a TD toss from Hirsch to All-American end Dave Schreiner to put the game out of reach.

While all appeared to go right for Stuhldreher's Badgers, everything seemed to go wrong for Brown's Buckeyes. Many players became ill from the drinking water on the train to Madison the day before. By Saturday afternoon, nearly half the squad was unable to play at full strength. Ohio State soon nicknamed the loss the "Bad Water Game."

When traveling to Wisconsin, the Ohio State team normally spent Friday evening in the small town of Janesville south of Madison. This trip, however, they stayed near the campus at the Park Hotel in downtown Madison. That evening, the hotel's elevators were not operating, causing the players to climb six flights of steps. Pep rallies were held Friday evening "until the wee hours," allowing most of the Buckeyes very little sleep. To top it off, the game was played on Halloween, with Ohio State seemingly haunted from start to finish.

Wisconsin moved to second place in the weekly *AP* poll behind Georgia as Ohio State fell to sixth. But matters changed very rapidly. The following week, Ohio State overwhelmed the Pitt Panthers 59-19 while Wisconsin was surprised by Iowa 6-0, and suddenly Ohio State, Illinois and Iowa were tied for first place in the league.

The next weekend, the Buckeyes reclaimed undisputed first place in the Big Ten title chase with a convincing 44-20 triumph over Illinois, before 68,656 half-frozen fans at snow-covered Municipal Stadium in Cleveland. The contest was officially an Illinois home game. The Illini were suffering from poor attendance, so when Cleveland alumni of both Illinois and Ohio State urged that the game be transferred from Champaign to Cleveland, authorities from both schools consented. A combined Ohio State-Illinois alumni rally was held Friday evening, with Cleveland Indians shortstop Lou Boudreau, an Illinois graduate, serving as Master of Ceremonies.

Following the Illinois win, the Buckeyes edged back to fifth place in the weekly *AP* poll. A win over fourth-ranked Michigan would assure them an outright league title since Ohio State had scheduled six league games to just five for the other contenders.

A rain-soaked Ohio Stadium crowd of nearly 72,000 saw the Buckeyes use the forward pass to perfection, defeating Michigan 21-7 to capture their first league crown since 1939. All three touchdowns came on passes from Horvath to Sarringhaus (20 yards), Sarringhaus to Shaw (60 yards) and Sarringhaus to Horvath (32 yards). It was Ohio State's first win over the Wolverines in five seasons.

FIRST NATIONAL TITLE

With the conference title assured, attention turned to the final game with the Iowa Seahawks and a possible shot at the national championship. The Seahawks were a Naval cadet service team comprised of former professional and college stars. Their starting 11 included three former Ohio State players: Jim Langhurst ('40 fullback and captain), Dick Fisher ('41 halfback) and Charlie Ream ('37 tackle).

> **F**ullback Gene Fekete's 89-yard touchdown gallop against Pittsburgh in '42 still stands as the longest rush from scrimmage in all of Ohio State football.

Entering its final game, the 8-1 Buckeyes were ranked third behind Boston College at 8-0 and Georgia Tech at 9-0. Showing no mental letdown following the Michigan win, they crushed a worthy Seahawk team 41-12. Sarringhaus led the ground attack with 114 yards and two touchdowns.

While Ohio State was winning its last game, Georgia stunned Georgia Tech 34-0. But the unbelievable upset occurred in Boston where unranked Holy Cross crushed top-ranked Boston College 55-12. The Eagles were so distraught they cancelled a celebration party which had been scheduled at the fashionable Cocoanut Grove in anticipation of a national title. Their loss to Holy Cross was probably a blessing in disguise as that evening, the Cocoanut Grove burned, killing more than 100 guests.

Ohio State was awarded its first national championship by a vote of 1,432 to 1,339 over second-place Georgia Tech in the *Associated Press* poll. Wisconsin (8-1-1) finished third and Michigan (7-3) ninth. Bob Shaw, Chuck Csuri and Lin Houston were selected All-Americans and Gene Fekete became the first Ohio State player to finish in the top ten voting for the Heisman Trophy, finishing eighth. Fekete also led the conference in both rushing and scoring. Csuri was selected the team's most valuable player.

WHAT MIGHT HAVE BEEN

Brown, who rolled to a 15-2-1 mark after two seasons, was selected one of the nation's ten "most outstanding young men." With the nation in the midst of World War II, most of the '42 squad soon entered the service. Following the '43 season, Brown was granted a Navy commission and reported to Great Lakes Training Center where he soon became the head football coach. From there he became coach of the Browns, Cleveland's new entry in the old All-American Conference. It became apparent the war had destroyed a college football dynasty in the making.

GRAVEYARD OF COACHES

Mild mannered Carroll Widdoes, a Brown assistant who had moved to Columbus with Brown from Massillon in '41, was named Ohio State's interim coach in 1944. Widdoes proved to be an outstanding replacement. OSU's squad of 44 players was made up of 31 freshmen, with only five seniors, three juniors and five sophomores. Former Sports Information Director Marv Homan labels the '44 season "one of the finest coaching jobs in school history."

Widdoes welcomed a big break when Les Horvath, who was enrolled in dental school, was given another year of eligibility under relaxed wartime regulations. It had been presumed his college career was over after his three seasons of 1940-41-42. Horvath was installed at quarterback and was joined by three freshmen — Dick Flanagan and Bob Brugge at the halfbacks and Ollie Cline at fullback.

The Buckeyes went 9-0 in '44 to capture the Big Nine title (the league was called the Big Nine after Chicago left in '39). In addition, Ohio State captured the "National Civilian Championship" and placed second to Army in the final *Associated Press* poll. Horvath became the first Ohio State player to win the coveted Heisman Trophy, finishing ahead of sophomores Doc Blanchard and Glenn Davis of Army. Carroll Widdoes was named the coach-of-the-year, the first Ohio State coach to receive this national distinction.

But Widdoes, a quiet, reserved man, soon grew tired of the limelight. He disliked the numerous speaking engagements and the evenings away from his family. After posting a very respectable 7-2 record in '45, he asked for his old job back as backfield coach. Widdoes recommended assistant Paul Bixler as his successor. Athletic Director L. W. St. John granted his request and, in a somewhat unusual move, Widdoes and Bixler switched positions.

But Bixler's stay was even shorter. After only one season (4-3-2 in 1946) he resigned under the "pressure of the Ohio State job" and accepted the head coaching post at Colgate. Many looked on the move as going from the "big time to the small time," and Ohio State was earning its reputation as the "Graveyard of Coaches."

FESLER AND THE FIRST ROSE BOWL TRIUMPH

With Bixler's resignation, Ohio State was again searching for a football coach, one who would become the fifth coach in just eight seasons. Many fans wanted Brown to return but the job went to former great Wes Fesler who had just completed his first season as head coach at the University of Pittsburgh.

After two years of building, Fesler's '49 team (7-1-2) tied Michigan for the Big Ten title and became the first Ohio State team to win the Rose Bowl, defeating California 17-14. This team was greatly strengthened by the addition of two fine sophomore halfbacks, Ray Hamilton and Vic Janowicz. Janowicz would soon be recognized as one of the finest all-around players in school history.

The 1950 season was very unusual. After losing the opener 32-27 to Southern Methodist, Ohio State won its next six and soared to the nation's number-one ranking. Then the roof caved in. The Buckeyes lost 14-7 at Illinois in the second to last game. Ohio State then closed its season at home against Michigan in the "Snow Bowl." Playing in blizzard-like conditions, Michigan won 9-3 without making a single first down.

Janowicz, then a junior, had an excellent season and became the second Buckeye to win the Heisman Trophy. But the pressure of the Ohio State coaching job was more than Fesler wanted, and in December he submitted his resignation. It was getting to be an old, old story — nobody seemed to want the job as Ohio State's football coach. But soon that would all change!

WOODY TAKES COMMAND

Ohio State was again looking for a football coach, and again many alumni and fans supported the return of Brown. Several nationally recognized names were rumored and the job was offered to Don Faurot of Missouri. Faurot accepted the position but two days later changed his mind and decided to stay at Missouri. Finally, 38-year-old W. W. "Woody" Hayes, a lesser known figure, was appointed Ohio State's 19th head football coach. Hayes came to Columbus after three seasons at Denison University followed by two years at Miami of Ohio.

Under Hayes' direction, the Ohio State program became one of the finest and most highly respected in college football history. His 28 seasons at Ohio State is surpassed in the Big Ten only by Amos Alonzo Stagg's 41 seasons at the University of Chicago (1892-1932) and Bob Zuppke's 29 years at Illinois (1913-1941). Hayes compiled a record of 205-61-10 at Ohio State. His teams won three national championships and 13 Big Ten titles or co-titles. Forty-two of his players were selected All-American one or more seasons.

Hayes' first Ohio

Coaching legend Woody Hayes

1954: Woody Hayes' first national championship

1955 co-captain Frank Machinsky

State game was a 7-0 victory over Southern Methodist in Ohio Stadium on September 29, 1951. Scoring the first touchdown by a Hayes-coached team was end Bob Joslin on a pass from quarterback Tony Curcillo. Janowicz added the conversion.

Hayes' fourth team in 1954 produced one of OSU's finest seasons in history. The Buckeyes captured the *Associated Press* national title with a 10-0 record which included a 20-7 Rose Bowl triumph over Southern California.

Ohio State won its second consecutive outright league championship in 1955, marking the school's first back-to-back titles since the Harley years of 1916-17. The key game was against Michigan, who needed a win over the Buckeyes to be Rose Bowl bound (Ohio State was ineligible with the no-repeat procedure in effect at that time). OSU's defense was superb as the Buckeyes won 17-0 for their first win at Ann Arbor since 1937.

The loss to Ohio State was doubly painful for Michigan, since intra-state rival Michigan State finished second in conference play and thereby earned the season-ending trip to Pasadena. "Hopalong" Cassady became the third Buckeye to win the Heisman Trophy after completing one of the finest careers in school history.

Ohio State's string of consecutive conference wins grew to a record 17 before the 1956 squad was beaten 6-0 at Iowa. Ohio State has twice equaled this mark (which stands yet today), first in the late 1960s and again in the mid-1970s. Guard Jim Parker completed an outstanding college career in 1956 becoming the first Buckeye to capture the Outland Trophy.

Woody Hayes' 1954 squad became the first Big Ten team to win seven conference games in one season since Amos Alonzo Stagg's Chicago Maroons won seven in 1913, the year Hayes was born.

After a surprising 18-14 opening game loss to Texas Christian, the '57 Buckeyes responded with nine consecutive wins to capture the Big Ten title and the *UPI* national championship. Their 17-13 win over Iowa has become one of the most talked about victories in Ohio Stadium history.

With 7:51 remaining in the final quarter, Ohio State took command at its own 32 trailing the Hawks 13-10. The Buckeyes put together a winning drive with sophomore Bob White carrying up-the-middle on seven of the eight plays for 66 of the 68 yards including the all-important touchdown. Ohio State concluded the season with a 10-7 Rose Bowl win over Oregon as Don Sutherin kicked a 34-yard field goal late in the game to break a 7-7 tie.

FACULTY COUNCIL SHUNS ROSE BOWL

Ohio State earned its next league championship in 1961. Texas Christian again spoiled a perfect season by posting a 7-7 tie in the opener. The Bucks then reeled off eight consecutive wins including a 50-20 season-ending triumph over Michigan in Ann Arbor. It was Ohio State's 400th all-time win with Hayes' offense amassing 512 total yards that afternoon.

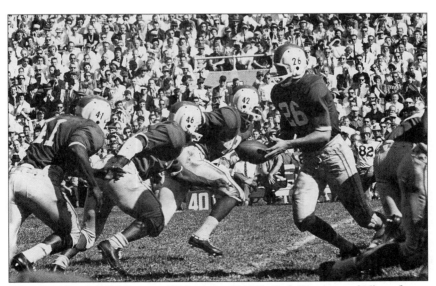

The 1961 backfield featured Matt Snell (41), Bob Ferguson (46) and Paul Warfield (42). Quarterback Bill Mrukowski had the enviable job of handing off to three of Ohio State's finest runners.

Ike Kelley (53) and Tom Bugel, two in Ohio State's long line of premier linebackers, played together from 1963-65

But the luster of the league title didn't last long. The following Tuesday, Ohio State's faculty council shocked the entire football world by voting against playing in the Rose Bowl. The council vote was 28-25.

Technically, the official Rose Bowl agreement between the Big Ten and the Pacific Eight had expired and partici-pants were selected by invitation. Sec-ond-place Minneso-ta then accepted the Rose Bowl's invite and responded with a 21-3 triumph over UCLA.

The disappointment and bitterness among the Buckeye players and fans requires few adjectives. To most it was a real shock, but apparently many of the faculty council felt the Ohio State football program was becoming too big. Many critics, however, felt it was inconsistent when the faculty council voted to accept its share of that year's Rose Bowl receipts after reject-ing an invitation to play.

THE BIG TEN'S LAST NATIONAL CHAMPION

Hayes greatly expanded his recruiting efforts outside Ohio in 1967 and assembled one of the most outstanding freshman classes in college history. The group became known as the "Super Sophomores of '68" and included such notables as cor-nerback Jack Tatum, middle guard Jim Stillwagon, quarterback Rex Kern and safety Mike Sensibaugh. The '68 team, which went 10-0, is the last Big Ten team to capture a national title. The first major test was a 13-0 thriller over top-ranked Purdue in the

The 1968 staff (kneeling, left to right) Lou Holtz, George Chaump, Rudy Hubbard, Bill Mallory, (standing) head coach Woody Hayes, Tiger Ellison, Lou McCullough, Earle Bruce, Esco Sarkkinen and Hugh Hindman

season's third game. The regular season concluded with a 50-14 blowout over Michigan, with fullback Jim Otis scoring four times.

The Michigan win set up one of the greatest Rose Bowls of all time — a head-to-head meeting between number-one ranked Ohio State and number-two Southern California. Southern California took a 10-0 lead early in the second quarter when O. J. Simpson electrified the crowd with a spectacular 80-yard run.

But Ohio State responded with 27 consecutive points to win 27-16. Rex Kern's ball-handling was excellent and often confused the NBC television camera crew. He passed for two touchdowns to Leo Hayden and Ray Gillian and was voted the game's MVP. Simpson visited the OSU locker room following the game and congratulated the Buckeyes on being "the greatest football team in the country."

The following two seasons were nearly as successful, but season-ending losses to Michigan in 1969 and Stanford in '70 prevented OSU from repeating as national champions.

1968: The most recent National Championship team for the Buckeyes

The Buckeyes' 22-game winning streak, longest in school history, came to a screeching halt in Ann Arbor when the Wolverines pulled the classic upset 24-12 in 1969. Bo Schembechler was in his first season as Michigan's head coach and the game set the stage for the ten-year "Woody and Bo War" which added greatly to an already strong rivalry.

Two of Ohio State's most devastating losses were played 50 years apart. Illinois kicked a 25-yard field goal with eight seconds remaining to hand Ohio State a 9-7 loss at old Ohio Field on Saturday, November 22, 1919. It was Chic Harley's last game as a Buckeye and the only loss of his brilliant three-year career. Ironically, *exactly* 50 years later, first-year coach Bo Schembechler led his Michigan Wolverines to a stunning 24-12 upset of Ohio State on Saturday, November 22, 1969.

The '70 Buckeyes swept through the season undefeated but were surprised by Jim Plunkett and the Stanford Cardinal in the Rose Bowl, losing 27-17. Even with this defeat, Ohio State had completed one of the most successful eras in all of college football. The Buckeyes had been 27-2 these three years with 11 different players being selected All-American one or more seasons. Jim Stillwagon won the Outland Trophy in 1970 and also received the Lombardi Award, which was first presented that same year.

ARCHIE ARRIVES

The next great chapter in Ohio State football was the four-year period, 1972-75, which is often referred to as "The Archie Griffin Years." The Buckeyes accomplished an outstanding four-year record of 40-5-1, won outright or shared four Big Ten titles, made four Rose Bowl appearances and twice just missed winning the national championship.

Freshmen became eligible for varsity competition in 1972. The second game of the season, against North Carolina, was quite significant. With the Buckeye offense stagnant that afternoon, Hayes elected to insert freshman Archie Griffin at tailback — that week's depth chart listed him with the fifth-team.

Before the day was through, Griffin had led Ohio State to a 29-14 victory and had established what was then a school sin-

Archie Griffin led some of the greatest teams in Ohio State history from 1972-75

gle-game rushing record of 239 yards. *Columbus Dispatch* sports editor Paul Hornung wrote, "There has probably never been so sensational a debut in the 50-year history of Ohio Stadium as that of 18-year-old Eastmoor grad Archie Griffin." Griffin was never out of the lineup the next four seasons.

The Buckeyes won a crucial contest over Michigan in '72, 14-11, mainly because of their defense. Twice the Wolverines were held on downs inside the OSU 1-yard line. Michigan led in total offensive yards, 344-192, but could muster only one touchdown.

The 1973 squad, which finished 10-0-1 was one of Ohio State's finest. It's doubtful if Ohio State ever had three better linebackers at one time than Randy Gradishar, Vic Koegel and Rick Middleton. The defense allowed only 64 points to lead the nation in scoring defense while the offense scored 413 for an average of 37.5 per game.

Ohio State and Michigan tied for the league title with identical 7-0-1 conference records after playing to a 10-10 tie in Ann Arbor. In 1973, the Rose Bowl representative was decided by a vote of the league's ten athletic directors if there was a tie for the league title. Ohio State was awarded the Pasadena trip by a reported vote of 6-4, and responded with a 42-21 victory over Southern California.

The '74 team finished 10-2 and once again the season's big game was a win over Michigan 12-10. Placekicker Tom Klaban, a walk-on, was the game's hero. Michigan had taken a 10-0 first-quarter lead before Klaban made good on four field goal attempts to earn the victory. Three of Klaban's kicks were in excess of 40 yards.

The Bucks were then beaten by Southern Cal 18-17, with the margin of victory being a successful two-point conversion late in the fourth quarter. Griffin was awarded the Heisman Trophy and for the second year was voted the Big Ten MVP.

In 1975, Ohio State went 11-0 during the regular season. Only a 23-10 Rose Bowl loss to UCLA cost the Buckeyes the national crown. Ironically, Ohio State had beaten UCLA 41-20 earlier that season.

The Buckeyes made a strong comeback in a 21-14 win over Michigan. Trailing 14-7 with just over seven minutes to play, Ohio State rallied for two touchdowns to earn a fourth consecutive trip to Pasadena. The last touchdown was set up by a fine interception and return by safety Ray Griffin.

Quarterback Cornelius Greene was selected the Big Ten MVP and Griffin became the only two-time winner of the Heisman Trophy. He also established a college record rushing for more than 100 yards in 31 consecutive regular-season games. He established an NCAA career rushing record with 5,177 yards which has since been topped only by Tony Dorsett of Pitt, Charles White of Southern Cal, and Herschel Walker of Georgia. Griffin's career rushing average of 6.13 yards per carry is still an NCAA record.

Hayes' last three teams from 1976-77-78 compiled a record of 25-9-2. His '76 and '77 squads were league co-champions with Michigan giving Ohio State a Big Ten record with six consecutive titles or co-titles. Two significant games were a 27-10 win over Colorado in the 1977 Orange Bowl, and a 29-28 loss to powerful Oklahoma in 1977.

The Hayes years were unquestionably one of the greatest eras college football will ever know. His dedication to his school, his players and people in general is unparalled. Schembechler perhaps said it best at the 1979 Big Ten media luncheon: "I really miss seeing Woody here. He did more for Big Ten football than any coach in our conference's history. I owe Woody a lot . . . we all do."

THE SUCCESS CONTINUES

One strong topic of conversation among Ohio State fans in the 1970s was "When will Woody retire?" and "Who will replace him?" Those questions were finally answered when Earle Bruce was selected as Ohio State's 20th head football coach in 1979.

Bruce, then head coach at Iowa State, was no stranger to Ohio State fans. An outstanding high school player, Bruce was recruited to play at Ohio State by Fesler in the fall of 1949. After a

Earle Bruce led the Buckeyes to an 81-26-1 record in his nine-year tenure as head coach

knee injury cut short his playing career, Bruce stayed on as a graduate assistant at the urging of Hayes. After graduating in 1953, Bruce began a very successful 13-year coaching career in the Ohio high schools (assistant at Mansfield, head coach at Salem, Sandusky, and Massillon). His combined head coaching record was 82-12-3 and three times he was selected the Ohio High School coach of the year. Bruce served six seasons as a Hayes assistant from 1966-71. In 1972 to went to Tampa before going to Iowa State the following season.

His first Ohio State team went 11-1, just missing the national title after losing to Southern Cal 17-16 in the Rose Bowl. Bruce was selected national coach of the year, the last Big Ten coach to receive this distinction.

Memorable wins during the 1980s included a 28-23 win over Pitt in the l984 Fiesta Bowl, a 45-38 come-from-behind triumph over Illinois in 1984 (with Keith Byars scoring all five TDs) and a 22-13 victory over top-ranked Iowa in l985. But maybe The best-remembered victory during the decade was Bruce's last one, a 23-20 win over Michigan in Ann Arbor.

The Monday prior to the 1987 Michigan game, President Edward Jennings announced Bruce was being dismissed as Ohio State's football coach. Later that afternoon, Athletic Director Rick Bay resigned in protest of Bruce's firing. That Saturday, the Buckeyes rallied from a 13-0 deficit to give their coach a significant victory in his last game for the scarlet and gray.

Bruce's nine-year record at Ohio State was 81-26-1 with two Big Ten outright titles (1979, '84) and two co-titles (1981, '86). His teams won five of eight bowl games and he was 5-4 against Michigan. Nine different Buckeyes were selected All-American one or more times including linebacker Chris Spielman who captured the Lombardi Award in '87.

John Cooper replaced Bruce as head coach in 1988. After going 4-6-1 his first season, his teams posted a very respectable 23-12-1 record the next three years. A thrilling 27-26 victory at Iowa in 1990 earned Cooper his 100th career victory.

OHIO STATE FOOTBALL ... THE GREAT TRADITION

During 102 seasons from 1890-1991, the Buckeyes have compiled an impressive all-time record of 641 wins, 261 losses and 51 ties (69.9 percent). Since joining the Big Ten in 1913, Ohio State has captured 25 league titles or co-titles.

But Ohio State football is much more than wins, losses, huge crowds and championships. It is a common denominator which binds friendships for a lifetime. Ohio State football is a *great tradition!* Its positive impact upon its players and countless fans will likely continue for many more generations.

Timeout

Ohio State's Ten Greatest Wins

1. 1968: Ohio State 13, Purdue 0 — Win over number-one ranked Boilermakers paves way for undefeated-untied season and national title.

2. 1954: Ohio State 21, Michigan 7 — Buckeyes earn Woody Hayes his first trip to Rose Bowl and first national title. Goal-line stand is one of finest moments in all of Ohio State football.

3. 1970: Ohio State 20, Michigan 9 — First time both teams enter season-ending game undefeated-untied. Win avenges '69 loss which cost OSU national title.

4. 1944: Ohio State 18, Michigan 14 — First time Ohio State-Michigan winner would be conference champion. Buckeyes' Les Horvath scores winning TD with 3:06 remaining. Ohio State finished 9-0.

5. 1968: Ohio State 27, Southern Cal 16 — Rose Bowl with #1 OSU vs. #2 Southern Cal led by O. J. Simpson. Buckeyes come back from 10-0 deficit.

6. 1957: Ohio State 17, Iowa 13 — With Buckeyes trailing 13-10 and 7:51 remaining, fullback Bob White leads 68-yard drive for winning TD to earn trip to Pasadena.

7. 1975: Ohio State 21, Michigan 14 — Both teams undefeated. Buckeyes rally for two touchdowns in last seven minutes to earn outright league title.

8. 1954: Ohio State 31, Wisconsin 14 — Hopalong Cassady's 88-yard interception return keys come-from-behind triumph over second-ranked Badgers.

9. 1985: Ohio State 22, Iowa 13 — Spirited Buckeyes knock undefeated Hawkeyes from their number-one ranking.

10. 1939: Ohio State 23, Minnesota 21 — Don Scott throws for three TDs as Buckeyes hand powerful Gophers their first conference loss at home in seven seasons.

Opening Games
1890 - 1991

		FIRST	LAST	OSU RECORD			
				W	L	T	TOTAL
1	Ohio Wesleyan	1890	1932	13	0	0	13
2	Western Reserve	1891	1891	0	1	0	1
3	Oberlin	1892	1892	0	1	0	1
4	Otterbein	1893	1912	12	1	2	15
5	Akron	1894	1895	1	1	0	2
6	Ohio Medical	1896	1897	2	0	0	2
7	Heidelberg	1898	1898	1	0	0	1
8	Case	1917	1917	1	0	0	1
9	Purdue	1924	1924	1	0	0	1
10	Wittenberg	1926	1929	4	0	0	4
11	Mt. Union	1930	1930	1	0	0	1
12	Cincinnati	1931	1931	1	0	0	1
13	Virginia	1933	1933	1	0	0	1
14	Indiana	1934	1954	5	0	0	5
15	Kentucky	1935	1935	1	0	0	1
16	New York University	1936	1936	1	0	0	1
17	Texas Christian	1937	1969	3	1	1	5
18	Missouri	1939	1949	7	0	1	8
19	Pittsburgh	1940	1985	2	0	0	2
20	Fort Knox	1942	1942	1	0	0	1
21	Iowa Seahawks	1943	1943	0	1	0	1
22	Southern Methodist	1950	1968	5	1	0	6
23	Nebraska	1955	1956	2	0	0	2
24	Duke	1959	1981	2	0	0	2
25	North Carolina	1962	1965	1	1	0	2
26	Texas A&M	1963	1970	2	0	0	2
27	Arizona	1967	1991	1	1	0	2
28	Iowa	1971	1972	2	0	0	2
29	Minnesota	1973	1974	2	0	0	2
30	Michigan State	1975	1976	2	0	0	2
31	Miami (Florida)	1977	1977	1	0	0	1
32	Penn State	1978	1978	0	1	0	1
33	Syracuse	1979	1988	3	0	0	3
34	Baylor	1982	1982	1	0	0	1
35	Oregon	1983	1983	1	0	0	1
36	Oregon State	1984	1984	1	0	0	1
37	Alabama (Kickoff Classic)	1986	1986	0	1	0	1
38	West Virginia	1987	1987	1	0	0	1
39	Oklahoma State	1989	1989	1	0	0	1
40	Texas Tech	1990	1990	1	0	0	1
TOTAL				**87**	**11**	**4**	**102**

2. Season Openers

OTTERBEIN MOST FREQUENT AMONG FOES

Season-opening games bring excitement, anticipation, enthusiasm and high expectations. The Buckeyes have enjoyed unusual success with their first 102 openers, winning 87, losing 11 and tying four (winning rate of 87.3 percent). They have outscored their opponents 2,686-719 for an average opening game score of 26.3-7.0. Ohio State has faced 40 different opponents on opening day with Otterbein College the most frequent (15 times: 1893 and 1899-1912).

Only seven of the 102 games have been played away from home including four of the first five from 1890-1894. Ohio State then opened at home for 79 consecutive years before launching the 1974 season with a 34-19 victory over Minnesota in Minneapolis. The '75 Buckeyes began with a 21-0 triumph over Michigan State at East Lansing in one of the most highly-publicized openers in Big Ten history. The last out-of-town starter was a 16-10 loss to Alabama in the 1986 Kickoff Classic at The Meadowlands in East Rutherford, N.J.

Twelve openers have involved Big Ten foes, all victories, with the most recent being a 49-21 win over Michigan State in 1976. The first opener against a league opponent was a 7-0 win over Purdue at Ohio Stadium in 1924. It was also the only opener against an opponent from outside Ohio during the Buckeyes' first 43 seasons from 1890-1932. Lopsided shutouts were very common as Ohio State usually found itself over matched against smaller Ohio Conference teams. Scores typical of this era were 55-0 over Otterbein (1912), 41-0 against Ohio Wesleyan (1918), 40-0 over Wittenberg (1926) and 59-0 against Mt. Union

(1930). The last opener against
an Ohio opponent was a 34-7
win over Ohio Wesleyan in 1932.

Ohio State's most one-sided
opening win was a 75-0 shellacking of Virginia in 1933. Nine
different players scored the 11
touchdowns as coach Sam Willaman substituted at will before a
record (at the time) opening
game crowd of 42,001. The Cav-
aliers recorded just one first

> **J**ohn W. Heisman, for whom college football's most highly respected award is named, assumed his first head coaching position at Oberlin College in 1892. The very first game of his coaching career was a 40-0 triumph over Ohio State.

down (on a penalty) and their only possession in enemy territory came after recovering a Buckeye fumble on the OSU 36 late in
the fourth quarter.

Western Reserve's 44-point victory (50-6) in 1891 remains
Ohio State's most lopsided opening game defeat (when touchdowns counted only five points). The second largest was 19-0 to
Penn State during Woody Hayes' last season in 1978. Buckeye
fans had speculated all summer who Hayes would go with at
quarterback—senior Rod Gerald, his starter the past two seasons, or highly-touted freshman Art Schlichter. Hayes started
both — Schlichter at quarterback and Gerald at split end. But
Joe Paterno's Nittany Lions were ready with a tenacious pass
rush which forced Schlichter to throw five interceptions. It was
the first time Ohio State had been shutout in an opening game
since a scoreless tie with Otterbein in 1901.

TCU GENUINE SPOILER

Twice the Buckeyes have won all their remaining games
after failing to win the season opener. Ironically, Texas Christian
did the damage both seasons. Hayes' 1957 Bucks captured the
UPI national title with a record of 9-1 after starting the season
with an 18-14 upset loss to the Horned Frogs. Hayes' 1961
squad finished 8-0-1 after tying TCU 7-7 in that season's opener.
In the '57 game, TCU's Jim Shofner (who later played with the
Cleveland Browns) keyed the outcome, returning a punt 90
yards for a six-pointer on the first play of the second quarter.
Shofner's run still stands as the longest punt return in Ohio Stadium history and the longest ever against an Ohio State team.

The 1922 opening game marked the first contest in Ohio

Stadium. The date was October 7 with Ohio State defeating Ohio Wesleyan 5-0 before 25,000 fans, the largest crowd ever to see a sporting event in Columbus. Captain "Butch" Pixley of Ohio State won the toss and Ohio State elected to receive and defend the south goal.

The Buckeyes' five-point margin of victory was much smaller than expected — coach John Wilce didn't want to show too much, saving most of his offense for the stadium dedication game two weeks later against Michigan. This was also the first Ohio State football game to be broadcast. The action was transmitted by radio station WEAO from the Robinson Laboratory on the Ohio State campus, by the Department of Electrical Engineering.

Ohio State opened the 1935 season with a 19-6 victory over a stubborn Kentucky squad. The attendance of 56,686 was, at the time, the largest opening day crowd in Ohio Stadium history. The Buckeyes played extremely well in the first and fourth quarters but stalled somewhat during the middle of the game. Captain Gomer Jones had an excellent afternoon with two interceptions and a fumble recovery. John Bettridge scored twice and Joe Williams once as the Buckeyes outgained the Wildcats in total offensive yards 331-159.

GETTING INSIDE CAN BE TROUBLESOME

Coach Paul Brown's first game was a surprisingly close 12-7 win over Missouri on September 26, 1941. The Tigers were coached by Don Faurot, who had aggressively sought the Ohio State head coaching position in 1941. That afternoon, Faurot unveiled an offensive formation, one that would revolutionize college football — the Split-T. Brown and his team were not totally prepared for this new concept but managed to survive for the five-point victory.

When the bus carrying the team and coaches arrived outside Ohio Stadium that day, Brown stepped off to say hello to Tink Ulrich and

The Buckeyes have only once opened facing the same opponent they played the final game of the previous season. The Iowa Seahawks (World War II service team) defeated Ohio State's "Baby Bucks" 28-13 in the 1943 opener. The Buckeyes had defeated the Seahawks 48-12 in the last game of 1942.

other friends from Massillon while the stadium gates were being opened. By the time Brown attempted to enter the stadium, the buses and their police escort had pulled inside. The guard at the gate did not recognize the new coach and asked to see his ticket. "I don't have a ticket. I'm the new coach," Brown told him. "Is that right? Well, I'm President Roosevelt, but you must have a ticket if you want to see today's game," said the ticket attendent.

Realizing the guard was serious, Brown walked over to the stadium's southeast corner below the Ohio State locker room and began throwing stones against the windows. As one of the trainers peered down, Brown yelled, "Send someone out here who can get me through that gate!" The trainer came down, explained that this man really was the Buckeyes' new coach and Brown was finally allowed to enter Ohio Stadium.

FIRST TV GAME FROM THE HORSESHOE

For pure excitement, it's hard to beat coach Wes Fesler's final two opening games. His 1949 squad opened with a thrilling 35-34 win over Missouri. It was the first game ever televised from Ohio Stadium and was carried in Columbus by WLW-C (now WCMH). The game was also broadcast nationally by veteran sportscaster Russ Hodges over the Mutual Radio Network.

This game also marked the football debut of senior end Dick Schnittker, a 6'5" All-American basketball player. Schnittker had joined the football squad just ten days earlier after injuries had depleted Fesler's end corps. Schnittker had been an all-Ohio end four years earlier at Sandusky High School.

The game was tied 14-14 at halftime. Ohio State's touchdowns were scored by fullback Curly Morrison on a two-yard plunge and by halfback Jerry Krall on a seven-yard scamper. Missouri scored first in the third period to lead 21-14 but the Buckeyes again tied the score, this time on a 31-yard pass from Krall to end Jimmy Hague. Ohio State finally took the lead 28-21 after quarterback Pandel Savic teamed with halfback Ray Hamilton on a 31-yard scoring toss.

> The 1950 opener featured opposing players who would finish the season as the Heisman Trophy winner and the runner-up — Ohio State's Vic Janowicz and Kyle Rote of Southern Methodist, respectively.

The touchdown was set up by Buckeye center Jack Lininger's interception return to the Missouri 31.

The Tigers scored again early in the fourth period but John Glorioso's all-important conversion attempt was wide, leaving the Buckeyes with a one-point lead, 28-27. The two teams then traded touchdowns to conclude the scoring at 35-34. OSU's TD came on another pass from Savic to Hamilton, this one covering 24 yards. But the Tigers still had a shot. With just eight seconds remaining and the ball at the OSU 26, Glorioso attempted a field goal which fell short, leaving the Buckeyes with a thrilling single-point win.

It was a tough loss for coach Don Faurot, whose Tigers had run 87 plays to Ohio State's 62 and had outgained the Buckeyes in total offensive yardage 507-430. But the visitors were signifi-

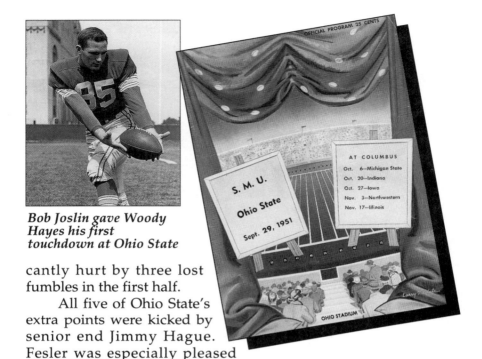

Bob Joslin gave Woody
Hayes his first
touchdown at Ohio State

cantly hurt by three lost
fumbles in the first half.

All five of Ohio State's
extra points were kicked by
senior end Jimmy Hague.
Fesler was especially pleased
with the play of two sophomore halfbacks, Hamilton and Vic
Janowicz, who were playing in their first varsity contests.
Hamilton rushed for 111 yards on five carries and caught five
passes for 115 yards and two touchdowns, while Janowicz was a
force defensively. He also singled out the play of Savic and tackle Jack Wilson, the Buckeye captain.

The 1950 opener produced one of the most miraculous
comebacks in Ohio Stadium history. With Fesler's Buckeyes
holding a 24-7 lead over Southern Methodist midway through
the third period, Mustang coach Rusty Russell inserted back-up
quarterback Fred Benners and instructed the lanky junior to
throw from the spread formation on every down. Benners really
responded! He threw for 325 yards — and four touchdowns —
during the game's last 20 minutes to single handedly pull the
Mustangs from behind to win 32-27.

Woody Hayes' first game at Ohio State was also against
Southern Methodist on September 29, 1951, with the Buckeyes
winning 7-0. The game's only touchdown came on a pass,
something Hayes earned quite a reputation for shunning in the
years ahead. In the third quarter, quarterback Tony Curcillo con-

nected with end Bob Joslin from 21 yards and Janowicz added the extra point.

In one of Ohio State's most thrilling openers, the Buckeyes edged Duke 14-13 to launch the 1959 football season before a nervous Ohio Stadium crowd of 82,834. The victory broke Duke's record of never having lost to a Big Ten opponent. Fans were generally pleased with Hayes' new wide-open attack, which featured an unbalanced line with split ends and flanked halfbacks.

Ohio State took the opening kickoff and drove 58 yards in eight plays to seize an early 7-0 lead. Sophomore left halfback Bob Ferguson (who would become an All-American fullback the following two seasons) bolted 15 yards through right guard for the touchdown. There was no further first-half scoring, but the Buckeyes suffered a real blow near halftime when starting quarterback Jerry Fields injured his right arm and was lost for the rest of the day.

With Fields injured, Hayes decided at halftime to try right halfback Tom Matte at quarterback. While most of the squad went to the dressing room under the guidance of the assistant

coaches, Hayes took Matte, center Jene Watkins and reserve halfbacks Dave Tingley and Ron Houck to the practice field outside the south end of Ohio Stadium. During this very impromptu rehearsal, Matte practiced taking snaps from center and running plays from the quarterback position.

Matte returned to his right halfback position for most of the second half. While sophomore quarterback Jack Wallace was unable to consistently move the Buckeyes, Duke scored twice to take a 13-7 lead. As Ohio State took possession at its own 37 with just over four minutes remaining, Hayes made his move and shifted Matte to quarterback.

In almost magical style, Matte courageously responded by driving his team 63 yards in nine plays for the winning score. Interestingly, the touchdown came on a fourth-down 22-yard rollout pass from Matte to end Chuck Bryant. Dave Kilgore converted to give Ohio State its one-point, come-from-behind win. Matte, a junior, continued at both positions throughout the 1959 season. He became Ohio State's starting quarterback the following year and was selected All-Big Ten at that position.

'68 OPENER HINT OF SUPERB SEASON

Ohio State opened its 1968 football season with great excitement and high expectations. The outstanding freshman class recruited by Hayes and his staff in 1967 was finally ready for its first taste of varsity competition (freshmen did not become eligible for varsity status until 1972). Additionally, the Buckeyes had finished their 1967 campaign with four consecutive wins including a 24-14 victory over Michigan in Ann Arbor.

The Buckeyes opened at home on September 28 against Southern Methodist. The visitors were coached by Hayden Fry, who was starting his seventh season with the Mustangs. Ohio State was aiming for its first Big Ten title since 1961 and its first Rose Bowl appearance since the 1957 season.

Ohio State started five seniors, eight juniors, and nine sophomores. The offensive line was anchored around senior center John Muhlbach and junior guards Alan Jack and Tom Backhus. Seniors Dave Foley and converted tight end Rufus Mayes started at the tackles and both would become All-Americans this season. The tight end and split end positions were filled by sophomores Jan White and Bruce Jankowski.

In the backfield, sophomore Rex Kern earned the quarter-

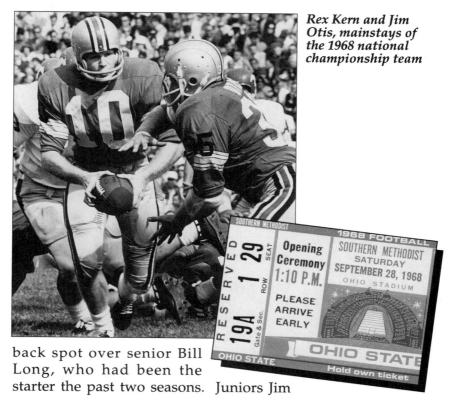

Rex Kern and Jim Otis, mainstays of the 1968 national championship team

back spot over senior Bill Long, who had been the starter the past two seasons. Juniors Jim Otis and Dave Brungard returned at fullback and left halfback while sophomore John Brockington started at the right halfback slot.

Defensively, sophomore Mark Debevec and junior Mike Radtke opened at the ends, juniors Paul Schmidlin and Brad Nielsen returned at the tackles and sophomore Jim Stillwagon edged veteran Vic Stottlemeyer at middle guard. The linebackers were seniors Mark Stier and Dirk Worden (team MVP in 1967). In the backfield, junior halfback Ted Provost was joined by three highly promising sophomores safety Mike Sensibaugh, cornerback Jack Tatum and halfback Tim Anderson.

Southern Methodist opened its season the previous Saturday with a 37-28 victory at Auburn where sophomore quarterback Chuck Hixson completed 28 of 40 passes. OSU assistant coach Esco Sarkkinen scouted the Mustangs and warned "They start passing when they get off the bus." The Buckeyes, ranked 15th nationally, entered the game as an 11-point favorite.

Southern Methodist moved the ball well on its first two

possessions but was unable to
score. Sensibaugh ended the first
threat intercepting a Hixson
pass at the OSU nine. On the
second drive, Bicky Lesser's 38-
yard field goal attempt was
wide right.

Ohio State's offense came
alive midway through the first
period with an 80-yard scoring

Ohio State's 62-0 season-
opening victory over Texas
Christian in 1969 was the
widest margin of victory for
any game during Woody
Hayes' 28 years as head
coach (276 games).

drive. Rex Kern went the final two yards untouched on an
option inside his right end. The drive's key play was a 44-yard
Kern-to-Brockington completion which moved the ball to the
SMU 27. Dick Merryman's conversion made it 7-0. Merryman, a
transfer from Miami (Ohio), had been with the team just nine
days.

Ohio State recovered SMU's fumble of the ensuing kickoff
and quickly moved 28 yards in seven plays to surge ahead 14-0.
Otis plunged over left tackle for the final eight-yards, carrying a
defender with him across the goal.

Hixson directed a 12-play, 70-yard scoring march early in
the second quarter to tighten things up at 14-7. Eleven passes
were thrown during the drive including an eight-yard strike to
end Ken Fleming for the TD. The scoring pass was a fine individual effort by Hixson who was almost trapped before zipping
the ball to Fleming as he was cutting across the end zone.

Next, versatile Dave Brungard exploded for two touchdowns to help give the Buckeyes a 26-7 halftime lead. His first
was a 41-yard sideline scamper to complete a three-play, 51-
yard drive, while his second came on an 18-yard pass from Kern
with just 35 seconds remaining in the half.

Kern's fine leadership ability become evident during this
last drive. With a fourth and ten at the SMU 41, he quickly
brought his team from the huddle while Hayes was trying to
send Sensibaugh in to punt. Kern made 15 yards on an exciting
option around right end to keep the drive alive. In his postgame
news conference, Hayes admitted it was one of the game's key
plays.

Southern Methodist put together three sustained drives to
start the second half. OSU's bend-but-don't break defense
stopped the first two with Mike Polaski recovering a fumble at

the OSU 19 and Stier intercepting a Hixson pass at the Ohio State two. But the Mustangs went the distance on their third possession with Hixson throwing six yards to Fleming to complete a 51-yard march and make it 26-14.

Southern Methodist nearly scored again early in the final period. Hixson drove his squad to the OSU 18 but the drive stalled on a fourth-and-eight play when Worden batted a pass at the Buckeye two. That series turned out to be the Mustangs' last threat. Hixson was later tackled by Debevec for a safety to increase OSU's lead to 28-14. Brungard then scored his third touchdown of the afternoon on a 20-yard pass play from Kern to make it 35-14.

The 73,855 fans in attendance had witnessed one of the most exciting (and offensive) openers in Ohio State history. With the two teams throwing 93 passes and running a total of 178 plays, the game lasted over three hours — at the time the longest in Ohio Stadium history.

Southern Methodist threw 76 passes (69 by Hixson and seven by back-up Gary Carter), completing 40 for 437 yards. It was the most passes ever thrown by one team in an NCAA game until Houston threw 78 (completing 46) against Arizona State on September 23, 1989. But Ohio State intercepted five of Hixson's tosses deep in Buckeye territory, ending drives at the OSU 12, 19, 18, 2 and 20.

OSU players presented the game ball to teammate Radtke, whose wife gave birth to twins during the game. Fry's Mustangs finished their 1968 season with a fine 8-3 record losing only to Texas and Arkansas. This opening game win over Southern Methodist was the beginning of one of the most successful seasons in Ohio State history. The Buckeyes became national champions, and concluded the season at 10-0 with a 27-16 Rose Bowl triumph over Southern California.

Ohio State opened at home in 1973 by overpowering Minnesota 56-7. Archie Griffin and Neal Colzie provided plenty of long range fireworks with Griffin scoring on a 93-yard kickoff return and Colzie on a 78-yard punt return. Junior fullback Harold "Champ" Henson, who led the nation in scoring the previous year, scored three times from close range. Sophomore Cornelius Greene played like a veteran at quarterback, directing the Buckeyes to touchdowns on four of their first six possessions.

NEW ERA BEGINS

The September 8, 1979, opener with Syracuse marked the first Ohio State game in 29 seasons without Hayes on the sidelines. The Buckeyes looked impressive, building a 21-0 halftime lead on the way to a convincing 31-8 triumph over the Orangemen. Greeting an over crowded room of newsmen after the game, coach Earle Bruce related he was a little relieved that the first game was a victory.

The first Buckeye to score for a Bruce-coached team was 6'8" tight end Ron Barwig on an 11 yard pass from Art Schlichter. Cornerback Mike Guess earned Big Ten Defensive Player of the Week honors with 11 tackles and a fumble recovery. Ohio State led 28-13 in first downs and 464-239 in total yards. The attendance of 86,205 was the 64th consecutive sellout in Ohio Stadium.

MOUNTAINEER OPENER PROVIDES EXCITEMENT

Fifth-ranked Ohio State relied heavily upon its defense to defeat neighboring West Virginia 24-3 in the 1987 opener. The game, played before a sellout crowd of 88,272, was just the fifth meeting between the two schools and the first since 1903. The Mountaineers had opened their season at Morgantown the previous Saturday with a 23-3 triumph over Ohio University.

Bruce arrived for the opening kickoff in a stylish gray suit, scarlet tie with gray O's and a light gray fedora. To everyone's surprise, Bruce had traded his normal coaching attire for a black suit and fedora at the Cotton Bowl the previous season. A pregame moment of silence was accorded the late Woody Hayes, who had passed away March 12.

West Virginia committed three turnovers on its first three plays to help Ohio State jump out to a quick 17-0 first quarter lead. Place-kicker Matt Frantz opened the scoring with a 47-yard field goal, at the time the longest of his career. Next, tailback Jaymes Bryant sped seven yards over right guard to cap a three-play, 21-yard drive. Later in the period, quarterback Tom Tupa drove the Bucks 65 yards with the touchdown coming on a 23-yard pass to flanker Everett Ross.

The Buckeyes' offense was dormant the next two periods. West Virginia made it 17-3 after three on a 27-yard field goal by Charlie Baumann. In the final quarter, William White scored on a 29-yard interception return with just over three minutes remaining. It was White's third interception of the afternoon, tying an OSU single-game record. Frantz's third conversion concluded the scoring at 24-3.

OSU's defense came up with six interceptions, just two short of the school single-game record of eight against Chicago in 1938. Linebacker Chris Spielman was as intense as ever with 19 tackles and two inter-

ceptions. Tupa, starting his first game at quarterback, had four punts of 60 or more yards.

Coach John Cooper's first game at Ohio State was an excellent 26-9 victory over Syracuse in the 1988 opener before an Ohio Stadium crowd of 89,768. The win snapped Syracuse's unbeaten streak at 14 games, which at the time was the nation's longest.

Quarterback Greg Frey made his first start a good one, completing 12 of 17 passes for 141 yards and one touchdown. After spotting Syracuse a 3-0 first quarter lead, Ohio State came back to lead 17-6 at the half and 23-6 after three quarters. For the first time since 1961, the Buckeyes did not have a penalty or commit a turnover. Kicker Pat O'Morrow had a fine day with four field goals, just one short of the school record held by Bob Atha.

Ohio State vs. Illinois

Highest Score in Series
Ohio State: 51-15 (1962, Champaign)
Illinois: 46-0 (1904, Columbus)

Highest Margin of Victory in Series
Ohio State: 44 points (44-0, 1961, Columbus)
Illinois: 46 points (46-0, 1904, Columbus)

Buckeyes' Most Significant Win
Trailing 24-0 early in the second quarter, Ohio State rallied to conquer Illinois 45-38 in the 1984 homecoming game. Tailback Keith Byars led the comeback, setting a school single-game rushing record with 274 yards in 39 carries and tying another school record with five touchdowns. The Buckeyes went on to become outright conference champions.

Buckeyes' Most Devastating Loss
Illinois dropkicked a 25-yard field goal with just eight seconds remaining to defeat Ohio State 9-7 in the final game of 1919. The loss denied the Buckeyes the conference championship and also marked the only defeat during Chic Harley's three illustrious seasons at Ohio State.

3. The Illinois Series

ILLINI'S 'FIGHT' ORIGINATED IN COLUMBUS

Ask any college football fan, "What is Ohio State's longest continuous series?" The likely reply would be "Ohio State and Michigan." The Buckeyes and Wolverines have met each season since 1918 in one of college football's strongest rivalries. But the Ohio State-Illinois series is even longer as the two have met each year since 1914 in what is the longest continuous series in all of Ohio State football. The two schools also played in 1902 and 1904.

Ohio State has a commanding lead in the series at 51-25-4 through 1991. The Illini prevailed throughout the early years allowing Ohio State only five triumphs during the first 18 games. The Buckeyes then went 43-8-2 over the next 53 seasons from 1930-'82. But recently the pendulum has swung back, with Illinois winning six of the last nine including the last four games.

Over the years, Ohio State has fared better at Champaign than in Columbus. The Buckeyes are 23-14-4 (61 percent) at home and 28-11 (71.8 percent) as the visitor. Ohio State's highest score against Illinois came during a 51-15 blowout at Champaign in 1962. The Buckeyes established a school single-game rushing record that afternoon with 517 yards (this record was tied in 1974, also against the Illini). Fullback Bob Ferguson's four touchdowns led Ohio State to a 44-0 win in 1961 — it is the Bucks' largest margin of victory in the series. Illinois' highest score was 46-0 in 1904 when touchdowns counted five points and field goals four.

Ohio State's first victory over Illinois propelled the Buckeyes to their first undefeated-untied season and first Big Ten title in 1916. With Illinois leading 6-0 in the game's final minute, sophomore halfback Chic Harley dramatically led the charge. With the ball at the Illinois 12, Harley went back to pass, then headed for the north sideline and desperately dove over the goal at the corner of the field to tie the game 6-6.

The famous shoes used by Chic Harley to kick the winning extra point in 1916 were given to him by his close friend, Joe Mulbarger, a former captain at East High School. The "block-toed" shoes had been made especially for kicking.

It was a rainy afternoon in Champaign and Harley's shoes were covered with mud. He went to the bench, put on a dry pair of shoes then calmly dropkicked the extra point to secure the Buckeyes a 7-6 triumph. Sportswriters called it "the most important victory during Ohio State's first 27 seasons of football." It was Illinois' first conference loss in three seasons.

HARLEY'S FINAL GAME

The Illini would return the favor. Harley was playing his last collegiate game against Illinois in Columbus in 1919 and the winner would capture the Big Ten crown. Nearly 17,000 fans jammed every inch of available space at Ohio Field and Athletic Director L. W. St. John estimated 50,000 tickets could have been sold. Halfback Ed Sternaman scored on a 50-yard run around end to give Illinois a 6-0 lead at halftime. Ohio State fans went wild late in the third period after Harley scored from the eight and kicked the extra point to give the Buckeyes a 7-6 lead.

Trailing by a point, Illinois faced a do-or-die situation taking possession at its own 20 with just two minutes remaining . Several Lawrence Walquist-to-Chuck Carney passes moved the ball to the Ohio State 20 as the clock ticked down. With just eight seconds remaining, sophomore Bobby Fletcher dropkicked a 25-yard field goal to give the Illini the verdict 9-7. It was Fletcher's very first field goal attempt — he was substituting for his older brother, Ralph, who was injured and unable to attempt the kick. This defeat was Ohio State's only loss during Harley's three glorious years with the Buckeyes.

The 1920 contest at Champaign provided a much happier locker room walk for Ohio State. Again the winner would capture the conference title — Ohio State was undefeated while Illinois had lost only once, to Wisconsin, the previous Saturday. The Illini played six conference games in 1920 and the Buckeyes played five. This afternoon also featured the very first college "Dad's Day" celebration.

It had been a very cold, nerve racking afternoon with each team holding the other inside the one-yard line to keep the game scoreless. The Buckeyes had the ball at the Illini 37 with just four seconds remaining and everyone expected Ohio State to attempt its highly successful passing combination of quarterback Hoge Workman to halfback Pete Stinchcomb. Workman dropped back to throw while the Illini covered Stinchcomb like a blanket, leaving end Cyril "Truck" Myers all alone. Workman threw to Myers who caught the ball at the 10 and scored untouched. Stinchcomb kicked the extra point and the Buckeyes pulled it out 7-0 in one of the most dramatic finishes possible.

THE "FIGHTING" ILLINI

The 1921 game produced one of college football's biggest upsets. It was the season's last game and the last collegiate contest played at old Ohio Field along High Street. Powerful Ohio State entered the game 4-0 in league play having shutout all four Big Ten opponents by a combined score of 76-0. A win would assure the Buckeyes at least a share of the 1921 Big Ten title. Illinois had lost all four of its league games having been outscored 51-8. The Illini had not scored a touchdown in these four games.

Illinois pulled off the impossible that afternoon, winning 7-0. Illinois coach Bob Zuppke used only 11 players in the game while OSU coach John Wilce used all 33 of his players in an attempt to wear down his opponent.

Sportswriter Harvey Woodruff, covering the game for the Chicago Tribune, was so impressed with the play of the Illini, he referred to them in his Sunday column as the "Fighting Illini." The name stuck and they have been known as the "Fighting Illini" ever since their monumental upset of Ohio State in 1921.

GRANGE'S LAST GAME A HORSESHOE CLASSIC

Ohio State's 1925 season-ending Homecoming clash with Illinois created an all-time demand for tickets and press box space. Sportswriters from across the country were flocking to

Columbus for the final collegiate appearance of Illinois' Harold "Red" Grange, one of the game's all-time greats. Among the notables were Grantland Rice of the *New York Tribune* and Joe Corcornn of the *Chicago American*.

Grange had made football history the previous season by leading Illinois to a 39-14 win over a Michigan team which had not lost in three years. In the game's first 12 minutes, he scored four touchdowns on runs of 95, 67, 56 and 44 yards.

The Ohio Stadium paid attendance of 84,295 was (at the time) the largest crowd to ever attend a sporting event in this country. Over 100 fans unable to purchase tickets spent Friday evening in the stadium's amphitheater before being removed Saturday morning by watchmen. Approximately 40 boys cleared the fences using a homemade "rope ladder." The athletic department announced 10,000 general admission tickets would go on sale one-half hour prior to kickoff — fans began assembling Friday evening and by noon Saturday, five lines stretched from Ohio Stadium's southeast corner to Neil Avenue.

Since each team had already lost two conference games, neither was in contention for the league title. Interestingly, both captains, Grange and OSU's Harold "Cookie" Cunningham, wore jersey No. 77. The Buckeyes gave their finest effort of the season before losing 14-9. Grange's all-around play definitely

made the difference as he electrified the crowd each time he touched the ball. His running set up a two-yard touchdown by fullback Earl Britton to put the visitors on top 7-0 early in the first quarter.

Ohio State scored a second-quarter safety when Illini center Robert Reistch missed a signal and centered the ball over his own goal. Later that quarter, Grange completed a 60-yard drive by throwing a 13-yard scoring toss to end Charles Kassell to give the Illini a 14-2 lead at

Illinois legend Red Grange removes his jersey for the last time

From 1919-33, the Ohio State-Illinois contest was the last game of the regular season for both teams. Ohio State and Michigan began the tradition of meeting in the season's final game in '35.

intermission.

The Buckeyes really made a game of it in the second half. Quarterback Windy Wendler passed 22 yards to halfback Elmer Marek, who beautifully sidestepped two defenders and dove across the goal to bring Ohio State within five late in the third period. But in the end, it was Grange's defensive play which made the difference. In the final quarter, he returned an interception 42 yards from his own 20 to end a threat. Two minutes later, Grange made another interception at midfield on the game's final play — a fitting conclusion to one of the most celebrated careers in all of college football.

Wilce was extremely proud of his team's play. His Buckeyes had given their best effort against one of the finest runners the sport has ever known.

Three-time All-American Wesley Fesler closed out his brilliant career by leading Ohio State to a 12-9 victory at Illinois in 1930. Normally an end, Fesler was shifted to fullback where his passing led to both Ohio State touchdowns. The Buckeyes had been shutout by the Illini the three previous seasons.

Illinois dealt Ohio State its only loss 14-13 during coach Francis Schmidt's first season in 1934. Trailing 14-0, the Buckeyes rallied for two fourth-quarter touchdowns but missed the first conversion attempt. The defeat prevented Ohio State from sharing the 1934 conference title with Minnesota.

WAR MOVES GAMES TO CLEVELAND

The 1942 and '44 games (both Illinois home games) were moved to Cleveland with very active support from the local alumni associations of both schools. Both became key Ohio State victories during championship seasons. The Buckeyes won 44-20 on November 14, 1942, and went on to capture the school's first national title with a 9-1 record.

Ohio State was victorious 26-12 on November 18, 1944, and earned the "national civilian championship" the following week after defeating Michigan, 18-14, to finish the year at 9-0.

The '44 game drew a Cleveland Municipal Stadium record

crowd of 83,627. The previous high was 80,184 when the Cleveland Indians dedicated the stadium in 1932. It also was the largest crowd to see a football game anywhere in 1944. A special radio booth was constructed for NBC's Bill Stern who broadcast the game nationally and to servicemen overseas.

It was a fine homecoming for Les Horvath and Bob Brugge, who both had grown up in suburban Parma. Brugge stunned Illinois when he unleashed his first collegiate pass, a 48-yard TD throw to end Jack Dugger for OSU's second score. The defense held Illini speedster Buddy Young to just 61 yards in ten carries. Tackle Bill Willis made one of the game's most exciting plays, catching Young from behind to prevent an apparent touchdown. Guard Bill Hackett was excellent on defense making tackles all over the field.

THE "FIFTH QUARTER" GAME

The 1943 contest at Ohio Stadium produced one of the most unusual endings in all of college football. With the game tied 26-26 and the ball at the Illinois 18, Ohio State quarterback Bobby McQuade threw an incomplete pass into the end zone on the game's last play. Both teams headed to their dressing rooms and most fans left the stadium with the understanding the game had ended in a tie. However, Illinois had been offside on the final down but few (including the other officials) had seen head linesman Paul Goebel signal the infraction. Coach Paul Brown was in the locker room delivering his post-game speech when he was informed his team would have "one additional down."

Nearly 20 minutes after McQuade's pass had fallen dead in the end zone, both teams returned to the playing field for one

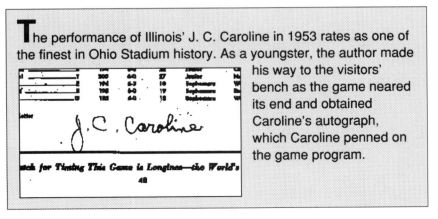

The performance of Illinois' J. C. Caroline in 1953 rates as one of the finest in Ohio Stadium history. As a youngster, the author made his way to the visitors' bench as the game neared its end and obtained Caroline's autograph, which Caroline penned on the game program.

final play. Sophomore Johnny Stungis then kicked a 33-yard field goal to give Ohio State a 29-26 "fifth quarter" victory. It was the first (and only) field goal attempt of Stungis' career.

Woody Hayes was 22-4-2 against Illinois and his teams won 13 of 14 in Champaign. His first squad in 1951 played the Illini to a scoreless tie, the only blemish on the Illinois schedule that season.

Ray Eliot's team routed the Buckeyes 41-20 in 1953 as two sophomore halfbacks, J. C. Caroline and Mickey Bates, teamed to provide one of the most explosive offensive performances ever witnessed in Ohio Stadium. The two ran the halfback counter play to perfection as Caroline rushed for 192 yards and two touchdowns and Bates scampered for 147 yards and four six-pointers. If anything, the setback was even more one-sided than indicated by the final score. Caroline had a long touchdown run called back by an offside penalty and the Illini blew another scoring opportunity losing a fumble on the Ohio State one yard line.

BUCKEYES STUN BUTKUS-LED ILLINI

With almost flawless coordination between its vibrant offense and conquering defense, fourth-ranked Ohio State

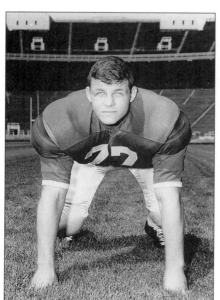

1964 team MVP Ed Orazen

shutout second-ranked Illinois 26-0 in 1964. It was one of Hayes' most impressive wins. The game was played at Champaign before a stunned Homecoming crowd of 71,227, the largest (at the time) to see a Big Ten game at Memorial Stadium. The Buckeyes had been six-point underdogs to the defending Big Ten champions whose returning starters included linebacker Dick Butkus and fullback Jim Grabowski.

The Buckeyes scored on their very first play from scrimmage with quarterback Don Unverferth bootlegging

24 yards on an option play around left end. The touchdown was set up when defensive back John Fill returned his first collegiate interception 47 yards to the Illini 24.

In the second period, fullback Will Sander plunged over from the one to cap an 84-yard march. The drive's big gainer was a 49-yard completion from Unverferth to end Bob Stock on first down from the OSU 16. Later in the quarter, Bob Funk connected on a 29-yard field goal to increase the lead to 16-0 at half-time.

Sander's four-yard touchdown run made it 23-0 in the third quarter. The score was set up when end Bill Spahr intercepted Fred Custardo's pass at the Illini 35. Funk's second field goal of the game in the fourth quarter concluded the scoring at 26-0.

Seldom has an Ohio State team been as well-prepared to play. A devastating pass rush led by Spahr, tackle Ed Orazen, guard Bill Ridder and linebacker Ike Kelley kept Custardo off-balance all afternoon. Hayes' diversified offense tied together his customary rushing attack with a more varied passing attack. Ohio State even used two tackle-eligible plays with Jim Davidson catching two passes for 37 yards.

Illinois never came closer to the red zone than the Ohio State 31. Coach Pete Elliott, who had been an All-American quarterback at Michigan in 1948, labeled the Buckeyes "as good as any Ohio State team I've ever seen."

The 1968 Buckeyes played their first road game at Illinois after opening with four wins in the friendly confines of Ohio Stadium. With Ohio State leading 24-0, the Illini opened with a new spread offense scoring three times and adding three two-point conversions to tie it at 24-24 late in the final period. Quarterback Ron Maciejowski then drove the Bucks 70 yards for the winning score, a four-yard burst by Otis. The key play of the drive was a 44-yard completion from Maciejowski to wingback Larry Zelina. Ohio State had won a tough one 31-24 and went on to capture the '68 national title.

The Illinois squad threatened to boycott the 1970 contest after their coach Jim Valek was fired the day before the game. Ohio State was given quite a struggle from the inspired Illini before winning 48-29.

Illinois was primed for an upset at Champaign in 1973 as both teams sported 4-0 conference records. With each team playing well defensively, Ohio State had to settle for a precarious 3-0 lead at halftime on a 25-yard field goal by Blair Conway. The Buckeye offense got on track in the second half as Archie Griffin scored from the one to boost the lead to 10-0 after three quarters. Cornelius Greene added two more scores in the fourth before freshman fullback Pete Johnson concluded the scoring with his first career touchdown. The final score was 30-0 as Ohio State's defense had held the Illini to 74 yards in total offense.

WOODY NOTCHES 200TH VICTORY

Griffin rushed for 146 yards to establish an NCAA record with 18 consecutive regular-season games of 100 or more yards during Ohio State's 49-7 triumph over the Illini at Ohio Stadium in 1974. The game also marked Hayes' 200th career victory which included 19 at Denison and 14 at Miami (Ohio) before coming to Columbus in 1951.

Ohio State had little trouble winning 40-3 at Illinois the following season. Griffin rushed for 130 yards giving him 30 consecutive games of rushing for more than 100 yards. Tom Skladany set a school record with a 59-yard field goal while Johnson set a Big Ten record with his 21st touchdown of the season breaking the record of 20 set by OSU's Champ Henson in 1972.

Earle Bruce was 7-2 against Illinois. His 1980 Buckeyes outscored the Illini 49-42 in one of the wildest games ever staged in the horseshoe. Ohio State jumped to a 28-0 advantage then almost let it get away as Illini quarterback Dave Wilson completed 43 of 69 passes for 621 yards and all six touchdowns. Art Schlichter had a pretty fair day himself, connecting on 17 of

Ohio State's 45-7 win over Illinois on November 11, 1978, was Woody Hayes' last victory in Ohio Stadium. Ironically, the Illini were coached by Gary Moeller, one of his 1962 co-captains and later head coach of the Michigan Wolverines.

21 tosses for 284 yards and four of the Buckeyes' seven TDs. The two teams combined for 91 points, 53 first downs and 1,057 yards of total offense.

BYARS LEADS GREAT COMEBACK

Bruce called it "the greatest comeback after the worst start I've ever been associated with." Down 24-0 early in the second period, the Buckeyes rallied to conquer Illinoi 45-38, in one of the most exciting games in the series. Junior tailback Keith Byars led the resurgence setting a school single-game rushing record with 274 yards in 39 carries. He scored five touchdowns to tie a school record established by Johnson during OSU's 32-7 win over North Carolina in 1975.

The game was played before a homecoming crowd of 89,973 — at the time, the second largest in stadium history. The two rivals were fighting for survival in the Big Ten title chase. The Illini entered with an overall record of 4-2 and 3-1 in the conference while eighth-ranked Ohio State was 4-1 and 2-1,

Buckeye Keith Byars gained a school-record 274 yards in 1984

after losing at Purdue the previous Saturday.

The Buckeyes were still smarting from a devastating 17-13 loss at Champaign in 1983. Illini quarterback Jack Trudeau had driven his team 83 yards for the

winning score with less than two minutes remaining. The setback eliminated the Bucks from title contention while Illinois went on to capture its first Big Ten championship in 20 seasons. It had been the Illini's first win over Ohio State since 1967.

Midway through the first quarter, Illinois took a 7-0 lead on a three-yard pass from Jack Trudeau to wide receiver Randy Grant. The Illini had driven 80 yards in 11 plays with the big gainer being a 38-yard gallop to the OSU five by fullback Thomas Rooks. On their next possession, Mike White booted a 26-yard field goal to increase the lead to ten.

Following the ensuing kickoff, quarterback Mike Tomczak took to the air on first down but the Illini's Mike Heaven intercepted and returned the errant pass to the OSU 21. From there it took Trudeau just four plays to increase the visitors' lead to 17-0. The touchdown was scored by split end David Williams on a nine-yard aerial from Trudeau. Williams had entered the game as the nation's leading receiver with 53 catches for 793 yards.

For Ohio State, it only got worse before it got better. Byars fumbled on first down, and safety Craig Swoope recovered for Illinois at the OSU 21. Six plays later, Trudeau connected with tight end Cap Bosco for an eight-yard touchdown and the Illini held a 24-0 lead just 13 seconds into the second quarter. Sportswriters were quickly reviewing their press guides to determine if Ohio State's "most one-sided loss in Ohio Stadium" might be in the making.

Ohio State finally began to move on its next possession but the drive stalled at the Illini 13 when a fourth-down pass fell

Octber 13 marked the date of Ohio State's gigantic 45-38 triumph over Illinois in 1984. Exactly 50 years earlier on October 13, 1934, Illinois defeated Ohio State 14-13 at Champaign. It was the only loss that season for the Buckeyes of first-year coach Francis Schmidt, and it prevented them from sharing the Big Ten title with Minnesota.

incomplete. After forcing Illinois to punt, the Bucks took over at their own nine and drove 91 yards in six plays for their first score with 4:13 remaining before halftime. Byars scored the touchdown from the 16. The drive's longest gainer was a 36-yard pass from Tomczak to freshman split end Cris Carter.

The Illini's Craig Swoope was ejected from the game following a flagrant dead-ball personal foul on the touchdown. Many observers felt this was the game's turning point — with the 15-yard penalty assessed on the ensuing kickoff, Ohio State decided on an onside kick from the Illini 45. Linebacker Joe Jenkins recovered for the Buckeyes at the Illini 31. On second down, Tomczak connected with Carter for a 30-yard touchdown, and Ohio State had scored twice within a span of 50 seconds. Rich Spangler's second conversion made it 24-14 and the Buckeyes were back in the ballgame.

Roverback Sonny Gordon set up Ohio State's next touchdown with a diving interception of a Trudeau pass at the OSU 38. Ten plays later, Byars dove four yards into the end zone to cut the Illini lead to 24-21 with just 23 seconds left before halftime.

Illinois' Ray Wilson fumbled the second half kickoff after being hit hard by Steve Hill. William White recovered and the Buckeyes were back in business at the Illini 26. Byars carried on four consecutive plays for his third touchdown as Ohio State took the lead at 28-24. The Illini came right back with a 46-yard Chris White field goal to cut OSU's lead to one.

But the Buckeyes kept right on charging. Byars scored his fourth touchdown on a 67-yard jaunt down the east sideline into the stadium's closed end to widen the lead to 35-27. The big tailback never broke stride, even after losing his left shoe near the Illini 40.

Illinois retaliated with a 63-yard scoring march capped by a nine-yard TD toss from Trudeau to Ray Wilson. Trudeau then rolled right for a two-point conversion to tie the game at 35 with 1:09 remaining in the third quarter.

The two weary opponents traded field goals in the final period. First, Spangler hit from 47 yards at the 10:21 mark. Later, Chris White booted a 16-yarder on a fourth-and- goal from the OSU one with just 3:18 remaining.

For the Buckeyes, it was now or never. After nearly 57 minutes of play and almost 1,000 yards in combined offense, the score was tied at 38. Ohio State met the challenge going 80 yards in 11 plays with Byars scoring the clincher from the three with just 36 seconds remaining. Spangler's fifth PAT made it 45-38 as fans had witnessed one of the most explosive and exciting games in all of Big Ten football.

Trudeau completed 32 of 52 passes for 313 yards and all four Illini touchdowns. Illinois led in first downs 27-23 and Ohio State led in total offensive yardage 564-509. The Buckeyes went on to win the '84 Big Ten title with a 7-2 league record and an overall mark of 9-3. Illinois finished at 7-4 overall and tied Purdue for second place with a 6-3 conference record.

Ohio State vs. Illinois

DECADE	W	L	T	POINTS OSU	ILL
1890	0	0	0	0	0
1900	0	1	1	0	46
1910	2	3	1	30	68
1920	3	7	0	29	94
1930	9	1	0	166	43
1940	8	2	0	230	141
1950	6	3	1	187	116
1960	7	2	1	297	107
1970	10	0	0	383	80
1980	6	4	0	245	247
1990	0	2	0	27	41
TOTAL	**51**	**25**	**4**	**1,594**	**983**

Ohio State at Home: 23-14-4
Ohio State on the Road: 28-11-0

Ohio State vs. Indiana

Highest Score in Series

Ohio State: 56-0 (1957, Columbus)
56-17 (1983, Bloomington)
Indiana: 41-7 (1988, Bloomington)

Highest Margin of Victory in Series

Ohio State: 56 points (56-0, 1957, Columbus)
Indiana: 34 points (41-7, 1988, Bloomington)

Buckeyes' Most Significant Win

Ohio State's 32-21 victory in the second game of 1942 propelled Paul Brown's Buckeyes to the Big Ten championship and the school's first national title.

Buckeyes' Most Devastating Loss

Indiana's 10-0 upset in 1937 cost coach Francis Schmidt's Buckeyes the Big Ten title. It was Ohio State's's only conference loss that season.

4. The Indiana Series

HAYES ASSISTANT REVIVES PROGRAM IN BLOOMINGTON

*I*ndiana University is no longer the doormat of the Big Ten Conference. The once lightly-regarded Hoosiers are 2-2-1 during their last five games with Ohio State (1987-1991), having outscored the Buckeyes 146-99. Their 41-7 win at Bloomington in 1988 is IU's highest score and largest margin of victory during the 69 games between the two schools.

Ohio State leads the overall series by a very comfortable margin of 52-12, with five ties. Fifty of the 69 games have been played in Columbus and four of Indiana's 12 victories came from 1901-05. Since joining the Big Ten in 1913, the Buckeyes' record against IU is 52-8-4. Interestingly, OSU's very first conference game was against Indiana at old Ohio Field on November 1, 1913, with the Hoosiers winning 7-6.

LOSS DENIES OSU LEAGUE CROWN

Indiana handed Ohio State its only con-

*N*ovember 4, 1933, was a disappointing day across the board for the Indiana Hoosiers. Bob Terry, student conductor of the Indiana Marching Band, recalls the truck carrying the band instruments broke down and did not reach Ohio Stadium until late in the second half, forcing the band to perform its halftime show after the game. Sophomores Dick Heekin, Stan Pincura and John Kabealo each scored touchdowns to help Ohio State defeat Indiana 21-0.

ference loss of the season, 10-0, at Ohio Stadium on November 6, 1937. The Buckeyes took the opening kickoff and drove 94 yards to the IU 1, only to lose possession on a fumble. The spirited Hoosiers then took charge, and Ohio State never again threatened. In the third quarter, Indiana quarterback Frank Filchock passed 12 yards to end Frank Petrick for the game's only touchdown. It was the first time in four seasons Ohio State had been shutout in league play.

This defeat cost Ohio State the '37 Big Ten title. The Buckeyes finished 5-1 in the conference, behind Minnesota at 5-0. It was the first time one of coach Francis Schmidt's squads had been defeated by more than a touchdown since Schmidt took over at Ohio State in 1934.

'42 WIN PAVES WAY FOR FIRST NATIONAL TITLE

Indiana invaded Ohio Stadium with one of its finest teams of all-time in 1942. Coached by the crafty "Bo" McMillan, the

Just a sophomore in '42, Gene Fekete became the first Buckeye to finish in the top ten in the Heisman Trophy balloting

Hoosiers featured two fine players in triple-threat back Billy Hillenbrand and linebacker Lou Saban, who that season was Indiana's MVP. Saban later spent many seasons as a coach in the college and professional ranks.

Ohio State outlasted the Hoosiers 32-21, with the lead changing hands five times. Indiana led 21-19 after three quarters. But on this hot October afternoon with the temperature in the low 90s, OSU's superior physical condition made the difference in the final quarter. Fullback Gene Fekete had a big day, scoring three of the Bucks' five touchdowns.

Coach Paul Brown called the contest "the greatest game I ever saw." Brown had substituted liberally because of the heat, and was extremely proud of his second and third stringers. This 1942 team went on to capture the school's first national title with an overall record of 9-1. The Hoosiers finished the season at 7-3.

Indiana handed first-year coach Woody Hayes a stunning 32-10 upset at Ohio Stadium on October 20, 1951. The Buckeyes lost four fumbles and tossed one interception, setting up three of Indiana's five touchdowns. Left-handed IU quarterback Lou D'Achille threw for two first-period touchdowns and kept the Buckeyes off balance with his pin-point passing. It was the only game Hayes would lose to Indiana, and it would be 36 years before the Hoosiers would again defeat Ohio State.

ENTER "HOPALONG" CASSADY

The Buckeyes opened the 1952 campaign with a 33-13 triumph over Indiana in one of the most celebrated openers in all of Ohio State football. In his first collegiate game, freshman Howard "Hopalong" Cassady scored three touchdowns and thrilled the sun-bathed Ohio Stadium crowd of 70,208 with his spirited running and pass receiving. The 18-year-old Cassady, who weighed just 168 pounds, was a product of Columbus Central High School where he excelled in football, basketball and baseball.

Woody Hayes introduced a new offense in this game — the Split-T formation — and selected sophomore John Borton, a fine drop-back passer from Alliance to lead his new attack. The Buckeyes led 6-0 early in the first period when Borton connected with fearless Fred Bruney on a 15-yard scoring toss. The Hoosiers then went ahead 7-6 later in the quarter. Cassady's first touchdown came midway through the second quarter, with a leaping 27-yard reception from Bruney. Indiana came back to tie it up 13-13 at halftime.

The third period was scoreless as the Hoosiers of first-year coach Bernie Crimmins hung tough. But the heavier Buckeyes really took command with a 20-point fourth quarter. Cassady got his second TD on a five-yard sweep around left end to make it 20-13.

Indiana came right back and drove to the OSU 3 but the Bucks' defense stiffened and held on downs. The key play was tackle George Jacoby's eight-yard sack of Lou D'Achille. The Buckeyes then put it away with two more touchdowns: a 27-yard burst over right guard by fullback John Hlay, followed by Cassady's final score of the game from the IU 3.

Hayes offered great praise for his team's spirited effort and the play of Cassady, Bruney and end Bob Joslin. Cassady's performance was just the beginning of one of the most outstanding careers in Buckeye history. In four seasons, he would help Ohio State capture a national title, two undisputed Big Ten championships and three triumphs over Michigan.

BUCKEYES' LAST SCORELESS TIE

Ohio State's last scoreless tie was against Indiana at Ohio Stadium on November 7, 1959. The Buck-

eyes managed just 127 yards of offense and seven first downs, while IU gained only 179 yards and 11 first downs. Hoosier coach Phil Dickens argued that fullback Vic Jones scored a touchdown in the second quarter but the officials spotted the ball just inches short of the Ohio State goal line.

Halfback Paul Warfield raced 75 yards to give Ohio State a 7-0 halftime lead in the 1962 game. But the Buckeye offense

Arnold Chonko's three fourth-quarter interceptions paved the way to victory in 1964

had trouble the rest of the afternoon and IU quarterback Woody Moore tied the game 7-7 on a one-yard sneak in the second half. Ohio State finally won, 10-7, with placekicker Dick VanRaaphorst booting a 27-yard field goal with just eight seconds remaining.

Ohio State rode the passing arm of Don Unverferth and the pass defending ability of cornerback Arnie Chonko to hold off talented Indiana, 17-9, in 1964. Interestingly, both Unverferth and Chonko would become honor graduates of The Ohio State University School of Medicine.

Ohio State led 17-3 after three quarters but the final period belonged to Indiana. Starting at their own 26, the Hoosiers moved deep inside OSU territory before Chonko picked off a Rich Badar pass at the OSU 6 to end the threat. After a short punt gave Indiana possession at the Buckeyes' 33, Badar quickly engineered a drive to tighten things up at 17-9. IU's touchdown came on a five-yard pass from Badar to Rudolph Keuchenberg. Badar's attempted two-point conversion pass was intercepted by Don Harkins.

Taking over at the OSU 24 after holding the Bucks, Badar moved his squad the length of the field, only to be interrupted by Chonko's second interception of the quarter at the goal line. Indiana again held and regained possession at its own 47. Badar directed his team to a first down at the OSU 3 — a touchdown and two-point conversion would tie the game. But there again was Chonko, inter-

Indiana has won two Big Ten football titles — outright in 1945 and a three-way tie with Minnesota and Purdue in 1967. The Hoosiers and Buckeyes did not meet either of these seasons.

cepting a pass thrown into the flat with just 14 seconds remaining. Chonko, whose three interceptions tied an OSU single-game record, was awarded the game ball.

WOODY'S FINAL WIN

In one of the most exciting and evenly-played games between the two schools, Ohio State came from behind to nip Indiana, 21-18, in the next-to-last reg-

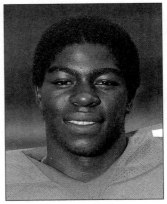

ular season game of 1978. The contest was played November 18 at Bloomington, with Woody Hayes' team at 6-2-1 overall and 5-1 in the conference. The Buckeyes had lost at Purdue earlier in the season and appeared to be out of Big Ten title contention until Purdue and Wisconsin battled to a 24-24 tie the previous Saturday. Ohio State realized a win over the Hoosiers coupled with a Michigan victory over Purdue that same afternoon would send the following week's Ohio State-Michigan winner to Pasadena — and that is exactly what occurred.

Mike Guess ended Indiana's comeback bid in 1978

Coach Lee Corso's Hoosiers were a better team than suggested by their 4-5 record. He had practiced his squad behind closed doors all week, in an attempt to register the school's first victory over the Buckeyes since 1951 — the Hoosiers were 0-21-1 in their last 22 meetings with Ohio State.

The Buckeyes took an early 7-0 lead, driving 83 yards in 13 plays on their very first possession. Fullback Paul Campbell scored the touchdown from the 4. On Ohio State's next possession, Hayes gambled and failed while attempting a fourth-and-one at the OSU 32. Indiana then went 32 yards in seven plays to tie the score, with Hoosier tailback Mike Harkrader plunging into the end zone from the 1.

The Buckeyes had great difficulty moving the ball the remainder of the first half. IU's David Freud kicked a 30-yard field goal in the second period to give the Hoosiers a 10-7 lead at halftime.

In the third quarter, Rickey Johnson and Ric Volley replaced an injured Campbell and Ron Springs at the running back positions. On their second possession of the quarter, the Buckeyes displayed one of Hayes' patented ball-control drives, moving 98 yards in 20 plays to take the lead at 14-10. Quarterback Art Schlichter scored the touchdown from the 3.

Early in the final period, Johnson raced 46 yards to increase OSU's lead to 21-10. Schlichter had caught Indiana in a nine-man front and Johnson had clear sailing into the end zone behind key blocks from wide receiver Rod Gerald and guard Ken Fritz. But the Hoosiers came right back, with sophomore quarterback Tim Clifford leading his team 72 yards in 14 plays for the score. A pass interference penalty against Ohio State advanced the ball to the 1. Tailback Darrick Burnett bolted across to cut the lead to five — Clifford then passed to Mike Friede in the corner of the end zone to make the score 21-18.

After forcing Ohio State to punt, the Hoosiers had one last opportunity for the upset. Pulling out all the stops, Corso called for a pass off an end-around-reverse, with split end Mike Friede throwing deep into Ohio State territory. But Mike Guess wasn't fooled, as he intercepted at the OSU 27-yard line to end Indiana's last threat with just 1:37 remaining.

A disappointed Corso was nevertheless extremely proud of his team's play. "We used everything we had," he said, "because we thought we had a shot at winning. We were going for the win all the way. Our game plan worked real well, but we just didn't have it at the end. We played the best we could and lost." The Hoosiers had used a number of reverses and even quick-kicked three times for 52, 66 and 76 yards.

As the game came to a close, Hayes had just coached his very last victory. Michigan would defeat Ohio State, 14-3, at Ohio Stadium the following week, and Hayes' coaching career would come to a close after a 17-15 loss to Clemson in the Gator Bowl. He had compiled a record of 205-61-10 during his 28 seasons at Ohio State, including 13 Big Ten titles and

Mike Harkrader, Indiana tailback from 1976-80, is the school's second all-time rushing leader with 3,257 yards. Harkrader's coach at Middletown (Ohio) Fenwick High School was his father, Jerry, who was a fine halfback under Woody Hayes and scored the final touchdown during Ohio State's 20-7 win over Southern California in the January 1, 1955, Rose Bowl.

three national championships (1954, 1957 and 1968).

Corso has fond memories of that afternoon in 1978 and of his association with Hayes. Corso's good friend, Al Carpenter, an avid Hoosier fan, attended all the games and most of IU's practices. Carpenter, who had cerebral palsy, watched most of the games from the IU bench.

During pre-game warm- ups in the '78 meeting, Carpenter asked Corso if it might be possible for him to meet Hayes. When the two head coaches met at mid- field, Corso told Hayes about Carpenter and recalls how Woody gladly went out of his way to talk with him. "It was heart-warming," Corso remembers. "He took such a sincere interest in speaking with Al and autographed his program. Al Carpenter couldn't have felt greater."

After Hayes finished, Carpenter graciously thanked Corso, who in turn kidded Carpenter by saying, "Al, I've known you for several years and you've never asked me for *my* autograph." "That's right, coach," a joyous Carpenter replied, "but then, you're not Woody Hayes!"

Corso also recalls when long-time Indiana assistant coach Howard Brown died in 1974, Hayes was the only other Big Ten coach to attend his funeral. Brown, a guard, had been selected the Hoosiers' most valuable player in 1945 and '47. A plaque recognizing Brown's dedication to Indiana football is proudly displayed in IU's Memorial Stadium.

Corso also remembers the day in 1982 when he was fired, following his 10th season with the Hoosiers. "Mrs. Anne Hayes was the very first person to call Betsy, my wife. Mrs. Hayes offered a lot of warmth and encouragement and wanted us to know it wasn't the end of the world. In our book, Woody and Anne Hayes were certainly two very special people."

It was the "Big Ten Game of the Week" when talented Indiana invaded Ohio Stadium to challenge the ninth-ranked Buckeyes on October 18, 1980. Ohio State and Indiana each entered the contest with 4-1 overall records, tops in the conference. Corso returned 39 lettermen from his '79 squad which went 8-4 for Indiana's first winning season since 1968.

Coach Earle Bruce's smoothly coordinated offense and defense combined for a 27-17 victory. Senior tailback Calvin Murray, who was celebrating his 22nd birthday, rushed for 224 yards and two touchdowns to lead the scarlet-and-gray attack. Murray's 224 yards is the fifth-highest single game total in Ohio State history.

Sophomore placekicker Matt Frantz's first collegiate kicks — three conversions and a key 43-yard field goal — paced the Buckeyes to a come-from-behind 24-22 win at Bloomington in 1986. Ironically, Frantz had won the job during practice that week and wasn't even listed on OSU's traveling roster.

Ohio State vs. Indiana

				POINTS	
DECADE	W	L	T	OSU	IND
1890	0	0	0	0	0
1900	0	4	1	28	60
1910	4	1	0	101	29
1920	2	1	1	27	12
1930	8	1	1	162	23
1940	5	2	0	151	68
1950	8	1	1	293	106
1960	7	0	0	124	40
1970	9	0	0	331	82
1980	8	2	0	335	208
1990	1	0	1	47	43
TOTAL	**52**	**12**	**5**	**1,599**	**671**

Ohio State at Home: 36-10-4
Ohio State on the Road: 16-2-1

Ohio State vs. Iowa

Highest Score in Series
Ohio State: 83-21 (1950, Columbus)
Iowa: 35-12 (1960, Iowa City)

Highest Margin of Victory in Series
Ohio State: 62 points (83-21, 1950, Columbus)
Iowa: 23 points (35-12, 1960, Iowa City)

Buckeyes' Most Significant Win
Ohio State defeated an excellent Iowa team 17-13 in the last home game of 1957 to capture the Big Ten title and eventually be selected national champions by the *UPI*. It was Iowa's only loss that season. The Buckeyes took possession at their own 32 with just 7:51 remaining in the game and Iowa leading 13-10. Sophomore fullback Bob White carried up the middle on seven of eight plays for 66 of the needed 68 yards and one of the most memorable touchdowns in Ohio State history.

Buckeyes' Most Devastating Loss
Iowa's 6-0 victory at Iowa City in 1956 snapped Ohio State's conference winning streak at 17 games, a league record. It eliminated any opportunity for the Buckeyes to capture a third consecutive outright Big Ten title, which instead was won that season by the Hawkeyes.

5. The Iowa Series

'50s MATCHUPS TRULY CLASSICS

Ohio State and Iowa have clashed 50 times through 1991 with the Buckeyes holding a commanding edge in the overall series at 34-12-3. The two first met in 1922 with Iowa winning 12-9 at Ohio Stadium. The Hawkeyes captured the Big Ten title that season with a record of 7-0. The two faced each other only 12 more times through 1949.

The Ohio State-Iowa games of the 1950s were some of the most significant of any decade in all of Ohio State football, starting with the memorable play of Vic Janowicz in the 1950 game at Ohio Stadium. It was truly one of the finest individual displays of talent in college football history. The Buckeyes won 83-21 before a Dads' Day crowd of 82,174, at the time the third largest in Ohio Stadium history. Sixth-ranked Ohio State was a three-touchdown favorite and entered the game at 3-1 while Iowa was 2-2. The Buckeyes had been introduced at an enthusiastic Friday evening pep rally by Ohio State football broadcaster Jack Buck, later the radio voice of NFL's Monday Night Football.

Janowicz kicked off ten yards beyond the end-zone line to start the game. Iowa's Jerry Faske fumbled on first down and Janowicz recovered at the Iowa 23. After the Buckeyes advanced the ball to the 11, Janowicz scored the game's first touchdown on a trap play through right guard. Janowicz kicked the extra point, making it 7-0 at the 13:05 mark.

Janowicz again kicked off beyond the end zone. After the Hawkeyes failed to register a first down, Glenn Drahn punted on fourth down. Janowicz took the punt on his own 39 near the east sideline, swirled to miss one tackler, dodged another, cut back and outran the others for his second touchdown. Veteran sportswriter Lew Byrer referred to Janowicz's return as "the finest bit of open field running I've seen since the days of Ohio State's Chic Harley (1919) and Illinois' Red Grange (1925)." Janowicz's second conversion increased the lead to 14 with 12:29 remaining in the first quarter.

Janowicz's kickoff again traveled well past the end zone. On second down, Hawkeye fullback Bill Reichardt's fumble was recovered by Janowicz at the Iowa 26. After Ohio State advanced to the 12, Janowicz fired a timing pass into the outstretched arms of Tony Curcillo for the Buckeyes' third touchdown.

1950 Heisman Trophy winner Vic Janowicz

Janowicz's extra point made it 21-0 with still 9:50 of the first period remaining.

Janowicz's game statistics included scoring two touchdowns, passing for four more and kicking ten extra points. He played very little in the second half as coach Wes Fesler emptied his bench for the fourth time that season. Bob Demmel's second-quarter touchdown on an 87-yard punt return is the longest in Ohio State history. Altogether, nine different players scored the Buckeyes' 12 touchdowns.

Ohio State's 83 points are the most scored by the Buckeyes in a Big Ten game. Also, the total of 104 points is the highest combined score of any game in conference history. Iowa's first touchdown was scored by halfback Bob Wilson. His father, John "Red" Wilson, lettered three seasons at Ohio State and scored the very first touchdown in Ohio Stadium against Oberlin on October 14, 1922.

21-POINT UNDERDOGS END TITLE HOPES

The Hawkeyes of first-year coach Forest Evashevski pulled off a major upset in 1952, defeating Ohio State 8-0 in Iowa City. For the three-touchdown underdog Hawkeyes, it was their first conference victory in two seasons and they were winless in their last ten games. Iowa led 2-0 at halftime and sealed the outcome with a touchdown early in the fourth period. Ohio State simply couldn't get its offense in gear, being held to 215 total yards including just 42 on the ground. A victory would have earned the Buckeyes the 1952 Big Ten title.

The 1954 contest was one of the most physical ever played between the two schools — it truly was a thriller to the very end. The Buckeyes were 3-0 and ranked fourth in the national polls and the 13th ranked Hawkeyes were 2-1. Iowa halfback Earl Smith, the Big Ten broad-jump champion, almost personally won the game for the Hawkeyes. Smith put Iowa on top 7-0 with a 67-yard interception return midway through the first quarter. But the Buckeyes came right back to tie, driving 61 yards with halfback Bobby Watkins getting the score.

In the second period, Ohio State ran its ground attack to perfection marching 72 yards with Dave Leggett scoring on a quarterback sneak. But early in the third quarter, Smith received a punt and weaved his way 75 yards to tie the game at 14-14. The Buckeyes regained the lead later that period with Leggett throwing 13 yards to end Dick Brubaker to cap a 64-yard drive. The score stood at 20-14 after the pass from center was fumbled on the all-important conversion attempt.

The Hawkeyes dominated the scoreless final period but simply couldn't put the ball in the end zone. With less than two minutes remaining, Ohio State preserved its perfect record by holding the Hawkeyes on downs inside the Ohio State 5-yard line. Woody Hayes' team, who went on to capture the national title with a 10-0 record, had survived its closest call of the season.

Ohio State beat another fine Iowa team 20-10 in the last home game of 1955. In his final Ohio Stadium appearance, Howard "Hopalong" Cassady carried for 169 yards and scored all three touchdowns. His first came on a 45-yard sprint off right tackle on his first carry of the afternoon. Cassady was jubilantly

The 1955 game featured the opposing play of the nation's two finest guards — Jim Parker of Ohio State and Calvin Jones of Iowa. Both were from Ohio (Parker-Toledo, Jones-Steubenville), both were consensus All-Americans, both would win the Outland Trophy (Jones-'55, Parker-'56) and both wore jersey No. 62.

carried off the field by his teammates much to the delight of the 82,701 spectators. The 1955 season was also the first year each home game drew more than 80,000 fans.

The Hawkeyes' 6-0 shutout of Ohio State in '56 may well have been the biggest win in all of Iowa football. The loss snapped the Buckeyes' conference winning streak at 17, longest in Big Ten history, and ruined Ohio State's opportunity to capture its third consecutive outright league title. After a scoreless first half, quarterback Kenny Ploen completed an 80-yard drive with a 17-yard third quarter TD toss to end Jim Gibbons for the game's only score. The hard-charging Hawkeyes, led by tackle Alex Karras, held Ohio State's falting attack to nine first downs and 147 yards in total offense.

The following Saturday, Iowa overwhelmed Notre Dame 48-8 while Ohio State lost to Michigan, leaving the Hawkeyes with the conference championship (their first since 1922). Iowa went on to its very first post-season bowl game, a 35-19 win over Oregon State in the Rose Bowl.

THE "WHITE BRIGADE"

The Ohio State campus was frantic the week prior to the November 16, 1957, clash between fifth-ranked Iowa and sixth-ranked Ohio State. The Hawkeyes were six-point favorites in

the game which would decide the Big Ten title. However, Buckeye spirits were somewhat dampened when it was learned halfback Don Clark would not play because of a leg injury suffered the previous week against Purdue.

Ohio State took an early 3-0 lead on a Don Sutherin field goal from the Iowa 15. Iowa came back to go ahead 6-3 on an eight-yard pass from Randy Duncan to end Bob Prescott. The Hawkeyes featured a flashy double-wing attack with multiple laterals and reverses.

Bob White gave visiting Vice President Richard Nixon a game to remember in '57

Ohio State drove 80 yards in the second quarter to take a 10-6 halftime lead. Frank Kremblas got the score on a one-yard quarterback sneak. The drive was highlighted by Kremblas' faking and ball handling and the powerful running of fullback Bob White. Iowa regained the lead in the third quarter 13-10, with Duncan scoring from the one to conclude a 70-yard drive.

Early in the final period, Iowa punted to Joe Cannavino who was downed at his own 32 at the stadium's north end. With just 7:51 remaining, the Buckeyes realized this might be their last chance. They were 68 yards away from the Big Ten title and a trip to Pasadena.

White plunged over right tackle for four yards and then over left guard for nine and a first down at the OSU 45. White next broke over right guard for 29 yards for a first down at the Iowa 26. By this time, the entire crowd was on its feet — the noise level was unbelievable.

Dick LeBeau carried for two, then White took it up the middle for six more. On third-and-two, White gained another ten for a first down at the Iowa eight. The powerful runner then hit the middle for three and followed it with a five-yard burst over left tackle for one of the biggest touchdowns in Ohio State history. White had carried on seven of the eight plays for 66 of the 68 yards.

Sutherin converted to end the scoring at 17-13. With just over three minutes remaining, Iowa mounted another drive but guard Bill Jobko ended the threat with a key interception at the Ohio State 32. Evashevski explained, "We knew what was happening but we were just powerless to stop it. It was fantastic." Most of the then-record crowd of 82,935, which included Vice President Richard Nixon, stayed long after the game to savor the win.

HAWKEYES COME BACK TO TIE FOUR TIMES

Iowa fielded one of its finest teams of all-time in 1958. The Hawkeyes defeated Oregon State 38-12 in the Rose Bowl to finish with an overall record of 7-1-1 and placed second to Louisiana State in the final *Associated Press* poll. Ohio State handed Iowa its only loss 38-28 in one of the most thrilling and dramatic games ever staged between the two schools.

The contest, which had been soldout since mid-September, was played November 15 before a then Kinnick Stadium record crowd of 58,463. Iowa had already secured the outright league title with a 28-6 win at Minnesota the previous week. The Buckeyes entered as 14-point underdogs. Interestingly, it was being strongly rumored coach Woody Hayes would be leaving Ohio State after the 1958 season to accept a position with the Ford Foundation.

The game's scoring pattern was incredible. Ohio State and Iowa alternated touchdowns until the fourth period when the Buckeyes finally went ahead to stay. Ohio State took the lead on each of its five touchdowns, yet Iowa responded after the first four to tie the game at 7-7, 14-14, 21-21 (halftime) and 28-28 (three quarters). Ohio State secured the win with ten unanswered points in the final period.

The play was fast and furious from the very start. White and Clark led Hayes' patented ground attack with 209 and 157 yards, respectively, and all five touchdowns. Clark scored both of his touchdowns on sweeps around right end, the first on a 25-yarder and the second from 37 yards out.

White powered 71 yards for his first score on a third-and-inches situation in the second quarter. His others were one-yard jaunts in the second and fourth periods. Dave Kilgore's 19-yard field goal completed the game's scoring with just 2:12 to play.

Hayes offered special praise for Ohio State quarterback Jerry Fields, who directed the Buckeye attack like a veteran while filling in for an injured Frank Kremblas. OSU's line play was superb with end Jim Houston, tackle Dick Schafrath and guard Ernie Wright playing the entire 60 minutes. Hawkeye quarterback Randy Duncan, the Big Ten's most valuable player in '58, set a then school single-game record completing 23 passes for 249 yards and a touchdown.

Ninth-ranked Iowa (4-1) posed the season's sternest challenge for fourth-ranked Ohio State (4-0-1) in 1961. The

Hawkeyes had beaten Ohio State the two previous seasons and no team had won three-in-a-row over Hayes' coached teams at this point in his career. Before a homecoming crowd of 83,795, at the time the largest in Ohio Stadium history, the Buckeyes came through, winning 29-13.

OSU's defense led the way to a 12-0 halftime lead. End Tom Perdue returned an interception 55 yards for the game's first score. Ohio State's second touchdown, an 18-yard pass from quarterback Joe Sparma to end Chuck Bryant, followed Dave Tingley's interception return to the Iowa 30.

The Buckeyes' last 17 points came in the fourth quarter. First, Sparma again connected with Bryant on a 63-yard scoring pass. VanRaaphorst kicked a 24-yard field goal before Bob Ferguson scored from the 11 to make it 29-7. Ferguson's TD followed a 53-yard interception by linebacker Gary Moeller down the west sideline to the Iowa 21.

Ohio State and Iowa were the only two Big Ten teams not to play each other in 1981. The other eight schools played a complete round-robin while the Buckeyes and Hawkeyes played only eight conference games. Ironically, Ohio State and Iowa tied for the league title with 6-2 records. Had the two met they would have been competing for the outright conference championship.

Hayes was extremely proud of his defense and especially the play of ends Perdue and Sam Tidmore. In later years, Hayes frequently referred to Bryant's 63-yard score as "one of the greatest individual efforts I have ever seen." Bryant had eluded seven different tacklers and carried an eighth over the goal line for the touchdown.

Ohio State ran its 1968 record to 8-0 at Iowa City but the win was anything but easy. Playing in the rain, the Buckeyes hung on for a 33-27 win after leading 26-6 at the end of the third period. Fullback Jim Otis led the attack with 166 yards and two scores while defenders Jack Tatum and Mark Stier each ended Hawkeye threats with interceptions.

ARCHIE SURPASSES OWN RECORD

The Bucks closed their home season with a 55-13 shellacking of winless Iowa in 1973. Archie Griffin established a new school single game rushing mark of 246 yards, breaking his old record of 239 yards against North Carolina the previous season. Fullback Bruce Elia netted just 11 yards in nine attempts but four of his carries were for touchdowns from inside the three.

In a near-perfect performance, Ohio State scored the first seven times it had the ball to win convincingly, 49-0, in 1975. Griffin led all rushers with 120 yards while quarterback Cornelius Greene completed all eight of his passes for 117 yards. One of his throws was a nine yarder to tight end Larry Kain for Ohio State's third touchdown. Freshman quarterback Rod Gerald entered the game in the fourth quarter and scored on runs of 45 and 14 yards — his only two carries of the afternoon.

BUCKEYES TOPPLE TOP-RANKED IOWA

In one of the school's all-time *great* victories, eighth-ranked Ohio State conquered the top-ranked Iowa Hawkeyes 22-13 before a national television audience and a rain-soaked Ohio Stadium record crowd of 90,467. The Hawkeyes, with a record of 7-0, entered the November 2, 1985, battle as a one-and-a-half point favorite. It was the first time Ohio State had been an underdog in its own stadium since the 1977 Oklahoma game, which the Sooners won 29-28.

The Buckeyes were 6-1 having lost at Illinois 31-28 when the Illini's Chris White kicked a 38-yard field goal on the game's last play. Ohio State owned the nation's longest home winning streak at 19. The Hawkeyes were the first number-one ranked opponent to appear in Ohio Stadium in 17 years dating back to October 12, 1968, when the Purdue Boilermakers were a 13-0 victim of a Rex Kern-led team that went on to capture the '68 national title.

The Hawkeyes, who had lost their last 11 games in Ohio Stadium dating back to 1961, were led by three All- Americans: quarterback Chuck Long, tailback Ronnie Harmon and linebacker Larry Station. Long entered the game as the nation's top passer having thrown for 1,984 yards and 21 touchdowns while surrendering only eight interceptions. Harmon was fifth nationally in all-purpose running averaging 170.4 yards per game.

Ohio State quarterback Jim Karsatos was the nation's fifth-ranked passer with 1,247 yards, 14 touchdowns and only four interceptions. The Buckeyes were leading the Big Ten in scoring averaging 35 points per game, but were ranked seventh in total

Sonny Gordon blocks a punt for a safety in the 1985 game

defense and ninth in pass defense.

The Buckeyes played without tail-back Keith Byars who had re-injured his right foot the previous Saturday against Minnesota. But the Dayton co-captain, who had one of the biggest games of his career against Iowa the previous year, delivered an inspirational pregame speech which ignited emotion into his team-mates. Byars became so excited he swiped a food tray from a table, broke a water glass and kicked a chair while giving his pep talk. Additional motivation was provided by a very uncom-plimentary article in the Saturday morning *Columbus Citizen-Journal* which belittled the secondary's chances against the nation's top passer — the Buckeyes were NOT impressed! With Byars out, freshman Vince Workman earned his first start at tail-back. Rich Spangler's 28-yard field goal and a blocked punt by roverback Sonny Gordon that went out of the end zone for a safety gave Ohio State a 5-0 first period lead, making the first time all season Iowa had been scored upon in the first quarter.

Meanwhile, the Buckeye defenders were confusing Long with their beautifully disguised pass defenses. Early in the sec-ond quarter, tailback John Wooldridge (who did not start because of bruised ribs) sped 57 yards on his very first carry to put Ohio State ahead 12-0. The touchdown was set up when William White intercepted a Long pass and returned it eight yards to the OSU 38. Later that quarter, Greg Rogan's theft of a Long pass set the table for Spangler's second field goal, a 26-yarder, to increase the Ohio State lead to 15.

The Hawkeyes finally got their offense on track driving 88 yards for their first touchdown with just 28 seconds remaining before halftime. Harmon scored from the three on the drive's 14th play. The drive had been kept alive when Long connected with David Hudson for 21 yards on a third-and-eight from the Hawkeye 25.

The third period was scoreless but the Hawkeyes had a golden opportunity when safety Jay Norvell intercepted Karsatos and returned the ball seven yards to the Ohio State 19. After two carries by Harmon moved the pigskin to the 11, he again tried the middle but linebacker Pepper Johnson slipped a block and nailed him at the 10. With coach Hayden Fry passing up a 27-yard field goal try, the Hawks again went to Harmon on fourth-and-one. But this time it was linebacker Chris Spielman who nailed him to the wet turf for no gain and the Buckeyes had met the challenge.

The two teams traded touchdowns in the final period with the Buckeyes scoring first on Workman's four-yarder over left tackle and Iowa's coming on a two-yard burst by Harmon.

Johnson and Spielman (with 19 tackles each) had led a vicious defense which forced Iowa to start its first seven possessions at its own 19, 17, 20, 21, 26, 12 and 20. Long (who was averaging 324 yards per game) had been held to 169 yards in 17 completions and was intercepted four times, two by Spielman. Seventeen of the Buckeyes' 22 points resulted from turnovers.

An elated Earle Bruce had just coached one of the finest games of his career. His team simply dominated Iowa. Also jubilant was Woody Hayes, who was especially impressed with Ohio State's defensive efforts. Hayes watched the game at his home where he was recovering from a heart attack.

Karsatos completed ten of 17 passes for 157 yards with two interceptions while fullback George Cooper rushed for 104 yards to become the first Buckeye fullback to rush for 100 or more yards since Vaughn Broadnax in 1982. Ohio State had just completed its eighth game without losing a single fumble. The

Buckeyes have won more than their share of *big* games over the years but few have been any bigger than the '85 triumph over top-ranked Iowa.

Iowa's next visit to Ohio Stadium two years later was not as pleasant for Bruce. With Ohio State leading 27-22 and Iowa facing a fourth-and-23 from the Ohio State 28, quarterback Chuck Hartlieb connected with tight end Marv Cook for a touchdown with just six seconds remaining to give Iowa the win 29-27. The home crowd was in total shock as Iowa had pulled off one of the most spectacular finishes of all time. The lead had changed hands six times as tailback Carlos Snow put Ohio State ahead 27-22 on a 14-yard run with just 2:45 left in the game. But Hartlieb then moved his team 54 yards for the victory despite being sacked once and incurring an 11-yard loss on a fumble.

Another photo finish at Iowa City in 1990 was much more favorable for the Buckeyes. Quarterback Greg Frey hit split end Bobby Olive on a three-yard scoring strike with just one second remaining to win 27-26. Ohio State trailed 26-14 with 11:00 to play. A gutsy Frey passed for three touchdowns and ran for another while outside linebacker Jason Simmons had three tackles for losses. It was coach John Cooper's 100th career victory and Olive and Simmons were selected Big Ten players of the week.

> **O**hio State's outstanding 22-13 triumph over top-ranked Iowa was played on November 2, 1985, the exact 50th anniversary of one of the most agonizing losses in Buckeye history, the famous Ohio State-Notre Dame game of November 2, 1935.

Ohio State vs. Iowa

				POINTS	
DECADE	W	L	T	OSU	IOWA
1890	0	0	0	0	0
1900	0	0	0	0	0
1910	0	0	0	0	0
1920	3	4	1	59	79
1930	1	0	0	40	7
1940	2	1	1	96	27
1950	6	3	0	232	137
1960	7	2	0	189	145
1970	9	0	0	338	78
1980	5	2	1	232	129
1990	1	1	0	36	42
TOTAL	**34**	**13**	**3**	**1,222**	**644**

Ohio State at Home: 23-8-1
Ohio State on the Road: 11-5-2

Ohio State vs. Michigan

Highest Score in Series
Ohio State: 50-14 (1968, Columbus)
50-20 (1961, Ann Arbor)
Michigan: 86-0 (1902, Ann Arbor)

Highest Margin of Victory in Series
Ohio State: 38 points (38-0, 1935, Ann Arbor)
Michigan: 86 points (86-0, 1902, Ann Arbor)

Buckeyes' Most Significant Win
Ohio State's 21-7 triumph in 1954 helped earn the Buckeyes the national championship, the outright Big Ten title and the school's first Rose Bowl appearance under Woody Hayes. With the score tied 7-7 early in the final period, Ohio State held Michigan on downs inside its own one-yard line, then marched 99 2/3 yards for the go-ahead touchdown. A 20-7 Rose Bowl victory over Southern California improved the Buckeyes' mark to 10-0. It had been one of the toughest schedules in Ohio State history.

Buckeyes' Most Devastating Loss
Michigan's 24-12 upset in 1969 broke Ohio State's all-time winning streak at 22 and prevented the Buckeyes from capturing their second consecutive national title. The Wolverines of first-year coach Bo Schembechler entered the game as 17-point underdogs.

6. The Michigan Series

COLLEGE FOOTBALL'S PREMIER ENCOUNTER

*T*he annual Ohio State-Michigan battle has rightfully been proclaimed college football's leading rivalry. Emotions among players, coaches and fans are nearly impossible to describe when the two clash each November.

Michigan leads the overall series 50-33-5 through 1991. The two met only 14 of the 21 seasons from 1897 through 1917, but have met continuously since 1918. It is the Buckeyes' second longest consecutive series (Ohio State and Illinois have met each season since 1914) and has been the last game of the regular season for each team since 1935.

The Wolverines completely controlled the early contests, compiling a 13-0-2 advantage in the first 15 games (spread over a 22-year period). Ohio State was shut out 11 of these 15 games and was outscored a whopping 369-21.

The two first clashed at Ann Arbor on October 16, 1897, with Michigan winning 34-0. It was the Wolverines' 18th season of football and the Buckeyes' seventh. The first touchdown was scored by Frederic Hannan and James Hogg kicked the first conversion (touchdowns were four points; conversions, two; and field goals, four). The second game in 1900, also at Ann Arbor, was a "moral victory" for Ohio State, as the game ended in a scoreless tie. The first contest played in Columbus was won by the Wolverines, 21-0, on November 9, 1901.

WHO WOULD HAVE BELIEVED?

Ohio State fans were excited about their chances as both teams entered their October 25, 1902, meeting with undefeated records. The Buckeyes had held their four opponents scoreless while Michigan had surrendered only six points during its first five games. To the complete disbelief of the 2,300 Ohio State rooters who had followed their team to Ann Arbor, the Wolverines completely annihilated the Buckeyes, 86-0. It could have been much worse — officials mercifully called the game with more than ten minutes remaining in the second half. Touchdowns counted only five points in 1902, so by today's scoring system the final score would have been 101-0.

> The Buckeyes' 86-0 setback at Michigan in 1902 is the most lopsided loss in Ohio State football. The 86 points is also the highest combined score in an Ohio State-Michigan game, even though the Buckeyes did not score. The second highest is 70 points (Ohio State 50 - Michigan 20, 1961).

Michigan's Albert Herrnstein scored six touchdowns that afternoon, the most ever scored by one player in an Ohio State-Michigan game. Ironically, Herrnstein coached Ohio State from 1906-09. His team in 1906 finished at 8-1, losing only to (you guessed it) Michigan.

Even though they again lost, the Buckeyes finally scored in the series' sixth game in 1904. Fullback Bill Marquardt picked up a Wolverine fumble early in the second half and rambled 44 yards for a touchdown to tie the game at 5-5. Ralph Hoyer's conversion attempt was good and the Buckeyes had taken the lead, 6-5. But the Wolverines soon retaliated with two touchdowns, two conversions and two field goals (first field goals in the series) to win convincingly, 31-6.

> Michigan withdrew from the Big Ten on February 1, 1908, after the conference adopted a series of "far-reaching regulations." The Wolverines were particularly opposed to a limitation of five games, which would sever their strong ties with Eastern teams. Michigan rejoined the conference on November 20, 1917.

The 1906 contest, eighth in the lengthy series, was the first to be decided by a field goal. With the game scoreless late in the fourth quarter, Johnny Garrels booted a 35-yard field goal to put the Wolverines in front, 4-0 (field goals counted four points from 1904-09). Michigan later managed a safety to take a 6-0 victory.

HARLEY TO THE RESCUE

The Buckeyes finally did it . . . they finally beat Michigan! Ohio State earned its first victory in the series, 13-3, at old Ferry Field in Ann Arbor on October 25, 1919. Both teams entered the game undefeated and unscored upon; the Buckeyes at 3-0 and the Wolverines, 2-0. Senior captain Chic Harley, Ohio State's sensational halfback, led the scarlet-and-gray-attack with one of his most gallant efforts.

In the first quarter, Ohio State tackle Iolas Huffman blocked a Wolverine punt and end Jim Flowers recovered in the end zone for Ohio State's first touchdown. Michigan's Clifford Sparks made it 7-3 at halftime with a 37-yard field goal late in the second quarter.

Three-time All-American Chic Harley

The Buckeyes struck quickly midway through the third period after holding Michigan on downs at the OSU 34. First, Pete Stinchcomb sped 24 yards to the Michigan 42. Harley then dashed around end, sidestepped two defenders and outraced the rest for Ohio State's second touchdown and the game's final score.

After finding OSU's line difficult to penetrate, Michigan took to the air. But Harley, in almost magical style, intercepted four of Michigan's 18 passes to erase any further threats. He also punted 11 times throughout the afternoon for a 42-yard average. This was Ohio State's only meeting with the Wolverines during Harley's three glorious seasons of 1916, '17, and '19.

Michigan coach Fielding Yost seldom visited an opponent's locker room after a game, but this date he toured the Buckeyes' dressing quarters, congratulating the victors for their brilliant play and excellent strategy. The Wolverines finished the season at 3-4, the only losing campaign during Yost's 25 years as head coach. Ohio State coach John Wilce's long hours of preparation had paid off. The crowd of 25,000 included approximately 5,000 Buckeye fans who had yelled themselves hoarse while watching their team do something no other Ohio State squad had ever done — beat Michigan!

The victory apparently set well for the Buckeyes; they also won the next two (14-7, Columbus, 1920; and 14-0, Ann Arbor, 1921). Beginning with Ohio State's initial win in 1919, there have been 73 games through 1991. The overall record for these 73 favors Michigan, 37-33-3, and the last 31 games are exactly even at 15-15-1. The Buckeyes hold a 20-17-1 edge over the 38 games from 1954-91, outscoring the Wolverines 623-566 during this span.

STADIUM DEDICATIONS HIGHLIGHT '20S

Ohio Stadium and Michigan Stadium were dedicated on October 21, 1922, and October 22, 1927, respectively, with the Wolverines and Buckeyes providing the opposition for each other's dedication. Michigan shut out Ohio State in both games, winning 19-0 in 1922 and 21-0 in '27. Halfback Happy Kipke was the star in 1922, scoring on a 26-yard run, a 38-yard pass interception and a 37-yard field goal. Kipke's kicking that after-noon was one of the finest in all of college football — he punted 11 times for a 47-yard average with nine of his kicks falling out-of-bounds inside Ohio State's eight-yard line. Kipke later coached the Wolverines from 1929-37.

The 1926 game at Ohio Stadium was one of the most mem-orable and electrifying of the series. The game had been sold out weeks in advance. The Buckeyes were undefeated at 6-0 and the Wolverines at 5-1 had been beaten only by Navy (10-0) two weeks earlier. Two thousand general admission tickets went on sale the morning of the game, but it is estimated another 15,000 could have been sold. With Ohio State unable to meet this tremendous demand, many fans stormed the gates and surged inside. The official attendance was announced at 90,411 but no one knew for sure how many people actually saw the game.

Ohio State took an early 10-0 lead but Michigan came back to tie 10-10 after Wolverine quarterback Benny Friedman kicked a 42-yard field goal from a very difficult angle near the west sideline right before the half. The Wolverines took the lead 17-10 early in the fourth quarter after the Buckeyes lost a fumble on a punt return deep in Ohio territory. Ohio State put on a scoring march of 69 yards with halfback Bryon Eby of Chillicothe sweeping left end for the final seven to make it 17-16. OSU's Myers Clark, a drop-kicker, was forced to hurry his extra point attempt as Michigan end Bennie Oosterbaan shot in from his left end position. The ball went through the uprights but below the crossbar, and Michigan had won a thriller, 17-16. It was Ohio State's only loss that season.

Oosterbaan, a three-time All-American end, moved to the backfield and threw for three touchdowns — all to Louis Gilbert — in the 1927 dedication game at Michigan Stadium. Gilbert also kicked the three conversions to score all of the Wolverines' 21 points. This was Ohio State's sixth consecutive loss to Michigan and fans were becoming highly vocal with their displeasure. The Buckeyes finally broke the streak with a 19-7 win over the Wolverines at home the following season.

Coach Sam Willaman posted a very respectable record of 26-10-5 during his five seasons from 1929-33, but his teams never finished higher than third in the Big Ten standings. Though his teams won two of five games against Michigan, Willaman resigned under pressure, even though his last squad went 7-1 — but that single setback was to the Wolverines, 13-0.

ONE LEG AT A TIME

The colorful Francis Schmidt replaced Willaman in 1934 and vowed his teams would beat Michigan. He told his players, "Why not? Those guys put their pants on one leg at a time, the same way you do." This remark sparked the formation of the Michigan Pants Club, which has continued at Ohio State since 1934. Each player and coach is presented with miniature

Coach Francis Schmidt and All-American Gomer Jones

gold pants following each victory over Michigan.

Schmidt's teams were extremely successful against the Wolverines his first four seasons, shutting them out by a combined score of 114-0. At Ann Arbor in 1935, Ohio State scored six touchdowns and had two called back on penalties to win 38-0. This game stands today as Ohio State's widest margin of victory over Michigan. Quarterback Tippy Dye returned a punt 65 yards for one of the scores — the first punt to be returned for a touchdown in an Ohio State-Michigan game.

Schmidt's last few squads were not as successful, losing all three meetings with the Wolverines. His final game developed into a very *long* afternoon in Ohio Stadium as Michigan's Tom Harmon (in his last collegiate game) led his team to a 40-0 shellacking. It was Ohio State's worst setback since losing to Michigan 40-0 in 1905. Harmon did everything that day but march in the band. Playing all but 38 seconds of the 60-minute game, Harmon scored three touchdowns and passed for two more, kicked four extra points, rushed for 139 yards, passed for 290 yards and returned three punts for 81 yards. He also punted three times for a 50-yard average. That season Harmon became the first Michigan player to be awarded the Heisman Trophy.

Ohio State and Michigan played to a 20-20 tie in 1941, the first deadlock in the series since 1910. The game was really a moral victory for Paul Brown's first team who had entered a 20-point underdog. The game was tied at 14 after three quarters. In the final period, the Buckeyes scored on a 52-yard pass from Jack Graf to Dick Fisher. John Hallabrin's conversion attempt was wide and the Buckeyes led by six. The Wolverines came back to score on their next possession with Bob Westfall getting the touchdown. Bill Melzow's extra point attempt also sailed wide, and the teams settled for the tie.

A rain-soaked Ohio Stadium crowd of nearly 72,000 saw the Buckeyes use the forward pass to perfection in 1942, defeating Michigan 21-7 to capture their first league crown since 1939. It was the Buckeyes' first win over the Wolverines in five seasons. Ohio State's three touchdowns came on passes from Les Horvath to Paul Sarringhaus (20 yards), Sarringhaus to Bob Shaw (60 yards) and Sarringhaus to Horvath (32 yards). This was an extremely key win for an Ohio State team that would capture the school's first national title.

HORVATH RETURNS TO PLAYING FIELD

With World War II going strong in the South Pacific and Europe, transportation problems, gas rationing and an acute shortage of players and coaches created vital problems for college football in the early 1940s. Most teams were comprised largely of freshmen too young for the draft, as well as a few older players who did not meet military physical standards (4Fs). Nevertheless, continuance of the game was highly encouraged for morale purposes by President Franklin D. Roosevelt.

1944 Heisman Trophy winner Les Horvath

Against this backdrop and under these conditions, coach Carroll Widdoes took command of the Ohio State football program in 1944, replacing 35-year-old Paul Brown who had been commissioned a lieutenant and had reported to Great Lakes Naval Training Base. It was understood Widdoes would be the "acting head coach" until Brown returned from the service (although Brown did not return to Ohio State after the war). Widdoes was a sound fundamentalist who had assisted Brown at Massillon (Ohio) High School before joining him at Ohio State in 1941. Other than Widdoes' stint as a junior high school coach, this was his first chance as a head coach.

Ohio State's 1944 squad of 44 players was made up of five seniors, three juniors, five sophomores and 31 freshmen. The Buckeyes got a big break when the Big Nine changed its rules allowing a fourth year of eligibility for any player on campus working toward a graduate degree. (The Big Ten became the Big Nine after Chicago dropped football in 1939. Michigan State filled the vacancy in '53). Les Horvath, the fine senior wingback on OSU's national champions of '42, was enrolled in Ohio State's School of Dentistry as part of an army specialized training program. When his unit was discharged from military obligations in August of 1944, the 24-year old Horvath returned to civilian status and returned to the gridiron for an additional season with the scarlet and gray.

The '44 Buckeyes ran from both the 'T' and single-wing formations. To make maximum use of Horvath's experience and abilities, Widdoes positioned him as his quarterback in the T and tailback in the single wing. Horvath was joined in the backfield by three 17-year-old freshmen — Bob Brugge and Dick Flanagan at halfback and Ollie Cline at fullback. Horvath and Brugge had grown up in Parma just two blocks apart.

The 1944 Ohio State-Michigan game was played in Columbus on November 25, the Saturday after Thanksgiving. The Buckeyes were 8-0 and had advanced to third in the *Associated Press* poll following an impressive 26-12 victory over Illinois in Cleveland the previous weekend. Michigan at 8-1 was ranked sixth and game tickets were at a premium. On Friday, 11,000 general admission tickets went on sale and a strong shoving match developed among the many fans who had stood in line but were turned away after the last tickets were sold.

Coach Fritz Crisler's Wolverines were 5-1 in the conference while Ohio State was 5-0. Michigan could capture the conference title with a win over Ohio State since the Wolverines had scheduled seven league games compared with OSU's six. It was the first time in league history the winner of the Ohio State-Michigan game would be the outright conference champion.

Ohio State won a thriller 18-14 before a homecoming crowd of 71,958, as the lead changed hands after each of the five touchdowns. Ohio State led 6-0 after one quarter on Ollie

OHIO STATE vs. MICHIGAN
1897 - 1991
Analysis of Victory and Point Totals by 25-Game Periods

Periods	OSU Wins	UM Wins	Ties	OSU Points	UM Points
First 25 (1897-1928)	4	19	2	103	492
Second 25 (1929-1953)	9	14	2	270	361
Third 25 (1954-1978)	15	9	1	393	307
Last 13 (1979-1991)	5	8	0	230	259
Total (88 Games)	**33**	**50**	**5**	**996**	**1,419**

No OSU-UM games 1898-99, 1913-1917

Cline's short plunge, which culminated in a 56-yard drive. Michigan took a 7-6 lead with just 22 seconds left in the half on a one-yard bolt by Dick Culligan. The score was set up with a 35-yard interception return to the Ohio State 25 by Ralph Chubb.

The Buckeyes regained the lead in the third period 12-7 with Les Horvath scoring from inside the one. Center Gordon Appleby had recovered a Michigan fumble at the OSU 23 to set up the drive. The Wolverines came back, driving 83 yards in the final period to regain the lead at 14-12. Culligan scored his second touchdown with just 8:29 left to play.

The ensuing kickoff went just 12 yards, going out-of-bounds at the Ohio State 48. It appeared to be an intentional onside kick, but Michigan coach Fritz Crisler denied it, stating, "It was just one of those things, but was not planned that way." The Buckeyes then drove 52 yards in 14 plays for the season's biggest touchdown. Horvath was like a "coach-on-the-field" during the drive by constantly encouraging the younger players. He scored the final touchdown himself from the one.

Michigan began another drive but Dick Flanagan intercepted a pass at the Ohio State 33 to end the threat and secure one of the biggest wins in all of Ohio State football. The Buckeyes had gone 9-0 for just the second undefeated-untied season in school history. Widdoes stated, "We played our best game of the season and Michigan was the toughest team we faced." He used only 16 players in the game with Horvath, Jack Dugger, Bill Hackett and Flanagan going the entire 60 minutes.

With the victory, Ohio State was invited to meet Southern California in the Rose Bowl. However, at this time the Big Nine did not allow post-season competition. A special vote of the schools was taken in Chicago on Sunday, November 26, but the member institutions voted against making an exception for Ohio State. Athletic Director L. W. St. John of Ohio State was quite disappointed but agreed to abide by the conference's decision. Tennessee then accepted the Rose Bowl committee's invitation.

The 7-7 deadlock at Michigan in 1949 is probably the sweetest tie in Ohio State football. Needing a win or tie to be Rose Bowl bound, the Buckeyes trailed 7-0 with nine minutes remaining and the ball on their own 20. An 80-yard scoring march, highlighted by a 47-yard Pandel Savic-to-Ray Hamilton pass, made it 7-6. Fullback Curly Morrison bolted across for the final four yards.

The situation at first looked quite gloomy when Jimmy Hague's all-important conversion attempt was wide to the right — but the Wolverines were ruled offside. Ohio State may never have benefitted from a more timely penalty! Hague's second attempt was good and the Buckeyes were smelling the Roses. Hague's right leg also figured prominently in the Rose Bowl. His late fourth-quarter field goal from the California Golden Bears' 18 broke a 14-14 tie and earned Ohio State its inaugural win in the New Year's Day classic.

THE UNBELIEVABLE "SNOW BOWL"

With the temperature hovering near ten degrees and winds whirling at 28 miles per hour, Columbus was completely paralyzed by one of the worst snowstorms ever to hit central Ohio. The date was Saturday, November 25, 1950, with Ohio State and Michigan meeting to decide the Big Ten title. Cars were snowbound for days following the game and many out-of-town fans did not arrive home until the following Tuesday. Ohio Stadium chief groundskeeper Ralph Guarasci often said, "I never saw anything like it and I hope I never have to see anything like it again." Guarasci's crew was faced with the impossible task of keeping the field clear of snow prior to kickoff. Amazingly,

Behind the blocking of Julius Wittman (67) and Chuck Gandee (32), Vic Janowicz plows ahead in the driving snowstorm during the '50 Michigan game

50,535 fans were unable to make it inside the horseshoe to witness one of the most unusual football games ever played.

Jack Park (left) with WJR's Warren Pierce and Tony and Bob Momsen, prior to the Ohio State-Michigan game in 1988

Michigan won the encounter 9-3 without registering a single first down. With the ground attacks all but halted by the conditions, both squads frequently punted on first or second down. Michigan's Chuck Ortmann punted 24 times for 723 yards and Ohio State's Vic Janowicz accounted for 685 yards on 21 kicks.

All scoring resulted from blocked punts. In the first period, OSU's Joe Campanella and Bob Momsen blocked an Ortmann quick kick and Momsen recovered at the Michigan six. Three plays then lost 16 yards and on fourth down Janowicz kicked a field goal from the 28-yard line to give the Buckeyes a 3-0 lead. Janowicz's three-pointer was truly a remarkable achievement considering the blowing snow, a difficult angle and kicking into the teeth of the whistling wind. Later that period, Michigan captain Al Wahl blocked a Janowicz punt which squirted out of the end zone for a safety. The Wolves had cut the margin to 3-2.

The first half's final 47 seconds produced an extremely controversial call — Ohio State had a third-and-six at the Michigan 13 when coach Wes Fesler instructed Janowicz to punt. Michigan center Tony Momsen blocked the kick and fell on it for the game's only touchdown. Harry Allis' extra point made it 9-3 and that was the ball game as there was no scoring in the second half. Tony Momsen was the older brother of OSU's Bob Momsen, whose earlier recovery set up Janowicz's field goal.

Fans still question Fesler's third down punt with only 47 seconds remaining. "We had two plays left," he said, "but too much time to close out the end of the period. So rather than take a chance of anything happening, I wanted to get the ball out of there."

MICHIGAN
OHIO STATE
HOMECOMING

NOVEMBER 22 1952
PRICE 25 CENTS

The game's final offensive statistics probably best describe the deplorable playing conditions. Ohio State rushed for 16 yards; Michigan totaled 27. The Buckeyes registered three first downs; Michigan, none. Ohio State completed 3 of 18 passes for 25 yards while Michigan was unable to connect on any of nine throws.

WOODY'S FIRST WIN OVER "THAT TEAM UP NORTH"

Led by an alert defense and the strong passing of quarterback John Borton, Ohio State closed out its 1952 season with a stunning 27-7 victory over favored Michigan before a jam-packed Ohio Stadium crowd of 81,541. It was Ohio State's first win over Michigan in eight seasons and the first of 16 for second-year coach Woody Hayes.

The Buckeyes' vicious tackling and well-executed game-plan forced eight Wolverine turnovers. Michigan, who had been averaging 25 points per game, was shutout until late in the final quarter. Fearless Fred Bruney, a senior halfback from Martins Ferry, Ohio, played brilliantly in setting an Ohio State single-game record with three first-half interceptions.

Borton had his finest game as a Buckeye. The sharp-shooting sophomore from Alliance, Ohio, threw for three touchdowns and scored another on a four-yard keeper. Borton's first two aerials were snagged by junior end Bob Joslin of Middletown, giving the Bucks a 14-0 advantage at halftime. His third went to Joslin's former high school teammate, senior end Bob Grimes. A Michigan victory would have earned the Wolverines the Big Ten championship and Rose Bowl berth. Instead, Purdue and Wisconsin tied for the title, with the Badgers getting the trip to Pasadena.

Prior to 1952, Ohio State had won only 12 of 48 encounters

with Michigan, but that trend was about to change. From 1952-75, Hayes-coached teams would be 16-7-1 against "that team up North" and 13 of those 24 games would have a direct effect on the conference championship.

GOAL-LINE STAND KEYS ONE OF GREATEST WINS

The Big Ten title and Rose Bowl berth were on the line when 12th-ranked Michigan invaded Ohio Stadium to challenge undefeated and top-ranked Ohio State in 1954. Coach Bennie Oosterbaan's Wolverines had lost only to Indiana in conference action and could force a tie for the Big Ten crown with a win over Hayes' Buckeyes. The game was nationally televised with former Michigan great Tom Harmon and veteran sportscaster Bill Stern handling the announcing. Press passes were issued to more than 500 media representatives, at the time the largest ever to cover a Big Ten game.

Michigan immediately took charge, driving 68 yards after receiving the opening kickoff for a 7-0 lead. Michigan surprised everyone with a new offensive formation that showed an unbalanced line with just one player — a tackle — on the left side of center. The Wolverines used a perfect blend of power, speed and

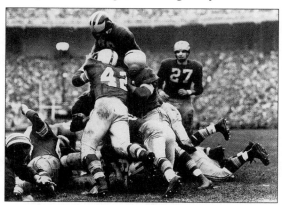

This goal-line stand keyed the Buckeyes' huge victory in 1954

deception with their multiple offense, scoring the touchdown on a seven-yard double handoff reverse around left end to halfback Dan Cline. Buckeye fans were already concerned!

The Wolverines dominated the first half but were unable to increase their lead. With just over three minutes remaining until halftime, Michigan quarterback Jim Maddock's pass was intercepted at the OSU 43 and returned to the 10 by linebacker Jack Gibbs. End Fred Kriss scored his first collegiate touchdown on a pass from quarterback Dave Leggett and suddenly it was 7-7. Gibbs, who had even been considered too small to play football at Columbus West High School, was a seldom-used player who had just entered the game.

Following a very poor Ohio State punt, the Wolverines drove to a first down at the OSU four late in the third quarter. With its backs to the wall, Ohio State's defense demonstrated great poise and confidence, holding Michigan on downs just six inches short of the OSU goal. Particularly effective during this memorable goal-line stand were guards Jim Parker and Jim Reichenbach, tackle Frank Machinsky and linebacker Hubert Bobo. Leggett then moved his team just six inches short of 100 yards in the other direction for one of OSU's biggest touchdowns of all time. End Dick Brubaker caught Leggett's second TD aerial for the six-pointer. Howard "Hopalong" Cassady scored during the game's last seconds and Tad Weed's third conversion finalized the scoring at 21-7.

Ohio State went on to a 20-7 win over Southern California in the Rose Bowl to capture the national title. Hayes would coach many additional *big wins* during the next 24 seasons — but none would be much bigger than the one over Michigan in 1954.

SPARTANS APPRECIATE BUCKEYES' EFFORT

The Big Ten title was again on the line when Ohio State traveled to Ann Arbor in 1955. Oosterbaan's Wolverines were 5-1 in the conference while Ohio State was 5-0. Michigan could capture the conference title and Rose Bowl berth with a win over Ohio State, since the Wolverines played seven league games compared with the Buckeyes' six. This engagement was Michigan's 600th all-time football game.

Michigan State also held a real interest in the game. The Spartans were 5-1 in the conference and had completed league play the previous Saturday. An Ohio State win over Michigan would place Michigan State second in the conference standings and send the Spartans to the Rose Bowl, since Ohio State could not return to Pasadena under the no-repeat rule in effect at that time. To help support the Buckeyes, one of the Spartan cheerleaders joined Ohio State's cheerleaders that afternoon at Michigan Stadium, while Michigan State was defeating the Marquette Warriors 33-0 at East Lansing.

The Spartans' support may have helped — Ohio State shutout the Wolverines 17-0, with the Buckeyes' defense allowing Michigan to cross the 50-yard line only once (on a penalty). On the following play, Ohio State's Jim Parker spilled the Wolverines for a loss, putting them back into their own territory. The game lost control at the end with penalties being assessed on almost every play. Two Michigan players were even ejected for unsportsmanlike conduct. Ohio State fans tore down both goal posts immediately following the game while numerous scuffles among opposing fans developed along the snow-covered sidelines.

Ohio State had thus captured its first win at Ann Arbor since 1937. The Buckeyes led in first downs 20-5 and in total offensive yards 337-109. Hayes had his team throw only three passes, completing one for four yards — the Buckeyes' first pass completion in three weeks. This afternoon marked the end of a fabulous collegiate career for Howard "Hopalong" Cassady, who rushed for 146 yards and scored the first touchdown. Ohio State had captured its second consecutive outright conference title, while Michigan State went on to represent the Big Ten with a thrilling 17-14 Rose Bowl win over UCLA.

400TH VICTORY QUITE SPECTACULAR

The 1961 game developed into one of the wildest and most offensive in the Ohio State-Michigan series. The Buckeyes entered Michigan Stadium with a record of 7-0-1 while coach

Calling the offensive plays during Ohio State's 50-20 triumph at Ann Arbor in 1961 was Buckeye assistant coach Bo Schembechler.

Bump Elliott's Wolverines were 6-2. Ohio State erupted for a 50-20 victory, even though the score was only 21-12 after three quarters. It was the Buckeyes' 400th all-time victory and the 50 points is Ohio State's highest point total against Michigan (it was equaled with a 50-14 OSU win in '68).

This game had everything! Fullback Bob Ferguson, playing his last collegiate game, rushed for 152 yards and four touchdowns to become the first Ohio State player to score four TDs in an Ohio State-Michigan game. Quarterback Joe Sparma and halfback Bob Klein connected on an 80-yard touchdown pass, the longest scoring pass play in the series. Michigan's Davey Raimey, from Dayton, Ohio, scored on a 90-yard kickoff return — the only kickoff to be returned for a touchdown in an Ohio State-Michigan game.

One of the day's most spectacular plays was executed by Paul Warfield. On a counter play right, the fleet halfback turned the end, cut back upfield, faked Michigan's safety off his feet and raced 69 yards for the second-longest scoring run from scrimmage in series history.

Altogether, Ohio State led in first downs 22-16 and in total offensive yards 512-271. With the score 48-20, Hayes elected to go for a two-point conversion, which was successful. When later questioned if he was deliberately running up the score, Hayes indicated long-time kicking coach Ernie Godfrey was celebrating his 70th birthday and he wanted the game's total points to equal 70 in Godfrey's honor. As might be expected, Wolverine fans were not so enchanted with Hayes' gift idea.

The 1963 meeting, scheduled for Saturday, November 23, was postponed one week following the assassination of President Kennedy on Friday, November 22. The announcement was not made until Saturday morning, just as the Ohio State squad was heading to Michigan Stadium from its hotel in Ypsilanti.

One of many unused tickets for the
1963 OSU-Michigan game which was postponed one week due to the
assassination of President Kennedy.

College football that weekend, including numerous traditional rivalries, was virtually forgotten.

The following week, a crowd of 36,424, smallest at Michigan Stadium in 20 years, saw the Buckeyes rebound from a 10-0 deficit to win, 14-10. Quarterback Don Unverferth connected with Warfield on a 35-yard scoring pass for the Buckeyes' first score just 41 seconds before halftime. Midway through the final period, Unverferth (who was known more for his passing than running) rolled out five yards around his left end for the other touchdown. It appeared the Wolverines might pull it out until their final drive stalled at the Ohio State six with under two minutes remaining.

> **M**ichigan won only one Big Ten title — 1964 — during Woody Hayes' first 18 seasons from 1951-68.

Michigan won a crucial meeting in Columbus the following season, claiming the conference title by shutting out the Buckeyes, 10-0. The temperature hovered near 20 degrees as severe winds whipped throughout the horseshoe. Ohio State finished the campaign at 5-1 in conference action compared with Michigan's 6-1. The Buckeyes were denied a share of the Big Ten title for the second straight season by playing one less conference game. Michigan and Ohio State both finished in the *Associated Press* top ten for the first time in 15 years, with the Wolverines fourth and the Buckeyes ninth.

Ohio State's 50-14 verdict at Ohio Stadium in 1968 concluded one of the Buckeyes' most glorious seasons. Both teams entered the contest undefeated and untied in league competition. Michigan had won eight straight after losing its opener to California, 21-7. The winner would claim the outright Big Ten title and trip to Pasadena. For Buckeye fans, it developed into one of the most glorious games in the series. The "Super Sophomores" broke it wide open in the last two quarters after leading 21-14 at the half.

Jim Otis led the attack with 143 yards and scored four of the seven touchdowns. The defense became stronger as the game progressed. Jack Tatum, Doug Adams and Art Burton each had interceptions while end Dave Whitfield had two tackles behind the line of scrimmage.

The victory earned Ohio State its first Big Ten championship since 1961 and its first Rose Bowl appearance since 1957. With the win, the Buckeyes moved to the top spot in the weekly *Associated Press* poll, dropping Southern California (their Rose Bowl opponent) to second. Ohio State defeated the Trojans 27-16 to complete the year with a perfect 10-0 record. It is the last season a Big Ten team has captured the national title.

WHAT A WAY TO START A WAR

The 1969 encounter could be characterized as Michigan's biggest win — *ever*, and Ohio State's most shattering loss — *ever*! The number-one ranked Buckeyes were riding the crest of a 22-game winning streak, longest in school history. They were averaging 46 points and 512 yards per game and needed one more win to break their own conference record of 17 consecutive victories. A win at Michigan would also assure Ohio State its second straight national title.

Former Hayes assistant Bo Schembechler had taken over

the Michigan program that spring after an impressive 40-17-3 six-year record at his alma mater, Miami of Ohio. His 12th-ranked Wolverines were 7-2 and had outscored their last four opponents 178-22. Nevertheless, Michigan entered the game a 17-point underdog.

Before a throng of 103,588, at the time the largest crowd ever to attend a regular-season college game, Ohio State grabbed a 6-0 lead on its second possession. Otis powered over from the one to cap a short drive after Larry Zelina returned a punt 35 yards to the Michigan 16. But then Michigan really took charge, scoring the next four times it had the ball. Fullback Garvie Craw's three-yard touchdown burst completed a 45-yard march and Frank Titas kicked the extra point to give Michigan the lead, 7-6. And for the first time all season, the Buckeyes were behind.

Ohio State recaptured the lead 12-7, moving 73 yards in 11 plays with Rex Kern throwing to Jan White for a 22-yard touchdown on the first play of the second quarter. But the Wolverines regained the lead for good on their next possession, driving 58 yards with Craw blasting across for his second touchdown from the one. The drive's big play was a beautiful broken-field run of 28 yards by sophomore Billy Taylor of Barterton, Ohio, Schembechler's hometown.

Next, Barry Pierson returned a punt 60 yards to the Ohio State three, and two plays later quarterback Don Moorhead sneaked over from the two and it was 21-12 Michigan. Pierson's punt return was probably the key play of the afternoon. It signaled the Wolverines were for real, and the Buckeyes were in deep trouble. Later that quarter, a Moorhead-to-Jim Mandich touchdown pass was nullified by a motion penalty, and Michigan had to settle for a 25-yard field goal by Tim Killian. The score was 24-12 with 1:15 remaining in the first half, and that's how the game ended.

Ohio State's defense stiffened in the second half, but so did

Michigan's. The Buckeyes moved past midfield only once in the final two quarters and the Wolverines virtually shut off the option play, forcing Ohio State to pass. The result was six interceptions, three by Pierson. The victory was really no big surprise for Schembechler. He began talking about beating the Buckeyes during practice the previous spring, and by late afternoon on November 22, it had turned to reality. The "Ten-Year War" was underway!

LITERALLY FOR A LIFETIME

What a difference a year makes! The Buckeyes captured the 1970 Big Ten title with a 20-9 triumph over Michigan and avenged one of the most difficult losses in all of Ohio State football. Hayes went to his office and began preparing for the return match the Saturday evening he returned from Ann Arbor in '69. His fifth-ranked Buckeyes entered the game with an 8-0 record while the fourth-ranked Wolverines were 9-0. It marked the first time both schools entered their season-ending struggle with undefeated-untied records. It also was the first time since 1905 that two undefeated-untied teams met to settle the Big Ten title —that year Chicago defeated Michigan 2-0 for the only•points scored against the Wolverines that season.

The atmosphere was ecstatic and Ohio State Sports Infor-

Generals Schembechler and Hayes exchange words during the "Ten-Year War."

mation Director Steve Snapp recalls that Ohio Stadium was virtually filled an hour before kick-off. The Buckeyes took an immediate 3-0 lead on Fred Schram's 28-yard field goal, following the recovery of a Michigan fumble on the opening kickoff. The Wolverines tied it up early in the second period on Dana Coin's 31-yarder.

Ohio State regained the lead when Kern connected with split end Bruce Jankowski on a perfectly thrown 26-yard pass play just before the half. The Buckeyes received a big break when a 72-yard punt by Michigan's Paul Staroba was nullified by a facemask penalty. Staroba's second punt was returned by Tim Anderson to the OSU 47, from where Kern drove his team 53 yards in ten plays for the go-ahead touchdown.

Tension really mounted in the third quarter as Don Moorhead guided his team 50 yards to a touchdown, with a pass to Staroba covering the final 13 yards. But Anderson blocked Coin's extra point attempt to leave the score at 10-9.

Schram's 27-yard field goal early in the final period increased the lead to 13-9. On the Wolverines' next series, OSU linebacker Stan White picked off a pass at the Michigan 23 and returned it to the nine. On third down from the four, Kern executed the option to perfection, pitching out to halfback Leo Hayden for the game's final touchdown. Schram's extra point completed the scoring at 20-9.

The Buckeye defense had been superb, yielding just 37 yards rushing to a team which had been averaging 247 per game. Hayes had surprised everyone with a two tight end offense. Hayden, who consistently gained yardage on a newly installed delay-type play, led all rushers with 117 yards.

In his postgame speech, Hayes referred to the win as the greatest game in Ohio State history. President Richard Nixon telephoned the jubilant coach within minutes after the victory to offer congratulations. In his pregame pep talk, Hayes had read an excerpt from an anonymous telegram which indicated, "This one is literally for a lifetime."

KICKERS TAKE CENTER STAGE

The kicking game had more impact in the Ohio State-Michigan series during the 1970s than any other decade. Michigan entered the 1971 game undefeated having sealed a Rose Bowl bid with a 20-17 win at Purdue the previous Saturday. The Buckeyes had already suffered three losses, but coach Woody Hayes had his squad superbly prepared for the possible upset that nearly materialized.

OSU's Tom Campana put on one of the finest displays of punt returning ever seen, bringing back five kicks for 166 yards. His 85-yard gallop for a third-quarter touchdown was a work of art, putting the Buckeyes on top 7-3. The Wolverines came from behind to win 10-7 on Billy Taylor's 21-yard end run in the final period, but Michigan had all it could handle.

The '72 contest at Ohio Stadium is remembered for the field goals that were *not* attempted. The game would determine the conference title with Michigan needing either a win or tie to be Pasadena bound, while the Buckeyes would go only if they won. Ohio State had gone ahead 14-3 early in the third period, after quarterback Greg Hare raced 33 yards on an option and freshman Archie Griffin raced the final 30 yards through the right side to score standing up. The Wolverines dominated the game's offensive statistics but finished on the short end of a 14-11 score. Ohio State won the game on two dramatic goal line miracles, twice holding Michigan on fourth down at the one. A fourth-down field goal on either drive would have tied the game at 14, thereby sending the Wolverines to Pasadena. For the afternoon, Michigan ran 12 plays from inside Ohio State's six-yard line, yet scored only one touchdown.

Schembechler was asked why he shunned the field goal attempt, particularly in the second opportunity. He replied, "No, I didn't go for the one-yard field goal because I thought we could score from there. We should have scored from the one!"

BO FIT TO BE TIED

Each team brought a 7-0 league record into their November 24, 1973, encounter at Michigan Stadium. Ohio State had outscored its seven opponents 297-27 while Michigan had been outscoring its seven, 235-48. The Buckeyes had not played Purdue (4-4) while Michigan did not meet Northwestern (4-4). Ohio

OHIO STATE vs. MICHIGAN 1897 - 1991				
Location	OSU Wins	UM Wins	Ties	Total Games	OSU Win %
Columbus	17	25	1	43	40.7%
Ann Arbor	16	25	4	45	40.0%
TOTALS	**33**	**50**	**5**	**88**	**40.3%**

State entered the game ranked No. 1 in the nation while Michigan was ranked fourth. The winner would be Rose Bowl bound, since the controversial "no-repeat" rule had been abolished prior to the '72 season.

The game began as a titanic defensive struggle with neither team able to sustain a drive in the first quarter. The Buckeyes then opened a 10-0 lead at halftime on Blair Conway's 21-yard field goal and Pete Johnson's five-yard touchdown plunge. The third quarter was scoreless, but Michigan took control late this period after holding Ohio State on a fourth-and-two at the Michigan 42.

The Wolverines then marched to the OSU 13 where Mike Lantry put Michigan on the scoreboard with a 30-yard field goal. Quarterback Dennis Franklin scored on the Wolverines' next possession to tie the game at 10-10. Lantry missed two field goals in the game's final two minutes, either of which would have broken the tie and earned Michigan the outright conference crown. Lantry's first try from the OSU 40 had the distance but was off target by inches. His second attempt from the 29 with 24 seconds left went wide to the right.

This 10-10 deadlock produced one of the most bitter controversies in Big Ten history. The two shared the league title with identical records of 7-0-1. Conference athletic directors voted to send Ohio State to the Rose Bowl, even though the Buckeyes had appeared in Pasadena the previous season. Michigan also had the better of the game's statistics, leading in first downs 16-9 and in total offensive yards 303-234. The reported vote was 6 to 4. Some felt the loss of Franklin with a broken collarbone hurt Michigan's chances of being selected. Schembechler was more than furious and strongly criticized the conference administration for its handling of the vote. The Buckeyes made the most of their opportunity, defeating a fine Southern California team 42-21 on New Year's Day.

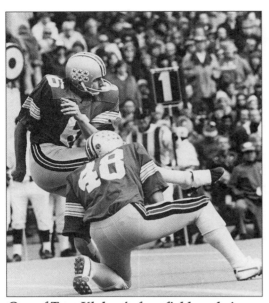

One of Tom Klaban's four field goals in 1974, held by Brian Baschnagel

The kicking game again was extremely prominent during Ohio State's 12-10 win in 1974. Michigan jumped out to a 10-0 first-quarter lead. Ohio State narrowed the gap to 10-9 at the half, as Tom Klaban, a walk-on, soccer-style kicker, booted three field goals of 47, 25, and 43 yards. A junior from Cincinnati, Klaban had settled in this country just ten years earlier when he and his family escaped from behind the iron curtain in East Germany.

Klaban's fourth three-pointer, a 45-yarder in the third quarter, put Ohio State on top and ended the scoring at 12-10. Much of the credit is also due Klaban's holder, wingback Brian Baschnagel. Two of the four snaps from center were extremely low, but Baschnagel was able to compensate, thus enabling Klaban's masterful feat.

With 18 seconds remaining in the game, Michigan had one final chance with the ball on the Ohio State 16. Lantry attempted a 33-yard field goal which not only would mean the difference between winning or losing the game, but also the league title and Rose Bowl trip. The left-footed Lantry's kick was wide to the left by a mere 18 inches, allowing the Bucks to preserve their two-point victory. OSU's defense had held Michigan scoreless the last three periods, largely because of some great individual defensive efforts and the long, booming kicks of punter Tom Skladany.

RAY GRIFFIN'S UNFORGETTABLE INTERCEPTION

The 1975 Ohio State-Michigan game was again the season's big one. Both teams entered the game with 7-0 conference records. For the seventh time in the last eight seasons, the league title and Rose Bowl were on the line. The Wolverines had not lost at home in their last 41 games. The 1975 season was also the first year Big Ten teams were permitted to play in bowls other than the Rose Bowl and the conference had arranged for the loser of the Ohio State-Michigan game to meet Oklahoma in the Orange Bowl.

Ray Griffin shifted to safety from tailback prior to the '75 season

Ohio State drove 63 yards on its first possession to take a 7-0 lead with Pete Johnson scoring on a seven-yard pass from Greene. Michigan scored on an 11-yard option pass from tailback Gordon Bell to wingback Jimmy Smith late in the second period to make it 7-7 at the half.

The third quarter was scoreless. Early in the fourth period, Michigan took over at the OSU 43 after forcing the Buckeyes to punt from their end zone. The Wolverines went the distance with freshman quarterback Rick Leach getting the touchdown from the one and Michigan was now in front 14-7 with 7:11 left in the game. Ohio State had not registered a first down since its early scoring drive.

But the Buckeyes soon made up for lost time. Starting from his own 35, Greene (after escaping near disaster while passing on first and second down) drove his squad 65 yards for the tying score. Johnson got the TD on a plunge from the one. The pressure was suddenly on Michigan with 3:18 left since a tie would send Ohio State to Pasadena.

Ohio State's 21-14 victory at Ann Arbor in 1975 was the first conference loss at Michigan Stadium for Bo Schembechler, who was in his seventh season as the Wolverines' head coach.

Michigan took over at its own 20 and came out throwing. On first down, Leach was spilled by middle guard Aaron Brown for a nine-yard loss, and his second down throw was incomplete. On third down, Ray Griffin intercepted Leach's pass at the Michigan 32 and streaked 29 yards to the three. From there, Johnson bolted over for his third touchdown, and the Buckeyes were

Pasadena bound. Ohio State really showed its class in what Hayes called "our greatest comeback and the greatest game I've ever coached."

> The Big Ten was really the "Big Two and Little Eight" from 1968-80. Ohio State and Michigan were each 6-6-1 against each other with each team scoring exactly 176 points over these 13 games. In addition, the Buckeyes and Wolverines were each 83-5 those 13 seasons against the "Little Eight."

Griffin's interception was one of the really significant plays in the history of the Ohio State-Michigan series. He was outstanding on defense with 14 tackles including ten solos. Two of his solos were safety blitzes which resulted in nine yards in losses for the Wolverines. The game had drawn a crowd of 105,543, at the time the largest ever to see a college football game.

JIM LAUGHLIN'S "BLOCK PARTY"

Coach Earle Bruce's first game against Michigan in 1979 went right down to the wire. Going into their November 17 showdown, the Buckeyes (10-0 overall) had moved into second place in the weekly *Associated Press* poll behind Alabama. Michigan, at 8-2, was ranked 13th. Tickets were at a premium, as Ohio State was shooting for its first undefeated regular season since 1975. The Michigan Stadium attendance of 106,255 was, at the time, the largest regular-season crowd in college football history.

After a scoreless first quarter, Vlade Janakievski put the Buckeyes on top 3-0 with a 23-yard field goal. Michigan then took the lead 7-3 with quarterback John Wangler teaming with Anthony Carter on a 59-yard scoring pass. Janakievski hit his second field goal, a 25-yarder, to make it 7-6 at the half.

Following intermission, Schlichter hit Chuck Hunter with an 18-yard scoring strike to put Ohio State ahead 12-7, but a two-point conversion attempt failed. Hunter's catch was the first Ohio State touchdown scored against Michigan since 1975. Later that quarter, Roosevelt Smith scored from the one and added a two-point conversion to put the Wolverines back in front 15-12 after three quarters.

With just over four minutes remaining and Ohio State's winning streak in jeopardy, linebacker Jim Laughlin came through with one of the biggest special team plays since the "Snow Bowl." Laughlin blocked Brian Virgil's punt, Todd Bell ran it in from the Michigan 18 and the Buckeyes had won a thriller, 18-15.

When later asked about the blocked punt, Laughlin said he knew he had a good shot at it as Michigan came to the line of scrimmage. "The Wolverine linemen were calling out who they were going to block, but no one called my number, so I felt there was a mix-up in their blocking assignments."

Each school has only once won the league title outright while losing to the other that same season. The Buckeyes were Big Ten champions in 1939, even with a season-ending 21-14 loss at Michigan. The Wolverines won the conference crown in 1982, but lost to Ohio State 24-14 in Columbus. The 1982 season has also been the only year the loser of the Ohio State-Michigan game has represented the Big Ten in the Rose Bowl. The Wolverines lost to UCLA 24-14 in Pasadena the following New Year's Day.

Laughlin went through the left side untouched to block the kick. Ohio State finished the regular season 11-0 earning its first outright league crown since 1975.

Field goal attempts played important roles in Bruce's final two Ohio State-Michigan games. The Wolverines needed a win in 1986 to earn a league co-championship with the Buckeyes and a berth in the Rose Bowl. Ohio State jumped off to a 14-6 lead at halftime but Michigan surged ahead 26-24 late in the fourth quarter. Matt Frantz's 45-yard field goal attempt with just 1:06 remaining was slightly wide to the left and Michigan had hung on for the two-point win. The Buckeyes really needed time for one more first down to allow Frantz a slightly shorter attempt.

During the 59 games from 1927-85, Ohio State and Michigan each scored 800 points. The Buckeyes held a very slight edge in these games at 29-27-3.

Frantz became one of the heroes in Bruce's last appearance. The Monday prior to the 1987 game, Ohio State President Edward Jennings announced Bruce was being dismissed as football coach. That Saturday, in support of their coach, every player wore white

Buckeye players show their support for Earle Bruce

headbands with the inscription "Earle." Ohio State rallied from a 13-0 deficit to take the lead at 20-13 midway through the third quarter, but Michigan then rallied to tie at 20-20. With just 5:18 remaining, Frantz kicked a 26-yard field goal to end the scoring and give his team a highly dramatic and historic victory. Eric Kumerow's recovery of a Michigan fumble on the Wolverines' next possession helped seal the win. Bruce had completed his Ohio State coaching career, winning five of nine against the Wolverines.

Ohio State vs. Michigan

				POINTS	
DECADE	W	L	T	OSU	UM
1890	0	1	0	0	34
1900	0	9	1	18	285
1910	1	3	1	16	53
1920	4	6	0	76	120
1930	5	5	0	148	86
1940	2	6	2	85	232
1950	5	5	0	133	120
1960	7	3	0	197	116
1970	5	4	1	111	129
1980	4	6	0	196	197
1990	0	2	0	16	47
TOTAL	**33**	**50**	**5**	**996**	**1,419**

Ohio State at Home: 17-25-1
Ohio State on the Road: 16-25-4

Timeout

Ohio State's Ten Most Difficult Losses

1. 1969: Michigan 24, Ohio State 12 — Wolverines end Buckeyes' 22-game winning streak. Loss costs Ohio State its second consecutive national title. Schembechler's first year at Michigan.

2. 1935: Notre Dame 18, Ohio State 13 — Both teams enter game undefeated. Down 13-0, Irish rally for three TDs in last quarter. Buckeyes' only defeat that season.

3. 1975: UCLA 23, Ohio State 10 — Rose Bowl. Season's only loss deprives Buckeyes of national title. Bruins score all 23 points in second half to avenge 41-20 regular-season loss to Bucks.

4. 1956: Iowa 6, Ohio State 0 — Hawkeyes snap OSU's conference winning streak at 17. Buckeyes' chance to capture third consecutive outright league title slips away.

5. 1970: Stanford 27, Ohio State 17 — Rose Bowl. Season's only setback eliminates opportunity for national championship.

6. 1919: Illinois 9, Ohio State 7 — Illini kick winning field goal with eight seconds remaining to hand Buckeyes their only loss during Chic Harley's three seasons.

7. 1979: Southern Cal 17, Ohio State 16 — Rose Bowl. Trojans drive 83 yards for winning score in last five minutes. Season's only setback as Buckeyes lose national title. Earle Bruce's first season.

8. 1926: Michigan 17, Ohio State 16 — Season's only defeat. Buckeyes' fifth consecutive loss to Wolverines.

9. 1974: Michigan State 16, Ohio State 13 — Spartans strike for two fourth-quarter scores to knock Buckeyes from number-one ranking.

10. 1977: Oklahoma 29, Ohio State 28 — Uwe von Schamann's 41-yard field goal with three seconds remaining seals OSU's fate.

Halftime

Ohio State football is more than a winning tradition and huge crowds in Ohio Stadium on a Saturday afternoon. It's also the love and loyalty of each Buckeye fan, the behind-the-scenes, person-to-person interactions, often humorous, always nostalgic, of those who share that special feeling for the Buckeyes.

WHOSE SIDE ARE YOU ON, ANYWAY?

Marietta College played at Ohio State on October 22, 1898. The Pioneers' traveling squad consisted of 12 players.

Midway through the second half, two Marietta players were injured and unable to continue play. Not wanting to forfeit the game, coach C. M. Showalter asked Ohio State coach Jack Ryder if he could "borrow" one of Ryder's players to finish the game. After pondering the situation for a few seconds, Ryder agreed and signaled to his bench for a substitute. The player assigned to the Pioneers is believed to have been halfback Bob Hager.

Ryder and his entire team were stunned when Hager sprinted 67 yards around end for a Marietta touchdown on his very first carry as Marietta won the game 10-0. The Pioneers were ecstatic over their very first victory in Columbus while Ryder *never* again loaned a player to one of his opponents.

UNDEFEATED AGAINST BIG TEN

Guard Bill Jobko, a three-year letterman, never played in a losing Big Ten game. He holds the distinction of being the only Ohio State player to have been a member of three teams which each won the Big Ten title outright. Jobko played on the 1954 and '55 squads which won back-to-back titles with league records of 7-0 and 6-0, respectively. He did not play in 1956 when Ohio State tied Michigan State for fourth in the conference with 4-2 marks. Jobko returned in '57 to help the Buckeyes win another outright championship with a 7-0 record. He also gained the team's most valuable player honor that season.

OHIO STATE-MICHIGAN: HOME FIELD OF LITTLE BENEFIT

The home field has apparently been of little advantage in the Ohio State-Michigan series. During the first 88 games played through 1991, the home team has won 42 and the visiting squad has won 41. Five other meetings ended in ties.

HAYES IN A HURRY

While opening his Lane Avenue barber shop one summer morning in the mid-1970s, Howard Warner spotted Woody Hayes driving to his campus office with his briefcase riding on top of his car. Apparently the coach had forgotten he had placed it there as he was leaving his home.

Howard immediately telephoned Mrs. Hayes, told her what he had just seen and jokingly expressed his concern that Woody's plans for the Michigan game might be inside. She called and relayed the message to the coach who went outside and found his briefcase still sitting on top of his car. The plans for the Michigan game were safe!

FOOTBALL BOOSTS ELECTION CAMPAIGN

At William G. McKinley's request, the Ohio State-Otterbein clash of 1896 was moved to McKinley's hometown of Canton, Ohio, as part of his "front porch" presidential campaign. The game was played October 17 near McKinley's home with the Buckeyes winning 12-0. The contest did not start until approximately 3:45 p.m. and by mutual agreement was called on account of darkness with about ten minutes remaining.

DOUBLE TROUBLE

The Michigan football team stayed at the same hotel near the Ohio State campus on the Friday evenings prior to their games in 1982 and '84.

A water main outside the hotel burst during the night in '82 and the entire hotel was without water Saturday morning. It's hard to believe but the same thing happened in '84 — a water main broke Friday night and the hotel was again without water Saturday morning. Steve Held, the hotel's maintenance manager, recalls that the Michigan players absolutely believed they had been sabotaged the second time.

As might be expected, Bo Schembechler selected a different hotel when his team returned to Columbus in '86.

HALFBACK CLARK LEADS '56 PASSING ATTACK

Woody Hayes had a strong reputation for shunning the forward pass. This was quite evident in 1956 when Ohio State's leading passer was not quarterback Frank Elwood but rather left halfback Don Clark, who completed 3 of 7 "halfback option passes" for 88 yards. Clark was also the team's leading rusher with 797 yards in 139 carries. Elwood was successful on seven of 20 passes that year for 86 yards.

VERSATILITY–PLUS

Matt Snell, one of Ohio State's 1963 co-captains, was a starter three consecutive seasons at three different positions. Snell started at right halfback in 1961, defensive end in '62, and fullback in '63.

SCRIPT OHIO — "THE REST OF THE STORY"

The Ohio State Marching Band celebrated the 50th anniversary of its famous "Script Ohio" in 1986. Its initial script was performed at halftime of the Indiana game on October 24, 1936.

But, according to George N. Hall, a 1935 graduate of Michigan, the very *first* Script Ohio was performed by the University of Michigan band four years earlier at the Ohio State-Michigan game of October 15, 1932. A member of Michigan's band that season, Hall provided the accompanying picture and an article which appeared in the *Michigan Daily* on Sunday, October 16, 1932, describing Michigan's script formation.

Reverend Joe Hotchkiss, another Michigan graduate and a longtime recruiter for the Wolverines, believes the Ohio State Department of Music asked each visiting band in 1932 to do a salute to the Buckeyes as part of its halftime show, since that season Ohio State was celebrating the 10th anniversary of Ohio Stadium. Michigan came up with Script Ohio then gave the band charts to OSU Band Director Eugene J. Weigel, since Michigan would no longer have a reason to use the formation.

The Michigan band "invents" Script Ohio

There are strong differences of opinion, however, as to whether Michigan really performed a moving script formation. Hall still loves to discuss the controversy. "I concede that Ohio people can both write and spell and that their brass band is reasonably good," he says, "but they weren't the first to do the script. We were!"

RAPID START

Tailback Tim Spencer raced 82 yards for a touchdown on the 1981 seasons's very *first* play from scrimmage, as the Buckeyes defeated Duke, 34-13. It is the third longest run from scrimmage in school history. Spencer finished his career in 1982 as Ohio State's second-highest all-time rusher with 3,553 yards.

WHAT SOME FANS WILL DO TO FOLLOW THE BUCKEYES!

Ohio State's great 13-0 victory over Purdue in 1968 was very significant in the life of one of the Buckeyes' most devoted fans — Ed Linser.

Linser grew up in New York City and joined the Navy in 1948 at age 19. While stationed at Great Lakes Training Center he became good friends with Bill Wade, an enlistee from Chauncey, Ohio, who was an avid Buckeye fan.

After Linser and Wade were discharged from the Navy, they roomed together for a short time in Columbus. Ed quickly became hooked on the Buckeyes even though he never attended a game. He met his wife, Shirley, and the two moved to New York City in 1951. Finally, after more than 17 years of keeping close account of the Buckeyes, the Linsers returned to Columbus to see their very first game in Ohio Stadium — the famous Purdue game of 1968. Ed went insane! He had never been part of anything as fantastic as an Ohio State football game.

The following spring, Linser, deciding he had to be closer to Ohio Stadium, made a decision that is almost beyond belief. He quit his job, sold his home and moved his family to Columbus. Friends told him he was crazy to give up a good job, especially when he had four school-age children to support and no job waiting in Columbus.

The Linsers lived with Shirley's parents until Ed found a job. They later purchased a home but Ohio Stadium became their "second home." Since 1969, Ed has missed only one game in the horseshoe (because of an illness) and Shirley now makes Scarlet and Gray musical Buckeye trees for other Ohio State fans.

"I'D RATHER DOT THE 'i' THAN BE PRESIDENT!"

ESPN college football analyst Beano Cook describes the dotting of the "i" in Script Ohio as one of college football's greatest thrills. "I'd rather dot the 'i' before I die than be president," he said, "because I believe it's a greater honor." Cook believes the Ohio State-Michigan series is the greatest rivalry in all sports. He attended Pitt's 21-14 win in Columbus in 1952 and recalls it was the first time the visitors tore the Ohio Stadium goal posts down since Notre Dame's 18-13 victory in 1935. Cook served as sports information director at Pitt from 1956-66.

ROUTE 88

Ohio State tailback Morris Bradshaw scored two touchdowns on 88-yard runs, one from scrimmage and the other on a kickoff return during the Buckeyes' 31-7 homecoming win over Wisconsin in 1971.

LOST BOY SCOUT

The Ohio Stadium grounds crew had an almost impossible task removing the canvas from the frozen surface so the 1950 "Snow Bowl" game between Ohio State and Michigan could get started. Many spectators, including several boy scouts, came down out of the stands to assist with clearing the field.

Soon after the game started, a rumor spread that one of the boy scouts had been caught and errantly wrapped in the canvas as it was being rolled from the field. The boy scout in question was Roy Case, who had fallen on the icy surface. Fortunately, the story proved to be a false rumor — Case had been able to roll aside after falling to avoid being caught in the rolling tarp.

Case is still involved with the boy scouts and the Buckeyes. For years he has been supervising the scouts who serve as ushers for each home game.

SUPER SLEUTH

A young lad enrolled at Ohio State in the fall of 1893 and practiced with the football team just long enough to learn the plays. After a few weeks, he dropped out of sight.

He was later spotted with the Kenyon College team when Ohio State played at Kenyon. Years later, when reminiscing about this game, Charles Wood, the Ohio State quarterback, recalled that "Kenyon just seemed to have all of our signals down pat."

Final score: Kenyon 42, Ohio State 2.

"JIM ZABEL, YOU STILL OWE ME ONE!" — JACK BUCK

Jim Zabel, sports director at WHO Radio in Des Moines, Iowa, is a legend in his own time. He followed Ronald Reagan as the sports voice at WHO and has broadcast every Iowa football game since 1950.

Zabel's first visit to Ohio Stadium in '50 developed into a *long afternoon* in more ways than one. He signed on the air for his pre-game show without taking into consideration the one hour time difference between Columbus and Des Moines. As the pre-game show progressed, Zabel soon realized he had an additional hour of air time to fill.

In the booth next to Zabel was Jack Buck, now the voice of the St. Louis Cardinals over KMOX Radio. Buck, an Ohio State graduate, was doing the Buckeyes' play-by-play on WCOL Radio in Columbus. Zabel first brought Buck into his booth for an interview. Then, during commercial breaks, Buck quickly arranged for other people in the press box to be Zabel's guests.

"It was a really long pre-game show," Zabel recalls, "but with Jack Buck's help, we made it."

Buck still remembers that afternoon in Ohio Stadium back in 1950. Today, when he's trying to fill air time during a rain delay with the baseball Cardinals, Buck's been known to say, "Jim Zabel, where are you when I need you? You still owe me one!"

For Zabel, the afternoon of his first trip to Ohio Stadium didn't get any better. Vic Janowicz did nearly everything possible on a football field that day to lead Ohio State to an 83-21 victory over the Hawkeyes.

WILL THE REAL JERRY MARLOW PLEASE COME FORWARD

Ohio State graduate Jerry Marlow, a pharmacist from New Philadelphia, Ohio, has had great difficulty obtaining tickets for Ohio State-Michigan encounters. Not wanting to miss any of the big games, Marlow has resorted to many gate-crashing antics at Ohio Stadium.

With a great deal of brashness and some very realistic costumes and props, Marlow has talked his way through the gates dressed as an OSU cheerleader, an ABC television camera operator, a game referee, an OSU band director and a nun. One year, he sat in a section designated for former Buckeye players by impersonating Tad Weed, Ohio State's placekicker in the early 1950s.

To prove his specialty is "all in fun," Marlow mails Ohio State a check each year which exceeds what he would have paid for the tickets.

HALL OF FAME

Two of football's greatest linemen have been Ohio State's Bill Willis and Jim Parker. Each has been inducted into both the College and Professional Football Halls of Fame.

Willis, who also ran sprints with the track team, played tackle on the Buckeyes' championship teams of 1942 and '44. He was an All-American his senior year and starred for eight seasons with the Cleveland Browns.

Parker, who excelled on both offense and defense, was an

integral part of the Buckeyes' championship squads of 1954 and '55. A two-time All-American in '55 and '56, he won the Outland Trophy his senior year. Parker spent his professional career with the Baltimore Colts.

Bill Willis

Jim Parker

LOOKING FOR CLUES AT 1711 CARDIFF ROAD

Dale Keitz, a defensive lineman at Michigan from 1976-79, played high school football at Upper Arlington in Columbus. During the summers, Keitz worked on one of the Upper Arlington Sanitation Department trucks, picking up garbage. One of his "customers" was the Hayes family at 1711 Cardiff Road. Keitz took a lot of good natured kidding about sorting through Woody's trash, looking for clues to Ohio State's game plan for the Michigan game.

Keitz also likely talked with his father, Dick, to gain an insight into Hayes' game-planning techniques. The elder Keitz played football under Hayes at Denison University in 1947-48.

SAM WILLAMAN – TOO GREAT A RECRUITER!

Prior to the Ohio State-Bowling Green game of September 12, 1992, the Buckeyes last encounter with an opponent from within the state of Ohio was at Western Reserve on November 3,

1934. The game was played at old League Park in Cleveland before a crowd of 11,000, with Ohio State winning 76-0.

The first of 11 touchdowns was scored by halfback Dick Heekin on the game's fourth play from scrimmage. First-year coach Francis Schmidt cleared his bench early in an attempt to keep the score as low as possible. It was a humiliating day for Western Reserve coach Sam Willaman, who coached the Buckeyes the five previous seasons and had recruited many of the Ohio State players his squad was facing that afternoon.

Ironically, Falcon coach Gary Blackney came to Bowling Green from Ohio State where he coached from 1984-90.

CARD TRICKS

Coach Francis Schmidt, master of the razzle-dazzle offense, was continually designing new plays for his offense. Tippy Dye, one of Schmidt's quarterbacks, recalls the Buckeyes had more than 300 plays which operated from seven different formations. With such a complicated offense, the quarterbacks wrote the number of each play on 3x5 cards to carry inside their helmets. During timeouts, they could quickly look through the cards to remind themselves of their many plays.

In the 1934 Michigan game, Dye was tackled pretty soundly, his helmet flew off and his play cards all scattered across the playing field. The curious Michigan players immediately examined some of Dye's cards but apparently they didn't learn much from them — Ohio State won the game, 34-0.

KNUTE ROCKNE TO THE BUCKEYES?

Soon after John Wilce retired as Ohio State's head coach in 1928, Athletic Director L. W. St. John was notified by Big Ten Commissioner John Griffith that Knute Rockne of Notre Dame had an interest in coaching in the Big Ten and would like to talk with St. John about the Ohio State coaching opening.

Rockne, who played at Notre Dame from 1910-13, had been head coach of the Irish since 1918, compiling an 11-year record of 86-12-5. Rockne, then 40 years of age, met with St. John at the American Football Coaches Association meeting in New Orleans in January of 1929. The two reached an agreement for Rockne to become Ohio State's new coach, under the condition Notre Dame would release him from his current contract. When Rockne returned to South Bend, however, he was convinced by Notre Dame officials to stay where he was.

Ohio State instead selected Sam Willaman, who had been a fine fullback on Wilce's first Big Ten team in 1913. Rockne guided Notre Dame to a 9-0 record in 1929 and a 10-0 mark in 1930 before losing his life in a plane crash over Kansas on March 31, 1931.

100-PROOF SOLUTION

The late Roger Stanton, publisher of the *Football News*, remembered the 1964 Ohio State-Michigan game as the coldest day of his 40-plus years covering football games.

"The Ohio Stadium press box was so cold that the copying machine wouldn't work," he said, "and the staff had no way of providing game statistics for the sportswriters. Finally, a resourceful individual poured vodka into the machine's gears. The 'lubricant' got it going and the machine hummed along reasonably well the remainder of the afternoon."

HAYES HONORED

Playing under Woody Hayes so greatly influenced end Tom Perdue, co-captain in '61, that Tom named his son Hayes Perdue in honor of his coach.

In addition to helping the Buckeyes capture the 1961 Big Ten title, Perdue was an All-American baseball player. His single-season batting average of .469 is still an Ohio State record. Perdue was also selected an Academic All- American his senior year.

'73 TEAM BEST OVERALL?

Some teams are remembered because of either a high-scoring offense or a stingy defense, but the 10-0-1 Buckeyes of 1973 were truly outstanding at both ends of the field. They outscored their opposition 413-64 and led the nation in scoring defense, surrendering only 4.3 points per game during the regular season. Except for a 10-10 tie at Michigan, their closest call was a 21-point Rose Bowl triumph over Southern California, 42-21. That season, Ohio State scored an average of 37.5 points, highest of any team in school history.

MOST ONE-SIDED WIN

The highest score and largest margin of victory in all of Ohio State football was a 128-0 drubbing of Oberlin College in 1916 at old Ohio Field along High Street. The Buckeyes scored 19 touchdowns and 14 conversions while amassing 1,140 yards in total offense. Ohio State went 7-0 in 1916 for its first undefeated-untied season and first Big Ten title.

STALEMATE

The 44 Ohio State-Michigan games from 1948-91 are exactly even at 21-21-2.

A GOAL FOR RETIREMENT

For nearly 25 seasons, Don Alexandre has been the host of WTVN Radio's Sportswatch which airs after each Ohio State game. The program provides game statistics, coaches' comments and scores of other games.

Interestingly, while he and his co-workers provide listeners with plenty of information about the Buckeyes, Alexandre himself has never attended an Ohio State game. His need to gather facts on other games from around the country keeps him at his studio where the broadcast originates.

FIRST COME, FIRST SERVE

The 1948 Ohio State-Michigan game at Ohio Stadium attracted media coverage from all over the country. The Wolverines had won 22 in a row and were aiming for their second consecutive national championship. Ohio State entered the game at 6-2 having lost only to Iowa and Northwestern.

In those years, three radio networks: CBS, NBC, and Mutual, each broadcast a "game of the week" nationally. Retired Sports Information Director Marv Homan remembers that each network normally followed an unwritten policy of notifying the home school by Monday if its game the following Saturday had been selected for broadcast.

CBS, with sportscaster Ted Husing, had selected the Ohio State-Michigan game weeks in advance. By Monday evening prior to the game, Wilbur Snypp (then SID) had not heard from NBC so he assumed it was going elsewhere. However, on Wednesday, Bill Stern, NBC's prominent sportscaster, called Snypp requesting a booth for the broadcast of Saturday's Ohio State-Michigan game. Stern was furious to learn that all radio booths had been assigned, and there was no space for him to air his broadcast.

With the press box full, Snypp had a temporary open-air platform erected, extending from the stadium's southwest corner and adjacent to 'C' deck. Even though the view of the playing field wasn't the greatest, it was from this platform overlooking the south end zone that Stern aired nationally the 1948 Ohio State-Michigan game won by the Wolverines 13-3.

REPEATS

Ohio State has twice captured consecutive, outright Big Ten titles: 1916-17 and 1954-55.

DOUBLE DUTY FOR BARBER

The famous Red Barber broadcast all of Ohio State's games in 1935 including the Notre Dame encounter. Just as Bill Shakespeare completed the winning touchdown pass, the spotter covering Notre Dame for Barber became so ecstatic, he ran from the radio booth and headed for the playing field to join in the wild celebration.

Notre Dame wore numbers only on the backs of their jerseys and Barber could not immediately identify the receiver. With his spotter gone, it took Barber several minutes to learn it had been Wayne Millner (#38) who had caught Shakespeare's final throw.

Brutus' Return

Former television reporter and news anchor Tom Burris considers the following story one of his favorites among the many Ohio State activities he covered for WSYX-TV in Columbus.

The date was Friday, November 16, 1984, the day before the Michigan game at Ohio Stadium. Eric Mayers, that season's Brutus Buckeye, was doing traffic reports that week at WSNY-Sunny 95 Radio as part of Michigan week activities. Early Friday morning as Mayers was leaving for the station, he discovered the Brutus head had been stolen from his car sometime during the night. Eric had a real problem as there was no other head available and the next day's big game was his last home appearance as Brutus Buckeye.

As part of Mayers' traffic reports that morning, WSNY announced a $500 reward for the return of Brutus' head. Mayers also joined Burris for his noon news telecast from the Ohio Union and described his predicament. An official from GTE joined them and announced GTE would add $1,000 to the reward fund. WSNY and WSYX-TV received numerous calls early that afternoon but none led to anything meaningful.

Finally around 3:30 p.m., a gentleman named Eli telephoned to report he had the missing head. After finding it in a trash dumpster near campus, he took it home to his children thinking it was a doll. Fortunately, his wife who had heard Burris and Mayers on the noon news recognized the item as the missing Brutus head. Eli returned it, collected his $1,500 reward, and described his find with Burris and Mayers live from Ohio Stadium on the 6:00 p.m. news.

Mayers couldn't have been more grateful. His Brutus head had been returned in time for the 7 p.m. Friday evening pep rally, and of course for the Michigan game Saturday —— which Ohio State won 21-6.

'57 Buckeyes Improve Quickly

"A football team improves more between the first and second games than any other time of the season!" That well-known quotation by Woody Hayes applied perfectly to his 1957 squad. After sustaining a discouraging 18-14 upset to Texas Christian in the opening game, Ohio State rebounded with nine consecutive triumphs to capture the *UPI* national championship. It is the only team in school history to have won the remainder of its games after losing the opener.

True To His Word

Will McClure, a freshman at Upper Arlington High School in 1986, was seriously injured while playing football. All-American linebacker Chris Spielman visited McClure at the hospital while he was recuperating and promised him an interception in Ohio State's next game against Illinois.

The following Saturday, Spielman made an interception during the Buckeyes' 14-0 victory over the Illini. He returned to the hospital and presented McClure with the ball, as promised.

Chinstrap Returns

Bob Ferguson and Jim Otis were two of the Buckeyes' finest fullbacks. Ferguson was a two-time All-American in 1960-61 and finished a close second to Ernie Davis in the Heisman Trophy balloting his senior year. Otis was an All-American in 1969 and his career rushing total of 2,542 yards is the highest of any fullback in Ohio State history.

Ferguson was fantastic in his last collegiate game, scoring four touchdowns while leading the Buckeyes to a 50-20 blasting of Michigan at Ann Arbor. Fifty points are the most ever scored by the Buckeyes against the Wolverines. On his way to the dressing room after the game, Ferguson gave his chinstrap to a young Ohio State fan who requested it as a souvenir.

Seven years later in 1968, Ohio State was preparing for its game with Michigan which would determine the outright Big Ten champion. Both teams entered the contest with 6-0 league records. At a huge pep rally on the Ohio State campus the Friday evening prior to the big game, the fan to whom Ferguson had given his chinstrap approached Otis, told him the history of the chinstrap and gave it to him.

The next day, Otis taped his new keepsake inside his shoulder pads as a measure of "good luck." In almost magical fashion that afternoon, Otis scored four touchdowns, just like Ferguson, and Ohio State again scored 50 points while defeating the Wolverines 50-14. Otis still treasures that famous chinstrap — the one that crossed the Michigan goal line eight times.

TWO-TIME LEADERS

There have been four two-time captains during the first 102 years of Ohio State football. The most recent is linebacker Thomas "Pepper" Johnson in 1984-85. The other three are linebacker Glenn Cobb (1981-82), tailback Archie Griffin (1974-75) and halfback Richard T. Ellis in 1891-92.

HAVE DESIRE, WILL PLAY

Ohio State's leading pass receiver in 1966 and '67 was end Billy Anders of Sabina, Ohio. Anders ranks fourth in career pass receiving with 108 catches for 1,318 yards and six touchdowns. Because his high school had been too small to field a football team, Anders never had the opportunity to play the game until his days at Ohio State. He and defensive halfback Sam Elliott were the Buckeyes' 1967 co-captains.

HOMEWORK WITH HAYES

Dick Guy, a fine tackle on Woody Hayes' teams of the mid-1950s, was a very outgoing individual who always liked to have fun at whatever he was doing. Hayes apparently thought Guy should take a little more serious approach to football. In the dressing room following practice the Monday evening prior to the 1955 Ohio State-Michigan game, Hayes told Guy, "You're moving in with me for a few days."

Guy spent the next three nights at the Hayes home. "Woody drilled me right up until bedtime every night," Guy recalls. Hayes would repeatedly ask, "What do you do on this play?" Then they would start all over again early the next morning. Thursday, Hayes finally allowed Guy to return to his campus room after he was convinced Guy knew all his assignments. "Man, was I glad to get out of there," Guy reflects. That weekend in Ann Arbor, Guy played one of the best games of his career as Ohio State beat Michigan 17-0.

TAILOR'S TALE

Bo Gallo of O.P. Gallo Tailoring and Formal Wear in Columbus remembers an incident which occurred approximately 25 years after the famous Ohio State-Notre Dame game of 1935. One Saturday morning, Gallo was getting ready to open his downtown store when a man knocked at the front door and asked if he could have a button sewn on his coat.

Gallo took the man inside and personally began to sew on the button. Since it was a football Saturday, Gallo asked him if he was in town to see the Ohio State game. "Why, yes," he replied, "I'm one of the officials who will be working today's game at Ohio Stadium."

The two introduced themselves with the man identifying himself as Mike Layden. Gallo asked him if he was related to the former Notre Dame football coach, Elmer Layden. "Yes, Elmer is my older brother," he said.

Gallo then recalled the '35 Ohio State-Notre Dame game, mentioning that his brother-in-law Frank Antenucci, had been a Buckeye fullback who played against the Irish that afternoon. "Frank made a great interception, then lateralled to Frank Boucher who sped 65 yards for Ohio State's first touchdown," he remembered.

Gallo then asked Layden if he had seen this game. Layden laughed a little, then said he not only had seen the contest, but that he had played football under his brother at Notre Dame, and had been one of the starting halfbacks that afternoon. With that, Gallo said, "Do you remember Frank's interception?" Layden replied, "Mr. Gallo, I remember it very well — I'm the one who threw the pass!"

CLUTCH KICKER

Ohio State posted a 7-2 record in 1965, but without the talents of placekicker Bob Funk, the record might have been 4-5. Three of Funk's eight field goals that season meant the difference between victory and defeat:

• A 27-yard field goal with just 59 seconds remaining earned Ohio State a 23-21 victory at Washington.

• An 18-yard field goal with 1:17 left gave the Buckeyes an 11-10 homecoming win over Minnesota.

• At Michigan, his 28-yard field goal with 1:15 remaining lifted Ohio State over the Wolverines 9-7.

KEEPING IT CLOSE

During the 60 Ohio State-Michigan games from 1931-90, each school scored a total of 883 points. The Wolverines had a very slight edge in these 60 games, 29-28-3.

NEIGHBOR'S REMARK MOTIVATES HAYES

While addressing the *Columbus Dispatch* Quarterback Club one evening during the 1975 season, coach Woody Hayes told of an event during the summer of 1954 which influenced his career. He recalled relaxing on his porch one Saturday evening while neighbors were having a small get-together nearby. Apparently they were talking about the Ohio State football program and Hayes overheard one neighbor state, "This is the year we get rid of Woody!"

Hayes' teams had a combined record of 16-9-2 and no Big Ten titles during his three previous seasons and the neighbor was wishfully thinking the coach would be gone after the '54 campaign. Hayes said that incident provided additional motivation for him to do his very best that fall. "I even got up an hour earlier each day so I could prepare all the more," he stated. As it turned out, the '54 season was the turning point for Hayes. His team went 10-0, through an extremely tough conference schedule, to capture the national title.

WRONG SIDELINE TWO YEARS RUNNING

Wes Fesler was the losing coach in the Ohio State-Pittsburgh games of 1946 and '47, even though he changed jobs between seasons.

Fesler was head coach at Pitt in 1946 when the Panthers lost to the Buckeyes 20-13 in Ohio Stadium. When Paul Bixler resigned the Ohio State job after the '46 season, Fesler accepted the opening. The following season, Pitt won only one game — Ohio State. The Panthers wanted revenge over their old coach and defeated his Buckeye squad 12-0 at Pitt Stadium.

THE HOUSTON BROTHERS

Occupying a rare chapter in Ohio State football are the Houston Brothers of Massillon — both were All-Americans and both played on national championship teams.

Lin Houston was a guard on Paul Brown's national title squad of 1942. That season, he was part of a unique guard-tackle-end All-American trio which included tackle Chuck Csuri and Bob Shaw.

Lin's younger brother, Jim, played end on Woody Hayes' national champions of 1957. He became an All-American the following two seasons and was the Buckeyes' captain in 1959.

REAGAN STUNNED BY COMEBACK

Columbus' Jimmy Crum received the Sertoma International Service to Mankind Award in 1984 in recognition of his lifetime of service to others. As part of this honor, Jimmy and his wife, Miriam, visited President and Mrs. Reagan at the White House.

When the conversation turned to Ohio State football, Reagan recalled being in Iowa City in 1935 to broadcast the Iowa-Indiana game on the same Saturday Notre Dame was playing at Ohio State. At that time, scores of other games were provided by Western Union ticker tape.

The entire nation was interested in the outcome of the Ohio State-Notre Dame game so Reagan frequently announced the score. Aware the Buckeyes had been leading 13-0 in the fourth quarter, Reagan received a tape showing the final score: Notre Dame 18, Ohio State 13. "I thought it was an error. I couldn't believe Notre Dame would have been able to score three touchdowns in so little time," Reagan told the Crums, "so I never announced the final score."

AIR WAR IN ANN ARBOR

Airplane banner towing over Ohio Stadium on a football Saturday is a popular means of commercial advertising and of conveying personal messages. Pilot Bill Watts, who has been towing stadium banners since 1969, recalls messages of "Joe Loves Sue," "Happy 50th Birthday, Harry," and "Judy, Will You Marry Me?"

One remarkable tow Watts recalls took place during Earle Bruce's first season in 1979. Enthusiasm was running high as the undefeated Buckeyes headed north to tangle with Michigan. Three Columbus businesses hired Watts to fly all the way to Ann Arbor that Saturday and tow a "Go Bucks Go" banner over

Michigan Stadium.

Watts' banner must have helped . . . Ohio State came from behind in the fourth quarter to win, 18-15, thereby capturing the outright Big Ten title and the trip to Pasadena.

SEVENTEEN NEAR-MISSES

Ohio State has had four undefeated-untied seasons:

| 1916 (7-0) | 1944 (9-0) |
| 1954 (10-0) | 1968 (10-0) |

Additionally, the Buckeyes have experienced 17 near-perfect seasons, winning all but one game:

Season	Record	Loss or Tie
1899	9-0-1	Ohio State 5, Case 5
1906	8-1	Ohio State 0, Michigan 6
1917	8-0-1	Ohio State 0, Auburn 0
1919	6-1	Ohio State 7, Illinois 9
1920	7-1	Ohio State 0, California 28*
1926	7-1	Ohio State 16, Michigan 17
1933	7-1	Ohio State 0, Michigan 13
1934	7-1	Ohio State 13, Illinois 14
1935	7-1	Ohio State 13, Notre Dame 18
1942	9-1	Ohio State 7, Wisconsin 17
1957	9-1	Ohio State 14, Texas Christian 18
1961	8-0-1	Ohio State 7, Texas Christian 7
1969	8-1	Ohio State 12, Michigan 24
1970	9-1	Ohio State 17, Stanford 27*
1973	10-0-1	Ohio State 10, Michigan 10
1975	11-1	Ohio State 10, UCLA 23*
1979	11-1	Ohio State 16, Southern Cal 17*

*Rose Bowl

JUMPING THE GUN

Long-time Buckeye fans Vic and Dot Ketcham recall overhearing a conversation between two football fans seated behind them at the 1935 Ohio State-Notre Dame game. The two appeared to be complete strangers, one cheering for the Buckeyes and the other for the Irish. The pair struck up a friendly conversation and the Ketchams overheard them make a $10 bet on the game.

Early in the fourth quarter (with Ohio State leading 13-0) the Notre Dame fan apparently gave up hope. "Here's your ten bucks," he said, handing the Ohio State fan a $10 bill as he headed for the exit. After the Irish completed their miraculous comeback to win (18-13), the Buckeye fan lamented, "What should I do with this guy's $10? I don't even know his name or have any idea where he lives."

The Ketchams recall another story, forty-two years later, when they were in New Orleans to see the January 2, 1978, Sugar Bowl between Ohio State and Alabama. At one of the hotel's social functions, Vic began talking with a gentleman who appeared to have a real interest in college football. Vic explained that he and Dot had gone to many exciting games over the years including the Ohio State-Notre Dame game of 1935.

Ketcham reminisced in detail about this particular game and the outstanding play of Notre Dame quarterback Andy Pilney. Pretty soon, Ketcham introduced himself. Much to his surprise, the other gentleman replied, "Vic, it's very nice to meet you. My name is Andy Pilney and I'm the Andy Pilney who played quarterback for Notre Dame back in '35."

Bo

Bo Schembechler (left), an Ohio State assistant coach for five seasons, poses with his 1962 tackles: Daryl Sanders (#76) and Bob Vogel (#73). Both were NFL first-round draft picks in '63, Sanders by the Detroit Lions and Vogel by the Baltimore Colts.

Varsity "O" At Last

Arthur Huntington, who lettered in 1895, finally received his award 53 years later.

Renick Dunlap, the 1895 captain, was reviewing a list of Varsity "O" members and realized Huntington's name was missing. Dunlap notified the athletic department and Huntington's monogrammed sweater was finally sent to him in 1948.

Ohio's "Other Team" Goes West

On an extremely cold and windy November afternoon at Ohio Stadium in 1964, Michigan shutout Ohio State 10-0 to emerge as the outright Big Ten champion and representative to the Rose Bowl.

Not surprisingly, all four of Ohio State's offensive backs that afternoon were from Ohio — quarterback Don Unverferth of Dayton, fullback Will Sander of Cincinnati and halfbacks Bo Rein and Tom Barrington of Niles and Lima, respectively.

Ironically, Michigan's entire offensive backfield was also from Ohio. All-American quarterback Bob Timberlake hailed from Franklin and halfback Jim Detwiler, who scored the game's only touchdown on a pass from Timberlake, was from Toledo. Fullback Mel Anthony and halfback Carl Ward were both from Cincinnati.

Ohio's "other team" represented the Big Ten well in the January 1, 1965, Rose Bowl, defeating Oregon State 34-7.

No More Mr. Nice Guy

The 1975 Buckeyes were 7-0 as they prepared for the season's eighth game — a meeting with Indiana at Ohio Stadium on the first Saturday in November. Ohio State had just completed an impressive 35-6 win over Purdue while Indiana lost to Michigan the previous week 55-7. The Hoosiers had won only two of their first seven starts.

Woody Hayes did something that week that, for him, was a first — he gave his players Monday off without practice. After seven games and with apparently not too tough an opponent the following weekend, Hayes thought the rest would be good for his squad.

That Saturday, Lee Corso's Hoosiers gave Ohio State the scare of the season. Indiana threatened to take the lead during the final quarter but the Buckeyes held, then scored late in the game to secure a 24-14 win. Ohio State had all it could handle before winning and the game was even closer than the final score suggests. Hayes was never known to again cancel a Monday practice.

TWO SCHOOLS, TWO NATIONAL TITLES

J.T. White has the distinction of not only earning a football letter at both Ohio State and Michigan but also playing on a national championship team at each school.

White played end on the Buckeyes' first national title squad in 1942. That year, he also played opposite his brother, Paul, during OSU's 21-7 win over Michigan. After returning from military service, White decided to finish his education at Michigan, where he was the starting center with the Wolverines' national champions of 1947. J.T. later served as an assistant coach at Penn State for several seasons under Rip Engle and Joe Paterno.

HAS THE SHELBYVILLE SCORE BEEN ANNOUNCED?

The following story is remembered by Dr. Chalmer Hixson, a 1937 graduate of Ohio State, an expert on NCAA football rules and a former professor of physical education at Ohio State.

The Buckeyes played at Notre Dame in 1936 and a group of Ohio State students decided to attend the game. They left Columbus and headed for South Bend, Indiana, early Saturday morning. Unfortunately, their car broke down near Shelbyville, Indiana, and they were forced to listen to the game on radio while their car was being repaired.

While driving back to Columbus that evening, and not wanting to tell their friends exactly what had happened, the group decided it would be fun to tell everyone they had gone to the "Shelbyville University" game against "Snake Valley Normal." In addition to inventing Shelbyville U., one student composed lyrics to an "Oh Shelbyville" fight song.

The following season, the group told their story to Leo Staley, Ohio Stadium public address announcer, and asked him to occasionally include Shelbyville when reporting other scores. Staley agreed and once or twice a season for the next several years he included the Shelbyville-Snake Valley Normal game when announcing scores from other games around the country. Shelbyville was usually a big winner — sometimes by as much as 55-0!

CLANCY'S ANNUAL RITUAL

A familiar happening for many seasons was the return of Clancy Issac at homecoming to lead his annual cheer, "Yea Ohio, Yea Ohio, Let's Go, Let's Fight, Let's Win!"

Issac was a cheerleader in the late-'30s and the originator

of the Block "O" card section in 1938. He got the idea after seeing a similar activity at the University of Southern California when the Buckeyes played there in '37.

Clancy returned for his familiar homecoming cheer for 40 consecutive years from 1939-78. His final appearance at the horseshoe was an emotional moment as the marching band spelled CLANCY as a tribute to his many years of loyalty and enthusiasm. The date was October 21, 1978, and Issac also remembers talking with Bob Hope, who was in Ohio Stadium that afternoon celebrating his 75th birthday.

In 1970, Issac was honored by his alma mater as "one of 100 distinguished alumni selected during The Ohio State University's first 100 years."

THE CENTURY MARK

Ohio State has had three coaches who have guided the Buckeyes for 100 or more games:
- John W. Wilce, 120 games (78-33-9), 1913-1928.
- Woody Hayes, 276 games (205-61-10), 1951-1978.
- Earle Bruce, 108 games (81-26-1), 1979-1987.

HEY, BUDDY, YOU'RE SITTING IN MY SEAT!

The beginning of the 1974 season was anything but normal. The Buckeyes opened with a 34-19 win over Minnesota at Minneapolis — Ohio State's first road opener in 80 years.

In the home opener the following Saturday, the Buckeyes blew out Oregon State 51-10. But some of the *real* action that afternoon came, not from the playing field, but up in the stands. As fans began arriving, portal chief Kenny Tinkler suddenly realized he had a big problem as all seats for section 9B had been double-printed and double-sold. In essence, two different fans each held identical tickets for each seat. Tinkler estimates nearly 700 seats had been duplicated. Obviously, most of the spectators were anything but overjoyed with the predicament.

Some fans were moved on top of the press box, others on temporary folding chairs placed on the running track while others simply sat in the aisles. Portal superintendent Dick Weber has remarked, "Those displaced fans probably can't recall the season, the opponent or the final score — but they'll always remember the confusion associated with the double-printing of the opening game tickets for section 9B."

SMALLEST GATHERING

Ohio State's 13-7 win over Wilmington in 1926 was played before a crowd of 5,482, smallest in Ohio Stadium history.

HAYES CALLED HIM THE BIG TEN'S BEST

He is one of the finest and most highly-recognized athletes in Ohio State history. Woody Hayes often introduced him as "the best quarterback in the Big Ten," yet he never took a snap from center or threw a single pass.

John Havlicek excelled as a football, basketball and base-ball player in high school and Hayes wanted Havlicek to join the Buckeyes at quarterback. Woody spoke at Havlicek's high school banquet and watched him play in the Ohio-West Virginia All-Star football game in the summer of 1958. Havlicek also made three visits to Columbus to discuss the Ohio State football program.

When he finally decided to concentrate on basketball, Hayes assisted basketball coach Fred Taylor with his recruiting. Havlicek became one of the Buckeyes' all-time greats and helped Ohio State capture the NCAA championship in 1960. Havlicek recalls, "Woody always left the door open for me to play football and he also kept his promise of not trying to per-suade me to change my mind."

Hayes' reference to Havlicek as the Big Ten's best quarter-back obviously refers to the success Hayes believes Havlicek would have enjoyed had he decided to play football.

ANOTHER VOTE FOR QB HAVLICEK

Woody Hayes wasn't the only one who realized Havlicek's quarterback potential. Havlicek's ability to pass the football became very apparent to WCMH-TV's Sports Director Jimmy Crum while he and former *Columbus Citizen-Journal* columnist

Kaye Kessler were covering an Ohio State football practice in 1960.

It was mid-October and the basketball team was using Ohio Stadium for physical conditioning. Quarterback Tom Matte had just come out of the dressing room when Havlicek yelled, "Tom, let me see the ball — I'll throw you one." Matte started down the field while Havlicek kept signaling him to go farther. Finally, Havlicek threw the football and Crum estimates it traveled at least 70 yards.

Havlicek innocently looked over at Crum and Kessler and said his arm was sore; normally he could throw even farther. No question about it — Havlicek could really pass the pigskin.

INAUGURAL LOMBARDI WINNER

Middle guard Jim Stillwagon won the Outland Trophy and the very first Lombardi Award in 1970, his senior year. A two-time All-American in 1969-70, Still-wagon is a member of the College Football Hall of Fame.

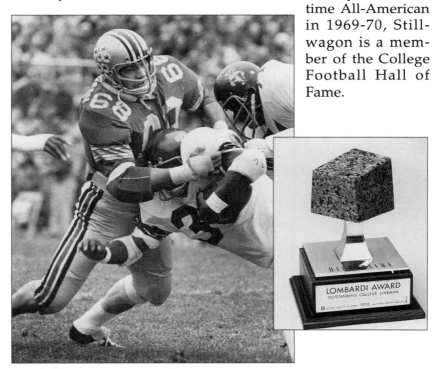

Jim Stillwagon

FULLBACK DELIGHT

Woody Hayes' love for his fullback-oriented offense was never more evident than during Ohio State's 28-0 shutout of Michigan in 1962. That afternoon, Hayes' three senior fullbacks scored all four of the touchdowns.

Dave Francis scored twice while rushing for 186 yards on 31 carries. The other touchdowns were scored by Bob Butts and Dave Katterhenrich. This game was also the final college game for Ohio State co-captains Bob Vogel, who later enjoyed tremendous success with the Baltimore Colts, and Gary Moeller, now head coach of the Michigan Wolverines.

Francis led the Big Ten in rushing that year even though he had carried only 14 times the two previous seasons while playing behind two-time All-American Bob Ferguson.

OHIO STATE'S FRIENDLIEST FRATERNITY

The great tradition of Ohio State is exemplified by its non-fraternity fraternity, SiU, a group dating back to the deep depression days of the 1930s. "It all began as a gag to impress coeds," related the late Nate Fraher, a 1937 graduate of Ohio State. "The name SiU was adopted from a wealthy fraternity at Kenyon College named Psi U. We hoped girls would assume we were from the same organization. Actually very few of the guys could afford to belong to a real fraternity. We all shared two circumstances — great friendship and an acute lack of money."

Smitty's Drug Store at 16th and High was a popular hangout for the football squads of the 30s. The basement was often used as a place to gather and socialize. Fraher was the store's soda clerk at the pretentious salary of fifteen cents an hour. He jokingly referred to Smitty's as the international headquarters of OSU's sidewalk fraternity.

Some twenty years later, Fraher and a few others decided it would be great fun if everyone could get together again, and a banquet was scheduled for the Friday evening prior to the Iowa game in 1957. The response was beyond belief as more than 200 returned for the first reunion. SiU has been meeting biannually ever since. "The popular reunions are so anxiously anticipated," says Fraher, "because we just have so much fun together."

Jim Smith, owner of Smitty's Drug Store and Bob Hill of the adjoining Hill Tailoring were honored at the first reunion as "SiU Men of the Year." Since then, the many individuals honored have included track star Jesse Owens, Governor James Rhodes, cartoonist Milton Caniff, quarterback Tippy Dye, Woody Hayes and Mrs. Anne Hayes. All four of Ohio State's Heisman Trophy winners were on hand to be honored at the 1985 banquet.

The SiU Motto tells it all: Never had a Charter, House, Pin or Dues. Never had a Formal Dance, Ritual or any Extra Money. ALL WE HAD WAS FRIENDSHIP.

Snow Bowl Attraction

Marilyn Soliday was one of many Buckeye fans who braved the weather to attend the infamous "Snow Bowl" between Ohio State and Michigan in 1950. She had a ticket for section 18C but sat in 18B because of the icy aisles.

During the second half, she noticed one of the portals seemed almost frozen from the cold and offered to share one of her two blankets with him. His name was Barney Atkinson. When Marilyn had to leave to catch a bus to her home in Bexley, Barney offered her a ride since he drove through Bexley on his way home to Pataskala.

Marilyn recalls that it took nearly three hours of driving through the heavy snow before he dropped her off at home. The long drive gave them a chance to get to know each other and the following Tuesday, Barney called and asked her to go out. They continued to date and the following May 11 they were married.

MVPs At Two Different Schools

Assistant coach Dick Fisher had the honor of coaching two noted players at two different schools who each became the Big Ten's most valuable player. Fisher (an excellent halfback himself for the Buckeyes in the early 1940s) became an assistant to coach Wes Fesler. Among his many players was Vic Janowicz, 1950 Heisman Trophy winner, who that season was also the Big Ten's

MVP. When Fesler moved to Minnesota as head coach in 1951, Fisher went with him. At Minnesota, Fisher coached one of the Golden Gophers' all-time greats, halfback Paul Giel, the Big Ten's MVP in both 1952 and '53.

SAFETY FIRST

Imagine completing a forward pass and having a safety scored against you — all on the same play. It happened in the 1955 Ohio State-Michigan game. The Wolverines, trailing 9-0 in the fourth quarter, had possession deep in their own territory. Quarterback Jim Maddock faded back into his own end zone then flipped a short pass into the flat to halfback Terry Barr. Before Barr could move up field, the Buckeyes' Bill Michael and Aurelius Thomas brought him to the ground for a safety. Ohio State won the game 17-0.

ENTERPRISING YOUNG GATE CRASHER

Fans unable to obtain tickets to Ohio State games sometimes resort to devious methods of entry. Some have tried slipping through the north gates with the marching band, others have tried the emergency exits inside the Stadium Scholarship Dormitories, and a brazen few have scaled the gates.

Frank Buffington, superintendent of gates, remembers a clever incident back in the early 1970s. A young boy, about 11, approached Gate 10 carrying a bag of ice on each shoulder. He explained that a concession manager had sent him out to obtain the ice. The ticket takers were somewhat suspicious of the boy's story but finally decided to let him through. Buffington recalls one of the gatemen saying, "Now let's see what he does."

After walking approximately sixty feet inside the stadium, the youngster suddenly dropped both sacks of ice and took off running at full speed. Buffington laughingly remarks, "What an *enterprising* young gate crasher! Just think, this youngster engineered his way inside Ohio Stadium for the cost of two 25-cent bags of ice!"

KING OF THE HILL NO LONGER

Nine times during the 22 seasons from 1969-90, Ohio State and Michigan have entered their season-ending game with one team undefeated in league play and the other with one loss. Seven of the nine seasons the team with the single league loss became the winner of the Ohio State-Michigan game. The two exceptions are 1979 and 1989.

	League Records Prior To Game		
Season	OSU	UM	Winner Of Game
1969	6-0	5-1	Michigan, 24-12
1972	6-1	7-0	Ohio State, 14-11
1974	6-1	7-0	Ohio State, 12-10
1976	7-0	6-1	Michigan, 22-0
1977	7-0	6-1	Michigan, 14-6
1979	7-0	6-1	Ohio State, 18-15
1982	6-1	8-0	Ohio State, 24-14
1986	7-0	6-1	Michigan, 26-24
1989	6-1	7-0	Michigan, 28-18

THE QUEEN THAT MOOED

The election of Maudine Ormsby as Ohio State's 1926 homecoming queen is one of the most remarkable college pranks of all time — Maudine was a pure-bred Holstein cow.

While the fraternities and sororities submitted the names of ten women candidates for queen, "Miss Ormsby" was sponsored by the College of Agriculture. A more crooked election was never held as Ohio State's enrollment was 9,300 students in 1926, yet more than 13,000 ballots were cast. Election committee members were unable to unravel the ballot-stuffing problem so they declared Maudine queen.

Maudine rode in the homecoming parade but university officials refused to let the bovine attend the traditional dance held at the Crystal Slipper, which was located on the north side of Lane Avenue across from where the French Field House now stands.

The candidate who would have been queen, had it not

been for Maudine, was Rosalind Morrison Strapp, a 1927 graduate. In later years, Strapp laughed and joked about the event, agreeing that it really was her claim to fame. After graduation she attended every Ohio State homecoming until her death in 1986. Strapp often joked that her epitaph should read: "But for Maudine, here lies a queen."

"Snow Bowl" Souvenirs

John Hummel was in charge of distributing football programs for many seasons at Ohio Stadium. He recalls that only about 4,000 of the 28,000 printed for the "Snow Bowl" were sold. After the heavy snow cleared the following week, Hummel arranged for a truck to haul away the remaining 24,000. "What a mistake. We later had many requests from people wanting to purchase one of them. Just think of the money the university lost by not having those available as collectors' items," he suggested years later.

It's Hard To Get Ahead Of Woody

Before freshmen became eligible for varsity competition in 1972, they normally sat together for all home games in section 17 directly behind the Ohio State bench. Two of the Buckeyes' most promising freshmen in 1961 were halfbacks Paul Warfield and Matt Snell. As the two reached their seats just prior to kick-off at the November 19, 1960, game against Michigan, both were instructed to meet with Woody Hayes in the Ohio State dressing room immediately after the game.

Approximately 45 minutes after the Buckeyes had defeated Michigan 7-0 and with the stadium basically cleared, the coach came back out onto the field with his two prized halfbacks dressed in sweat suits. Senior quarterback Tom Matte (OSU's MVP in '60) had just played his last collegiate game and Hayes was already considering a shift of either Warfield or Snell to quarterback. Also, Hayes was not breaking any NCAA rules since practices could be held through the day of the season's last game.

The two worked out about an hour passing and practicing handoffs. The following season, Warfield and Snell had moved into the starting halfback positions with John Mummey and Bill Mrukowski basically sharing the quarterback chores along with the Buckeyes' best passer, Joe Sparma. The Buckeyes went 8-0-1 in '61 and finished with a 50-20 victory at Michigan.

Better Late Than Never

Fred and John Zimmerman, whose firm publishes the Ohio State football programs, had a few anxious moments prior to one of the 1983 home games. The Zimmermans guarantee the programs will be at the stadium on time — otherwise they pay for the programs (at $2 apiece).

The programs are printed in Dayton and the schedule calls for the delivery to reach the stadium by noon Friday. One particular Friday morning, Fred received a call from the printer telling him he should be concerned about the condition of the truck which just left for Columbus with the programs.

Soon Fred received another call. The truck was stuck with a

broken axle on Interstate 70, about one-half hour east of Dayton. When Fred reached the scene, he discovered the truck driver unloading the programs onto the ground, even though there was a strong threat of rain.

Another truck was acquired and loaded and the programs finally reached Ohio Stadium around 7 p.m. By this time, the stadium maintenance crew that normally unloads the truck had gone home and the stadium was locked. The only opening was a ticket window near gate 28, just wide enough for one box to be handed through. So, one by one, all 500 boxes (weighing 20 pounds each) were passed through this window. Tired, sore and hungry, Fred and his crew finished about 11 p.m.

VICTORY BELL

Ohio State's victory bell has been sounding after every home win since 1953. A gift from the class of '43, the bell is located in the south east tower of Ohio Stadium. The original plans called for the bell to be located on the oval and sounded after every athletic victory, not just football. After the bell was cast nearly ten years later, it was placed in its present location.

84-12-6

Ohio State has had 84 winning seasons, six at an even 50 percent winning rate and only 12 losing seasons during its first 102 years through 1991. The most recent losing season was 1988 (4-6-1); the Buckeyes have not had consecutive losing years since 1923 (3-4-1) and 1924 (2-3-3). Following is a summary by time periods:

Seasons	Winning	.500	Losing	Total
First 30 (1890-1919)	22	4	4	30
Second 30 (1920-1949)	23	2	5	30
Third 30 (1950-1979)	28	0	2	30
Last 12 (1980-1991)	11	0	1	12
TOTALS	**84**	**6**	**12**	**102**

MEMORABLE SCRIPT

Tom Hamilton, former sportscaster with WBNS Radio in Columbus and now play-by-play voice of the Cleveland Indians, was the color commentator with the University of Wisconsin football radio network in 1983. Hamilton's first game in Ohio Stadium was the Buckeyes' 1983 homecoming game against the Wisconsin Badgers.

"I was doing a halftime interview," remembers Hamilton, "when suddenly the crowd's applause became so deafening, I simply couldn't continue with the interview. We all looked out of the radio booth to see what was happening down on the field — Woody Hayes had just dotted the "i" in Script Ohio."

SMALL TOWN, U.S.A.

Don Hoaglin of Battle Creek, Michigan, enjoys showing Ohio State fans a copy of the State of Michigan's 1979 Official Transportation Road Map. The layout engineer became very creative when he inserted "new towns" just south of the Michigan-Ohio line. One labeled "beatosu" is placed on Route 66 between Archbold and the Ohio Turnpike. The other, "goblu," is located on Route 2, just east of Toledo.

ONLY THE BEST FOR WOODY'S COACHES

Dave Diles, former anchor for ABC's college football studio telecasts, covered sports for the *Associated Press*, both in Columbus and Detroit, before moving to New York with ABC.

Diles recalls that Woody Hayes agreed to speak at the 1954 high school football banquet in Middleport where Diles grew up. When Ohio State found itself headed for the Rose Bowl, though, Hayes asked if they could re-schedule the banquet for after January 1, and the school agreed. "The place was filled to capacity that night," Diles recalls, "and Woody really captivated them."

Hayes met Diles' parents that evening and a strong friendship developed over the next several years. The coach would call when he was going to be in the area and ask Mrs. Diles to bake one of her lemon meringue pies. When assistant coaches Ernie Godfrey and Esco Sarkkinen spoke at Middleport banquets in later years, Hayes insisted they first stop and have a piece of "Lucille Diles' lemon meringue pie — the world's finest!"

PRESS DAY

Buckeye fans of all ages attend Ohio State's annual press day to obtain autographs, take pictures and preview the forthcoming season with players and coaches. Jane (left) and Julie Park pose with quarterback Jim Karsatos at the '83 gathering.

LOYALTY PLUS

Bob Schlegel has been a diehard Buckeye since seeing his first game at age seven in the late-1930s. He and his wife Pete have attended numerous games over the years, even while living in Cincinnati, Chicago, Toronto, Tokyo and Elkhart, Indiana.

When daughter, Deb, graduated with honors from "that school up north," Bob wore a gray sport coat and red slacks to the president's reception. After Deb accepted a job in Japan, Bob gave her a "one way ticket to Tokyo."

GETTING IN WAS HALF THE FUN!

Reverend Ted Lilley, a 1927 graduate of Ohio State, is a retired minister living in Cedar Rapids, Iowa. As a youngster growing up in Columbus, Lilley and his friends devised creative ways of getting inside old Ohio Field on Saturday afternoons. Scaling the fences surrounding the field, known as fencing, was the most popular method.

Another good routine was known as blanketing. The players would run to Ohio Field from the old Athletic House near 16th and High with their blankets either being carried or worn cape-like over their shoulders. As the players approached the gate, young fans would dart under a blanket and go through with one of the players.

Still another way was called gate-crashing. Timing was key and Lilley learned that the best time to strike was near kickoff when impatient fans crowded through the turnstiles. Looking back, Lilley has pleasant memories of seeing Chic Harley, Pete Stinchcomb and other great players of the time but admits getting into old Ohio Field was half the fun.

Ted's father's cousin was Alexander S. Lilley, Ohio State's first football coach in 1890.

A THANKLESS JOB

Former Ticket Director Bob Ries recalls an incident when Ed Weaver was ticket director. Weaver had taken a group to lunch and had parked his car on High Street near downtown Columbus. When he returned he found his front windshield heavily soaped with the message, "I can't see from my seats, either!"

TONGUE TWISTERS

"Ladies and gentlemen, welcome to Ohio Stadium and Ohio State Football," was the familiar introduction used by Ron Althoff, stadium public address announcer from 1969-88. Althoff spent considerable time each week learning to correctly pronounce all the players' names. Among those which required a little extra time were:

John DiFeliciantonio - Illinois
Ali Haji-Shiekh - Michigan
Ralf Mojsiejenko - Michigan State
Olatide Ogunfitidimi - Michigan
Manu Tuiasosopo - UCLA

ORANGE AND BLACK BUCKEYES

Orange and black were first chosen as Ohio State's colors in 1878. When the selection committee learned that Princeton had already selected these colors, the committee instead picked scarlet and gray.

OFF YEAR FOR RIVALS

The Ohio State and Michigan football programs have both been extremely successful over the years. Only once during the 88 seasons Ohio State and Michigan have met through 1991 have both teams finished a season with losing records — 1959. The Wolverines' record was 4-5 in '59 while the Buckeyes' was 3-5-1.

A GREAT ICE BREAKER AT PARTIES

An Ohio Stadium tradition since the early 1980s is Orlas King's neutron dance in section 11B.

When the Ohio State-Michigan contest is at Ann Arbor, King hosts a party at his home to view the game. If Ohio State wins, King immediately dives into a pond in his backyard with nothing on but his Brutus Buckeye underwear. It was so cold the day of the Buckeyes' 14-9 win in 1981, King had to crack the ice before he could take a dip. When asked if this tradition could be a little hard on his health, King responded,"The thrill of beating Michigan is so great, I don't feel a thing!"

SPORTSMANSHIP AT ITS BEST

With Ohio State leading Southern California 20-7 late in the 1955 Rose Bowl, Woody Hayes began sending in players who had not yet been in the game. One such player was co-captain John Borton, who had lost his starting quarterback position that season to Dave Leggett. As Hayes called upon Borton to relieve Leggett, Borton very unselfishly suggested that third-team quarterback Bill Booth be inserted instead. Borton was aware that Booth's father, Dick Booth, had played fullback for the Pitt

Panthers against Stanford in the 1928 Rose Bowl. Hayes proudly shook Borton's hand, then beckoned Booth who quarterbacked the last three plays of the game.

Borton was Ohio State's only able-bodied player not to see action that afternoon, but his thoughtfulness will always be remembered by Booth as "the greatest act of sportsmanship I have ever seen." Booth's proud father was in attendance that day and they became the first father-son combination to have appeared in a Rose Bowl.

FAR AWAY PLACES

Dr. Norman Burns of Bryan, Ohio, carries the Ohio State spirit with him everywhere he goes. While visiting China in 1983 with five other dentists and their wives, Burns found time to take pictures of the Great Wall of China after decorating it with a large Ohio State pennant. Retired, he now has more time for one of his favorite activities — covering Ohio State football. During the football season, Burns serves as a photographer and stringer for the *Bryan Times* and also produces a sports program on WBNO Radio in Bryan.

THE DUGGER BROTHERS

Brothers Jack and Dean Dugger had a lot in common. Both played end for the Buckeyes, both were All-Americans and both played on undefeated-untied national championship teams.

Jack was All-American in 1944 under Carroll Widdoes when Ohio State compiled a 9-0 record and was declared the national civilian champion. Ten years later, Dean earned All-American honors. That season, Woody Hayes' Buckeyes went 10-0 to capture the 1954 national title.

THE SERGEANT AND THE PROFESSOR

Pat Harmon, historian/curator at the College Football Hall of Fame, tells a story about Woody Hayes driving all night to get home from Philadelphia after the evening's last flight was cancelled. Hayes was not too happy and as he was making arrangements for a rental car, a young Air Force sergeant named David Buller overhead him and asked if he could ride with him. Hayes readily agreed as Buller explained his need to get to Dayton to make a connection to his home in Ogden, Utah.

The two drove all night and as they reached the outskirts of Columbus about 3 a.m., Hayes called John Mummey, one of his assistant coaches, and asked Mummey to drive Buller on to Dayton. As Mummey started for the Dayton airport, Buller indicated how impressed he was with Hayes' knowledge of history and how enlightening it was to talk with him.

With that, Mummey asked, "Do you know who you were riding with?" "He said his name was Hayes," Buller replied, "and he sure sounded like a history professor." Mummey asked, "Are you aware this Mr. Hayes is coach Woody Hayes of Ohio State?" "You're kidding, *the* Woody Hayes? He never once even mentioned football," the open-mouthed sergeant answered. "I can't believe it. Just wait until I tell my parents!"

Mummey drove Buller to Dayton then headed back to Columbus for an 8 a.m. coaches' meeting — and there was Woody, eager to get started after only a couple hours sleep.

NEVER MISSES A BEAT

One of the most recognized performers at each season's alumni band appearance is Drum Major Deve Kesling. Well-known for his twirling ability and general showmanship, Kesling was Ohio State's drum major in 1947 and '48 and hasn't missed an alumni band weekend since the first one in 1966. "I just love coming back each fall," he says. "It's always such a thrill."

THE FIRST LADY OF BUCKEYE FOOTBALL

Dan Heinlen, director of alumni affairs, and his wife have had seats in 16B for several years, and have become close friends with many of the portal workers in this section. One Saturday in the early 1980s they were greeted by a new portal worker dressed in the standard red cap and coat, who was really having a good time helping people find their seats — Mrs. Anne Hayes. Dan recalls the fun and excitement she was creating and how many people were coming into the section specifically to talk with her.

WAKE-UP CALL

The Ohio State Marching Band spent Friday evening at a Toledo hotel before continuing on to Ann Arbor for the Michigan game in 1949. Band members Jimmy Thompson and Merv Durea recall that the trumpet section decided to provide the Saturday morning wake-up service. Scattered throughout the hotel, all 40 of the trumpeters sounded revelry promptly at 6 a.m. The other members of the band were quickly awakened as were all of the hotel's other guests.

PREOCCUPIED WITH FOOTBALL

Coach Francis Schmidt was totally preoccupied with football 365 days a year. He was never without his 3x5 cards and stubby pencil and he would continually make notes to himself whenever he thought of a new play.

One morning, Schmidt and Athletic Director L. W. St. John decided to go hunting east of Columbus. Schmidt, who was driving, stopped for gasoline. St. John went inside to purchase some food while Schmidt stayed in the car to work on some new plays for next season. When the service station attendant was through, Schmidt paid him and drove away. He was several miles down the road before realizing he had left St. John (his boss) back at the station.

LUCKY BUCKEYE

Ohio State fans Bill and June Kuhn of Bucyrus carry Buckeyes, gathered from a special tree, to each home game. One evening in 1967, Woody Hayes spoke at the OSU Mansfield Campus where June was a student. She remembers the effectiveness of Hayes' talk which stressed desire and dedication and she was thrilled to receive a small Buckeye tree from the coach as a token of friendship and pride.

"That was one of the most significant evenings in my life,"

she recalls. "Woody Hayes gave us the encouragement and confidence to reach our goals." The Kuhns proudly planted the tree; it's been providing Buckeyes ever since.

WHAT A THRILL!

Buckeye fan Jimmy Park talks football with Ohio State's four Heisman Trophy winners: Vic Janowicz, Les Horvath, Hopalong Cassady and Archie Griffin prior to the 1988 Ohio State-Michigan game.

REAL SUCCESS

For three consecutive years, one of Woody Hayes' former players finished first in the Ohio State College of Medicine's first-year class — Arnie Chonko in '66, Don Unverferth in '67 and John Darbyshire in '68.

OUTSTANDING ACCOMPLISHMENT UNDER TRYING CONDITIONS

Carroll Widdoes took over as acting head coach in 1944 after Paul Brown was granted a Navy commission and reported to Great Lakes Training Center. Widdoes was a soft- spoken, reserved individual whose relaxed style of coaching contrasted sharply with Brown's more dynamic approach. He was born in the Philippine Islands, the son of missionary parents and later lived at the United Brethren Home in Lebanon, Ohio. Since Lebanon High School had no football team, Widdoes played his very first football at Otterbein College where he became an excellent all-around athlete.

In '44, Widdoes performed one of the greatest tasks of

coaching in Ohio State history, guiding the Buckeyes to a 9-0 record and the National Civilian Championship. Few people realized, however, the personal stress in Widdoes' life at that time. Knowing that his parents had been captured by the Japanese and were being held as prisoners-of-war, Widdoes spent the entire season wondering if he would ever see them again. Fortunately, they were rescued by U.S. Paratroopers when the war was over in 1945.

ON THE AIR AND OUT THE WINDOW

Rick Rizzs, former sports director at WBNS Radio and now play-by-play voice of the Detroit Tigers, was broadcasting the Ohio State-Wisconsin game from Madison in 1981. Rizzs' color commentator that season was former Buckeye great Jim Stillwagon.

"Jim was really great to work with," recalls Rizzs. "He was a very enthusiastic broadcaster with a tremendous knowledge of the game. That afternoon, while vigorously protesting an official's call, Jim pounded the table in front of us so hard his microphone flew out of our radio booth's open window — while we were on the air." Rizzs continued to talk while Stillwagon used the cord to pull his microphone back into the booth.

Wisconsin won that afternoon 24-21. It was the Badgers' first victory over Ohio State in 22 seasons.

FAMILY TIES

Tom Skladany, three-time All-American punter from 1974-76, is the only specialty team player in Ohio State history to be selected a co-captain. Skladany averaged 42.7 yards on 160 career punts and also holds the school record for the longest field goal, a 59-yarder at Illinois in 1975.

Tom's father, Tom Skladany Sr. of Pittsburgh, was one of four brothers to play professional football during the 1930s. Tom's uncle, Joe Skladany, was one of the Pitt Panthers' all-time greats as a two-time All-American end in 1932 and '33.

THANK YOU, MRS. GRIFFIN

A popular bumper sticker in 1975 simply read, "Thank You, Mrs. Griffin," acknowledging the contributions three of her sons were making on the football field that fall. Archie won his second Heisman Trophy that season, Ray was the starting defensive safety and Duncan (then a freshman) was a member of the Buckeyes' specialty teams.

BUSH HELPS THE BUCKEYES

One of Ohio State's volunteer assistant coaches in 1892 was Samuel P. Bush, grandfather of President George Bush. Samuel Bush was a successful industrialist, civic leader and sportsman who organized an amateur baseball league in Columbus and helped develop the Scioto Country Club golf course.

SWEET SOUND OF VICTORY MISSING

The sound of the Victory Bell was conspicuously absent following Ohio State's 38-0 triumph over Iowa in the last home game of 1965 — the bell's clapper had been stolen. Some students did their best by hitting the bell with a hammer but the sound was too faint to be heard outside the stadium tower.

The following week, the clapper was discovered hanging from a rope around the William Oxley Thompson statue in front of the Main Library.

Ohio State vs. Michigan State

Highest Score in Series
Ohio State: 54-21 (1969, Columbus)
Michigan State: 35-20 (1912, Columbus)

Highest Margin of Victory in Series
Ohio State: 42 points (42-0, 1979, Columbus)
Michigan State: 25 points (32-7, 1965, East Lansing)

Buckeyes' Most Significant Win
Ohio State's 21-0 opening-day triumph at East Lansing in 1975 avenged the prior season's loss to the Spartans and propelled the Buckeyes to an 11-0 regular season and outright Big Ten title.

Buckeyes' Most Devastating Loss
Michigan State's 16-13 win at East Lansing in 1974 was Ohio State's only conference loss during the 1973-74-75 seasons. This setback dropped the Buckeyes from the nation's number-one ranking, a position they held for seven consecutive weeks. It also allowed Michigan to tie Ohio State for the league title with a 7-1 record.

7. The Michigan State Series

SPARTAN SERIES WILD, CONTROVERSIAL

"*T*hrilling" and "controversial" describe this series, even though through 1991 the Buckeyes and Spartans have met only 26 times. It is the fewest games between Ohio State and any of the nine active members of the Big Ten Conference. Michigan State joined the league in 1953, replacing Chicago who withdrew after the 1939 season.

Michigan State carried the nickname "Aggies" when the two first met Thanksgiving afternoon, 1912, at old Ohio Field. Approximately 3,000 spectators saw Ohio State lose, 35-20, after leading 20-14 through three quarters. OSU's first touchdown was scored by sophomore Honus Graf, who would become an excellent fullback the next two seasons. The 35 points are the most ever scored by Michigan State against the Buckeyes. It would be 39 years before the two would meet again.

"TRANSCONTINENTAL" DEALS WOODY FIRST SETBACK

Michigan State football reached a new high under coach Clarence "Biggie" Munn, who guided the Spartans to a 54-9-2 mark from 1947-53. Munn brought his number-one ranked Spartans to Ohio Stadium on October 6, 1951, to meet the seventh-ranked Buckeyes. It was just the second game for first-year coach Woody Hayes, whose team had defeated Southern Methodist, 7-0, in the previous week's opener.

It was an extremely hard-fought contest, with Ohio State holding a 20-17 lead late in the final period. The Buckeyes then lost a fumble on their 45. Michigan was soon faced with a fourth-and six at the OSU 28, as Munn inserted reserve quarterback Tom Yewsic, a sophomore, at left halfback. Quarterback Al Dorrow lateraled to Yewsic, who ran to his right — stopped suddenly — then passed back across the field to Dorrow, who eluded two defenders before falling into the end zone with the winning touchdown. The Spartans had won a real thriller, 24-20.

This miraculous play, known as the "transcontinental pass," had been formulated on the sideline by Munn just seconds before it was executed. It was Yewsic's very first collegiate pass. Two of Ohio State's touchdowns were scored by end Ray Hamilton on a 19-yard pass from halfback Vic Janowicz and a 25-yard toss from quarterback Tony Curcillo. The Spartans (9-0) placed second behind Tennessee in the final '51 Associated Press standings. Ohio State and Michigan State did not meet in 1952 when the Spartans (again 9-0) captured the national title and outscored their opponents, 312-84.

Ohio State's best effort of the 1953 season just wasn't enough as the superior Spartans had all they could handle with a hard-earned 28-13 win in the season's seventh game. MSU's speedy "pony backfield" of Yewsic, halfbacks LeRoy Bolden and Billy Wells and fullback Evan Slonac weighed just 180, 163, 175 and 170 pounds, respectively. The elusive Bolden gained 128 yards in 18 carries and dazzled the Ohio Stadium crowd of 82,328 with touchdown runs of 37, 20 and 3 yards.

Early-arriving fans at the 1953 game wondered what was flying from the flagpole at the stadium's open end. Assistant coach Ernie Godfrey's practice pants had been hoisted to the top of the pole.

The Buckeyes, who trailed just 14-13 after three quarters, lost any hope for an upset after failing to convert two golden opportunities in the final period. First, George Rosso intercepted an Earl Morrall pass and returned it to the OSU 45. But the Buckeyes soon surrendered the ball on downs at the Spartan 20 after four consecutive rushes gained only nine yards. Then Dave Leggett picked off Yewsic and returned the ball to the Michigan State 23. However, Tad Weed's field goal attempt on fourth down from the MSU 27 was blocked, killing any chances of a Buckeye win.

Anne Hayes gave her husband some helpful advice preceding the 1960 game. After reading a *Sports Illustrated* article, she told him how a Texas coach praised Ohio State's use of the "trap play." Woody decided to put it back into his offense and Bob Klein raced 45 yards on a "halfback trap" for the game's first touchdown.

Michigan State went on to defeat UCLA in the Rose Bowl, 28-20, after tying Illinois for the '53 Big Ten crown.

MATTE GUIDES FIRST WIN

Junior Tom Matte, starting his first game at quarterback, led Ohio State to its first victory over Michigan State, 30-24, in Ohio Stadium in the sixth game of the 1959 season. It was the Buckeyes' best effort of the year as Matte fired two scoring passes to end Jim Houston and a third to halfback Billy Wentz. The loss cost Michigan State the Big Ten title as the Spartans finished second with a league record of 4-2 behind Wisconsin at 5-2.

The following year, Ohio State made its first appearance in East Lansing a memorable event, winning 21-10 before a then record Spartan Stadium crowd of 76,520. Halfback Bob Klein (a native of Athens, Michigan) scored first on a 45-yard halfback trap in the second quarter. Later that period, fullback Bob Ferguson plunged 3-yards to cap a 21-yard drive, following end Tom Perdue's blocked punt. Late in

End Jim Houston caught two touchdowns in the '59 game

the third quarter with the ball at the MSU 25, Matte connected with end Bob Middleton, who evaded two tacklers and continued untouched into the end zone for the Buckeyes' final score.

SPARTANS SPECTACULAR DURING MID-'60s

Michigan State fielded one of the strongest teams in Big Ten history in 1965. Coach Duffy Daugherty's Spartans were led by defensive end Bubba Smith, linebacker George Webster, halfback Clint Jones and receiver Gene Washington. That season in East Lansing, Michigan State dealt the Buckeyes one of the worst setbacks during Woody Hayes' career. The Spartans won, 32-7, while holding Ohio State to minus-22 yards rushing. This game ultimately decided the '65 Big Ten title — MSU finished 7-0 in league play, Ohio State 6-1.

The next year in rain-soaked Columbus, inspired Ohio State nearly pulled off the season's biggest upset before bowing to the nation's number-one team, 11-8. The Buckeyes took an 8-3 lead on the first play of the fourth quarter on a well-executed 47-yard touchdown pass from quarterback Bill Long to end Bill Anders. But the Spartans pulled ahead driving 84 yards in the closing minutes with fullback Bob Apisa scoring MSU's only touchdown on fourth down from inside the OSU 1-yard line.

Among Spartan coach "Biggie" Munn's 1953 assistant coaches were Bob Devaney, who later built a powerful program at Nebraska; Dan Devine, who went on to success at Missouri, Notre Dame and with the Green Bay Packers; and "Duffy" Daugherty, who became head coach following Munn's retirement after the 1953 season.

Ohio State's 1966 record of 4-5 was the second and final of two losing seasons during Woody Hayes' 28 years in Columbus. Michigan State finished the year at 9-0-1 after tying Notre Dame 10-10 in one of college football's most highly-publicized contests that season.

After starting 1967 at 2-3 (all three losses at home), the Bucks finally jelled with a 21-7 win at Spartan Stadium. Fullback Paul Huff provided most of the offensive power, churning for 120 yards in 35 carries and scoring twice on short plunges. Long had one of his best days, completing 9 of 11 throws for 129 yards.

After being presented the game ball, Hayes said, "I never appreciated a ball more," confirming the frustration his team had experienced its first five games. This victory marked the beginning of a 22-game winning streak, longest in Ohio State football, which would not end until the final game of 1969 at Michigan.

SUPER SOPHOMORES' "CLOSEST CALL"

Ohio State was pushed to the limit before earning a 25-20 victory over upset-minded Michigan State on November 2, 1968. The five-point win was the Buckeyes' closest call that season. Hayes started six sophomores on offense and five on defense before a Parents' Day crowd of 84,859, at the time the largest in Ohio Stadium history. Coach Hugh "Duffy" Daugherty's 16th-ranked Spartans (4-2) had upset Notre Dame 21-17 the previous week. The Buckeyes were ranked second with a 5-0 record.

Ohio State confused Michigan State from the start, running plays in sequence without a huddle or having them called by quarterback Rex Kern at the line of scrimmage. Mixing their

running and passing very effectively, the Buckeyes took a 7-0 lead with fullback Jim Otis plunging across from the 1 to complete an 83-yard drive following the opening kickoff. They increased the lead to 13-0 early in the second period when Kern fired a 14-yard scoring toss to split end Bruce Jankowski to climax a 64-yard drive. The Spartans tightened things up at 13-7, holding the ball for 19 plays until Bill Triplett scored on a quarterback sneak from the 1.

Mike Radtke was singled out for his excellent defensive effort in 1968.

Kern severely sprained an ankle in the second quarter and was sidelined for the remainder of the afternoon. "Super Sub" Ron Maciejowski replaced Kern and immediately guided his team 83 yards in 13 plays to boost OSU's halftime lead to 19-7.

Otis scored his second touchdown, this time from the 3.

Michigan State's offense took charge in the third period when Triplett directed a 57-yard scoring drive to bring MSU within five at 19-14. The Buckeyes then marched 70 yards, with Maciejowski rolling out around left end for the TD to make it 25-14. Later that quarter, MSU's Frank Waters returned Mike Sensibaugh's punt to the Ohio State 31; the Spartans again were threatening. Halfback Tommy Love dove over the middle for the final yard and a 25-20 score.

In the hectic and scoreless final quarter, Ohio State's defense made the difference. Defensive end Mike Radtke was particularly impressive, first by blitzing Triplett and forcing a fumble which OSU end Dave Whitfield recovered at the MSU 31. On their next possession, the Spartans were forced to give up the ball after Radtke spilled Triplett for a 14-yard loss on a key third-and-six at midfield. Finally, Radtke blindsided Triplett and forced the game's last fumble with less than two minutes remaining. Whitfield again recovered, this time at the MSU 20.

After the game, Hayes praised the efforts of both teams, and complimented defenders Radtke, Bill Urbanik, Jim Stillwagon and Jack Tatum for their fine efforts. Turnovers helped spell the difference — the Spartans threw three interceptions and lost four fumbles. It was a gigantic win for the Buckeyes, who were within four victories of capturing the 1968 national title with a 10-0 record.

The following season, a vigorous defense and the dazzling quarterback play of Kern guided top-ranked Ohio State to a 54-21 thrashing of the 19th-rated Spartans. The home win extended the Buckeyes' three-season winning streak to 17.

The 54 points were the most against Michigan State during Daugherty's 19 seasons as the Spartans' head coach (1954 -72). The point total also was the most given up by Michigan State since a 55-0 shutout at Michigan in 1947.

Ohio State's superb defense throttled the Spartans' triple-option veer attack and immediately took control of the game. End Mark Debevc intercepted a Triplett pass, returning it 14 yards for OSU's first touchdown. Triplett had made a hasty toss from his own end zone while being pressured by Stillwagon.

After recovering a Spartan fumble, Ohio State drove 26 yards for its second score with Kern taking it across from the 1. Wingback Larry Zelina then returned a punt 73 yards for the

Bucks' third touchdown and a 20-0 lead after just six minutes of play. After Michigan State got on the board with a 76-yard Triplett-to-Frank Foreman pass play, Kern scored his second touchdown from the 4 to make it 27-7 after one quarter.

With MSU's defense geared to halting Hayes' famed ground attack, Kern took to the air for OSU's next three scores. First, he connected on a 24-yarder to tight end Jan White, followed by a 13-yard strike to Jankowski. Kern's last toss was a beautifully-executed, 29-yard connection with sophomore halfback Tom Campana. Reserve quarterback Kevin Rusnak passed five yards to Campana for OSU's final touchdown late in the fourth quarter.

Hayes used 59 players in this game including 10 ballcarriers and eight receivers. The 1969 season was the 100th anniversary of college football, and the '69 Buckeyes left little doubt they were one of the finest teams the game had ever seen.

TWO BIG TEN LOSSES OVER FOUR SEASONS

Michigan State dealt Ohio State its only two conference defeats during the four seasons from 1972-75 — 19-12 in '72 and 16-13 in '74, both in East Lansing.

The week prior to the 1972 contest, Michigan State upset conference co-leader Purdue, 22-12, following Daugherty's announced retirement (effective at the end of the season) on the eve of the game. This added incentive apparently carried over to the following week for the 3-4-1 Spartans, who ran 81 plays to the Buckeyes' 57 and outgained the visitors, 356 to 176 yards in total offense.

Placekicker Dirk Krijt, a junior college transfer from the Netherlands, booted four field goals to lead the Spartan attack. Krijt, who was playing in his first varsity game, had never kicked a football before joining the team from the soccer squad earlier that fall. Ohio State and Michigan shared the Big Ten title that season with 7-1 conference records.

The 1974 game produced one of the most unusual endings in college football history. With the number-one ranked Buckeyes holding a 13-3 lead midway through the fourth quarter, Michigan State struck for two quick scores to lead 16-13. The final TD came on a first-down, 88-yard sideline sprint by fullback Levi Jackson — second longest rushing play ever by an Ohio State opponent.

The Buckeyes then marched to the Spartan 5 where fullback Champ Henson plunged to within inches of the goal line. Just 29 seconds remained and Ohio State had used all its timeouts. MSU's defenders were very slow to get up following Henson's plunge and Ohio State had difficulty getting off another play. Finally the ball was snapped — it squirted between quarterback Corny Greene's legs and was picked up and carried into the end zone by wingback Brian Baschnagel. Head linesman Ed Scheck signalled touchdown but field judge Robert Dagenhardt indicated time had run out before this last play.

To say that confusion followed is a strong understatement. Nearly 40,000 of the 78,533 fans were still in the stadium when, 46 minutes later, Big Ten commissioner Wayne Duke announced Michigan State had won the game, 16-13. Referee Gene Calhoun informed Duke time had run out before OSU's last play. Calhoun also stated the Buckeyes would have been penalized because they did not come to the required one-second set before the ball was snapped.

Ironically, Ohio State launched the 1975 season at East Lansing. With memories of the '74 debacle still very vivid, Ohio State hammered the Spartans, 21-0, in one of the most highly regarded openers in Big Ten football. The 62-year-old Hayes was especially thrilled with the play of his young defense, which returned only three regulars from 1974. The Buckeyes held the explosive Spartans to just 11 first downs and 173 yards in total offense. Senior defensive halfback Craig Cassady (son of '55 Heisman winner Hopalong Cassady) tied a school single-game record with three interceptions in his first collegiate start. Fullback Pete Johnson scored twice on bursts of 6 and 9 yards and Greene connected with Lenny Willis on a 64-yard pass play for the other TD. Senior Archie Griffin took a big step toward capturing his second Heisman Trophy, leading all rushers with 108 yards in 29 carries. It marked Griffin's 22nd consecutive regular season game of rushing for more than 100 yards.

OWNING MSU'S PLAYBOOK

Beginning in 1975, Ohio State won all eight of its games with Michigan State through 1984. Redshirt freshman quarterback Jim Karsatos led Ohio State to a 21-11 rain-soaked win at Ohio Stadium in 1983. It was his first collegiate start while replacing the injured Mike Tomczak.

Ohio State appeared to have the '84 game well under control, leading 16-6 after three quarters in East Lansing. But MSU struck with two long fourth-quarter scores, the first a 75-yard pass from Dave Yarema to Mark Ingram; the second a 93-yard kickoff return by Larry Jackson. With Ohio State leading 23-20 and only six seconds remaining, placekicker Ralf Mojsiejenko's 43-yard field goal attempt sailed low and to the right. The three-point win was a narrow escape for Earle Bruce's squad, who had dominated the game's statistics but nearly let it slip away at the end.

Ohio State vs. Michigan State

DECADE	W	L	T	POINTS OSU	POINTS MSU
1890	0	0	0	0	0
1900	0	0	0	0	0
1910	0	1	0	20	35
1920	0	0	0	0	0
1930	0	0	0	0	0
1940	0	0	0	0	0
1950	1	2	0	63	76
1960	4	2	0	136	101
1970	5	3	0	211	73
1980	5	2	0	167	103
1990	1	0	0	27	17
TOTAL	**16**	**10**	**0**	**624**	**405**

Ohio State at Home: 9-6
Ohio State on the Road: 7-4

Ohio State vs. Minnesota

Highest Score in Series
Ohio State: 69-18 (1983, Columbus)
Minnesota: 37 points, 41-37 loss (1989, Minneapolis)

Highest Margin of Victory in Series
Ohio State: 51 points (69-18, 1983, Columbus)
Minnesota: 27 points (27-0, 1949, Columbus)

Buckeyes' Most Significant Win
Ohio State's 23-20 victory at Minneapolis in 1939 paved the way for OSU's first outright Big Ten title in 19 seasons. The Golden Gophers had been league champions the two previous years. This was their first conference loss at home in seven years.

Buckeyes' Most Devastating Loss
Minnesota dealt Ohio State its only setback in 1949, 27-0, at Ohio Stadium. The Buckeyes bounced back to tie with Michigan for the league title and went on to defeat California 17-14 in the Rose Bowl.

8. The Minnesota Series

POSSIBLE CLASSICS NEVER HELD

The Ohio State-Minnesota series could be described as "some of the finest Big Ten games *never* played." The Golden Gophers were national champions in 1934, '35, '36, '40, '41, and '60. Minnesota faced Ohio State only once during these six campaigns, defeating the Buckeyes 13-7 at Ohio Stadium in 1940. Ohio State was 7-1 in both 1934 and '35, 5-3 in '36, 6-1-1 in '41, and 7-2 in '60.

The Buckeyes won national titles in 1942, '54, '57, and '68, and did not meet Minnesota any of these four seasons. During these years the Golden Gophers were 5-4 (1942), 7-2 ('54), 4-5 ('57), and 6-4 ('68).

Ohio State has won 29 of the 35 games between the two through 1991. The winning rate of 82.9% is the highest between Ohio State and any of the other nine active members of the Big Ten. The Buckeyes and Golden Gophers squared-off only ten times from 1921-50, with Ohio State winning six and losing four. The series resumed in 1965, and the two have played continuously since '69.

Ohio State and Minnesota first clashed before an overflow crowd of 18,000 at old Ohio Field in 1921. The Buckeyes were magnificent, winning with surprising ease, 27-0. But the Gophers returned the favor in 1931, outplaying Ohio State in every department to win, 19-7, during a "charity game" at Minneapolis. With the country in the midst of the great depression, approximately 30,000 fans con-

> Ohio State and Minnesota shared the 1935 Big Ten title with identical 5-0 league records.

tributed $46,000 to the Big Ten's fund for unemployment relief. The Buckeyes couldn't control fullback Jack Manders, who ran for 121 yards and played an important role in each of the Gophers' three touchdown marches. Clearing a path for Manders was Minnesota's All-American guard, Clarence "Biggie" Munn, who later enjoyed great success during the early 1950s as head coach at Michigan State.

SCHMIDT'S BIGGEST VICTORY

One of Ohio State's finest all-time triumphs came at Minneapolis in 1939, as the courageous Buckeyes of coach Francis

Schmidt twice came from behind to defeat powerful Minnesota, 23-20. The game was played October 21 before a stunned Homecoming crowd of 53,000. Ohio State blended a spectacular passing offense with excellent blocking and execution to overtake the Gophers' gallant rushing attack. The action-packed contest left both squads emotionally and physically exhausted.

It was just Minnesota's third loss in its last 33 conference games over seven seasons and its first home conference defeat since a 3-0 shutout to Michigan in the final game of 1932. Coach Bernie Bierman's teams had compiled a 44-8-4 record during his first seven seasons. Schmidt, affection-

Quarterback Don Scott threw for all three touchdowns in the '39 contest in Minneapolis

ately known as master of the razzle-dazzle offense, had compiled an overall mark of 29-10-1 during his first five seasons in Columbus.

The two schools had not met since 1931. The Buckeyes entered the game with a record of 2-0, the Gophers were 1-1-1. Minnesota won the toss and chose the west goal with the wind at its back — Ohio State elected to kickoff. Midway through the first quarter, Ohio State's Jim Strausbaugh fumbled a punt on his own 13. Three plays later Joe Mernik slipped around OSU's left end for the game's first touchdown — his conversion gave Minnesota a 7-0 lead.

Six plays into the second quarter, Buckeye quarterback Don Scott combined with end Esco Sarkkinen on a 31-yard touchdown pass to cap a 74-yard drive. Sarkkinen caught the ball at the seven and scampered across the goal untouched. Scott's extra point attempt was blocked, leaving Minnesota with a one-point lead.

After holding the Gophers on downs, Ohio State took over at the Minnesota 48. Four plays later at the 28, Scott completely fooled the Gopher secondary by floating one into the arms of fullback Jim Langhurst for his second touchdown pass of the quarter, and Ohio State's first lead of the day at 13-7.

Next, Minnesota really got its running game on track. George Franck returned Scott's kickoff 50 yards to the Buckeye 48 before Strausbaugh chased him out-of-bounds. On third-and-one, Harold VanEvery broke over left tackle, shook loose from two defenders and raced 39 yards to paydirt. John Bartelt's extra point put the Gophers back on top, 14-13.

It was now the Buckeyes' turn. Near halftime an Ohio State drive stalled at the Minnesota 14. On fourth down and from a very difficult angle, tackle Charlie Maag booted a crucial field goal from the 21 to give Schmidt's team a 16-14 lead at intermission.

The game became even more nerve-wracking in the second half. Five plays after receiving the kickoff, Minnesota's Martin Christiansen bolted through center for ten yards, then tried to lateral to VanEvery — his pitchout was wild and Langhurst recovered for Ohio State at the Gopher 45. After the ball was advanced to the 34, the elusive Scott again took to the air. After drifting back near the 50-yard line, he floated the ball perfectly into the hands of end Frank Clair, just as Clair was crossing the Minnesota goal. Scott's third touchdown pass and second conversion increased Ohio State's lead to 23-14.

Early in the final quarter, a short punt gave Minnesota excellent field position at the OSU 39. On first down, VanEvery passed to Bruce Smith who caught the ball at the three and carried Scott across the goal line for the Gophers' third touchdown. Mernik's attempted conversion was blocked by Fritz Howard, leaving the score at 23-20.

After an exchange of punts, the Buckeyes took over at their

own 19. On first down, Langhurst bolted through right guard and raced 81 yards for an apparent touchdown, but the play was called back and Ohio State was penalized five yards for backfield-in-motion. Schmidt protested the call, but the penalty stood.

Langhurst lost a yard on first down from the Gopher 14. Dick Fisher then fumbled on an attempted end sweep and Mernik recovered at the Ohio State 15 as the Gopher fans went wild. Schmidt again protested the call, claiming Fisher had been run out-of-bounds prior to the fumble.

After three rushing plays gained nine yards, Minnesota was penalized back to the OSU 21 for holding. With fourth-and-16, the Gophers lined up for a field goal. A complete silence fell over the huge crowd as Mernik's kick rose slowly, hit the crossbar, wobbled momentarily, then lazily fell back onto the playing field. Ohio State partisans breathed a sigh of relief — but the game was still far from complete.

After Ohio State was unable to sustain a drive, Minnesota took over at its own 43 with less than a minute remaining. OSU's Jack Graf then intercepted a VanEvery pass which was intended for Earl Ohlgin, but the Buckeyes were penalized for defensive holding, giving the ball back to the Gophers at the OSU 44. VanEvery intended his next long aerial for Franck, but Graf again intercepted at the five as the game came to a close.

Veteran *Columbus Citizen* sportswriter Lew Byrer called it "one of the greatest football games ever played anywhere by any two teams. I've never seen an Ohio State team show better blocking than the Buckeyes exhibited against the Gophers." Outstanding on the line were center Steve Andrako and guard Vic Marino, who played the most outstanding games of their careers. It was the first come-from-behind win for the Buckeyes since the Chicago game of 1935. Ohio State finished the '39 season as the outright Big Ten champion, with a league record of 5-1 and an overall mark of 6-2. It was the Buckeyes' first outright conference championship since 1920. Scott and Sarkkinen were selected All-Americans, and Andrako was chosen the team's most valuable player.

ONLY SETBACK FOR EVENTUAL ROSE BOWL WINNER

Minnesota overwhelmed the Buckeyes 27-0 at Ohio Stadium for Ohio State's only loss in 1949. It was the season's fourth game and the Buckeyes hardly resembled the team that would go on to capture the school's first win in the Rose Bowl. OSU's strong rushing attack was held to just 53 yards. The Gophers were paced by the bruising play of two All-American linemen, center Clayton Tonnemaker and tackle Leo Nomellini. Minnesota's MVP that season was end Bud Grant, later head coach of the NFL's Minnesota Vikings. Ohio State made only one serious threat that afternoon, being held on downs at the Gopher four in the second quarter.

The 1950 game at Minneapolis was a complete reversal, with Ohio State routing Minnesota 48-0. This game was even more one-sided than suggested by the final score. Seven different players scored OSU's seven touchdowns, as coach Wes Fesler cleared his bench early in the second half. The Buckeyes led in first downs, 19-5, and in total yardage, 472-92. Halfback Walt Klevey led all rushers with 89 yards in 11 carries. Minnesota Athletic Director "Ike" Armstrong classified the Buckeyes as "the greatest college football team I ever saw." Interestingly, Armstong hired Wes Fesler as Minnesota's head coach the next year after Fesler resigned the Ohio State position following the 1950 season.

After a 14-year absence, Minnesota returned to the Ohio State schedule for the 1965 homecoming game at Ohio Stadium. The tension-filled afternoon was highlighted by a "fake kick" and a "real kick." With the Gophers leading 7-0, OSU quarterback Don Unverferth passed 25 yards to Nelson Adderly for a second-quarter touchdown. Placekicker Bob Funk lined up to apparently kick the extra point. The ball was centered to holder Arnie Fontes, who then swept around right end for a very unexpected two-point conversion and an 8-7 lead.

Minnesota went back on top in the third quarter on a 32-yard field goal by Deryl Ramey. With just 1:31 remaining in the

A prankster apparently sneaked into Ohio Stadium the Friday evening before the 1965 Minnesota game and strung a web of fine nylon fishing line between the uprights of the north goal posts. Fortunately, stadium superintendent Ralph Guarasci noticed the mesh glistening in the sun Saturday morning and had it removed. It was through this goal that Bob Funk's fourth-quarter field goal lifted Ohio State to an 11-10 victory.

fourth period, pressure really mounted when Woody Hayes elected to go for a field goal on a fourth-and-inches situation at the Gopher one. Funk's kick was perfect and the Buckeyes led, 11-10. But Minnesota quickly moved 63 yards to the OSU eight, then used its final time-out with just 17 seconds remaining. Ramey's field goal attempt from the 15 was barely wide to the left, leaving the Buckeyes with the only single-point win in the Ohio State-Minnesota series.

Ohio State's 56-7 opening day win over the Gophers in 1973 gave strong indication the Buckeyes were embarking upon one of their finest seasons. Archie Griffin and Neal Colzie provided plenty of long-range fireworks with Griffin scoring on a 93-yard kickoff return and Colzie on a 78-yard punt return. Junior fullback Harold "Champ" Henson, who led the nation in scoring the previous year, scored three times from close range. Sophomore Cornelius Greene played like a veteran at quarterback, directing the Buckeyes to touchdowns on four of their first six possessions.

Two years later, Ohio State clobbered Minnesota, 38-6, in the '75 home finale. Each member of Ohio State's talented backfield of Griffin, Greene, Brian Baschnagel, and Pete Johnson scored at least once to lead the attack. Griffin gained 124 yards during his last appearance in Ohio Stadium, going over 100 yards for the 31st consecutive regular-season game. The Buckeyes had won 24 in a row in the horseshoe dating back to the 1972 opener against Iowa.

BRUCE'S BUCKEYES PULL IT OUT

First-year coach Earle Bruce directed Ohio State to an impressive 31-8 win over Syracuse in the 1979 opener. But the following week at Minneapolis, Minnesota won everything but the final score. Using a surprise double-winged-T offense, first-year coach Joe Salem's Golden Gophers led in first downs 26-12, and in total offensive yardage 505-295. But the injury-plagued Buckeyes hung in there to win, 21-17. The difference was Art Schlichter, who executed brilliantly on key downs while accounting for 238 of his team's 295 yards.

Art Schlichter's 32-yard scamper brought the Buckeyes to victory in '79

Minnesota scored on its first two possessions to take a 14-0 lead before Ohio State could get untracked. Schlichter then connected with Tyrone Hicks on a 38-yard TD pass to make it 14-7. The Gophers scored a second quarter field goal to lead 17-7 at halftime.

Calvin Murray scored from the one in the third quarter to cut the Gophers' lead to 17-13. In the final period, Schlichter hit end Chuck Hunter for 29 yards before scrambling the final 32 himself for the game's final touchdown. He then connected with tight end Bill Jaco for a two-point conversion to seal the victory.

The Gophers took advantage of OSU's porous pass defense for a come-from-behind 35-31 win in 1981. The Buckeyes appeared to be in control after tailback Tim Spencer scored on a 73-yard sprint to put Ohio State on top, 14-0, on the last play of the first quarter. But the game soon changed direction as Gopher quarterback Mike Hohensee threw for all five touchdowns while establishing school records with 37 completions in 67 attempts for 444 yards. It was the last game between the two at old Memorial Stadium on the Minnesota campus.

GALLANT COMEBACK AT METRODOME

One of the series' most thrilling games saw Ohio State come-from-behind to win, 23-19, in 1985. Second-year Gopher coach Lou Holtz, a former Woody Hayes assistant, had been pointing toward Ohio State all season. The ninth-ranked Buck-eyes and 20th-ranked Gophers each entered the nationally tele-vised contest with records of 5-1. The tremendous noise created by the record homecoming crowd of 64,455 at the Metrodome frequently disrupted the signal-calling of OSU quarterback Jim Karsatos.

Two Chip Lohmiller field goals of 36 and 50 yards gave the Gophers an early 6-0 advantage. Ohio State then took the lead, 7-6, driving 80 yards with tailback Keith Byars getting the score on a two-yard option pitch around right end. Rich Spangler's 38-yard field goal increased the lead to 10-6.

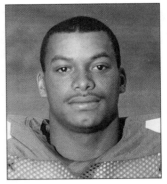

But the momentum really shifted when Gopher quarterback Rickey Foggie, master of the triple-option attack, scored from the two just nine seconds before halftime to put Minnesota back on top, 12-10. Early in the third period,

Injuries to Keith Byars and John Wooldridge made a hero out of Vince Workman in '85

Foggie completed an 89-yard drive with a one-yard plunge, increasing the lead to 19-10, and the Gophers could smell the upset.

With its back to the wall, Earle Bruce's squad marched 90 yards to narrow the deficit to 19-17 early in the final period. Karsatos, who kept the drive moving with a 28-yard strike to Doug Smith, connected with tight end Ed Taggart on a one-yard toss for the touchdown.

Cornerback William White helped quiet the crowd by pick-ing off a Foggie pass (Foggie's first interception of the year) at the OSU 47. With Byars and John Wooldridge both injured, freshman Vince Workman entered the game at tailback. After Karsatos moved his team to the Gopher 16, Workman swept around left end for the winning touchdown behind key blocks by guard Jim Gilmore and tackle Larry Kotterman.

But Holtz's squad was far from finished. Starting from their own nine, the Gophers moved to a fourth-and-inches at the Ohio State 12 with just 48 seconds remaining. Unfortunately for Minnesota, Foggie had been injured on the third-down carry and was replaced on fourth down by Alan Holt. The reserve quarterback handed the ball to halfback Valdez Baylor on a straight ahead dive play, but linebacker "Pepper" Johnson was there to meet him for no gain, and the Buckeyes could finally breath a little easier.

With the lead changing hands four times, Bruce was extremely pleased with the poise exhibited by his team. Linebacker Chris Spielman played one of his finest games, leading the defense with 13 solo tackles.

Freshman tailback Carlos Snow celebrated his 19th birthday by scoring four touchdowns during Ohio State's 42-9 Homecoming win over Minnesota on October 24, 1987.

TURNAROUND TIES NCAA MARK

The Buckeyes rallied for an unbelievable 41-37 win at the Metrodome in 1989 after trailing 31-0. Carlos Snow finally crossed the Gopher goal for OSU's first score just ten seconds before half-time. Quarterback Greg Frey led the second-half comeback, passing for 362 yards and three touchdowns. The winning score came on a 15-yard pass to flanker Jeff Graham with just 51 seconds remaining. Ohio State tallied twice on fourth-down situations and made three two-point conversions. This victory tied an NCAA record for the largest turnaround in a major college game. Maryland had rallied from a 31-0 deficit to defeat Miami (Fla.), 42-40, in 1984.

Ohio State vs. Minnesota

				POINTS	
DECADE	W	L	T	OSU	MINN
1890	0	0	0	0	0
1900	0	0	0	0	0
1910	0	0	0	0	0
1920	1	1	0	27	9
1930	1	1	0	30	39
1940	3	2	0	100	70
1950	1	0	0	48	0
1960	2	1	0	52	34
1970	10	0	0	292	108
1980	9	1	0	369	156
1990	2	0	0	87	29
TOTAL	29	6	0	1,005	445

Ohio State at Home: 16-2-0
Ohio State on the Road: 13-4-0

Ohio State vs. Northwestern

Highest Score in Series
Ohio State: 70-6 (1981, Columbus)
Northwestern: 28 points, 40-28 loss (1982, Evanston)

Highest Margin of Victory in Series
Ohio State: 64 points (70-6, 1981, Columbus)
Northwestern: 21 points (21-0, 1958, Evanston)

Buckeyes' Most Significant Win
The conference title was at stake when the two undefeated teams met in the season-ending game of 1916 at old Ohio Field. Ohio State defeated Northwestern 23-3 to capture its first conference championship and complete its first undefeated-untied season.

Buckeyes' Most Devastating Loss
Northwestern pulled an upset 21-0 at Evanston in 1958 to hand the Buckeyes their only loss of the year. It was OSU's only conference setback in two seasons and prevented Woody Hayes' squad from capturing its second consecutive Big Ten title.

9. The Northwestern Series

'CATS COMPETITIVE DURING '40S

Ohio State has dominated the Northwestern series with an overall record of 47-13-1 through 1991. The Wildcats' last win was a 14-10 upset at Ohio Stadium on November 13, 1971. The Buckeyes' highest score and largest margin of victory was 70-6 in 1981, as coach Earle Bruce used 80 different players (including ten different ball carriers) in a futile attempt to hold down the score. Northwestern's highest output came during its 42-28 loss at Evanston in 1982. That afternoon, freshman quarterback Sandy Schwab passed for 393 yards and three touchdowns in a losing effort.

Ohio State and Northwestern first met at old Ohio Field in the season-ending game of 1913, the year Ohio State joined the Western Conference (now the Big Ten). The Buckeyes won 58-0, registering their very first conference victory after losses to Indiana and Wisconsin.

'16 WIN PRODUCES FIRST LEAGUE TITLE

The 1916 game, played at old Ohio Field, was likely the most significant between the two schools. It was Homecoming and both teams entered this season-ending contest with 6-0 records — the winner would emerge with the school's first conference championship. The game matched the league's two leading halfbacks, Ohio State's Charles W. "Chic" Harley and Northwestern's John "Paddy" Driscoll.

In the opening quarter, Harley kicked a 34-yard field goal to give the Buckeyes a slender 3-0 halftime lead. Northwestern had several strong marches in the third period but simply couldn't score. The game's turning point came as Ohio State held the Wildcats on downs at the 2-yard line. Early in the final quarter the visitors tied the game 3-3, when Driscoll drop-kicked a low bullet from the OSU 38 that just cleared the cross-bar.

But the remainder of the afternoon belonged to Harley and his talented teammates. First, he sent the crowd into an uproar with a 63-yard touchdown run around right end. The blocking was excellent, enough that coach John Wilce often referred to this run as "the perfect play." Harley scored again on a 15-yard sweep and set-up fullback Frank Sorensen's 2-yard touchdown plunge with a 28-yard pass to Clarence McDonald. This 23-3 triumph earned Ohio State its first league title, and Harley and senior tackle Bob Karch became the school's first All-Americans.

The '36 game at Evanston was also for the Big Ten title but this time it went to Northwestern, 14-13. Quarterback Nick Wasylik hit halfback Mike Kabealo with a 19-yard scoring toss to put Ohio State on top 6-0, but the conversion attempt by Merle Wendt, which was to be the eventual margin of defeat, was wide. Two weeks later, the Wildcats defeated powerful Minnesota 6-0, ending Minnesota's four year string of 28 games without defeat. Northwestern finished at 6-0 in the conference while Ohio State and Minnesota were each 4-1.

PAUL BROWN'S "EYE FOR TALENT"

Northwestern dealt first-year coach Paul Brown his only loss of the 1941 season by a 14-7 count in Columbus. But Brown made an important discovery that afternoon that would quite favorably affect his football coaching career.

The Buckeyes entered the game 3-0 while the Wildcats were 2-1. NU coach Lynn "Pappy" Waldorf had not won

Northwestern tailback Otto Graham

at Ohio Stadium in three previous tries. Ohio State's attack was weakened with fullback Jack Graf, the 1941 Big Ten most valuable player, sidelined due to a knee injury.

Northwestern played at Ohio Stadium on November 3 in both 1945 and 1951, and the Buckeyes benefitted from fourth-quarter field goals to win both games. Max Schnittker's 32-yard field goal in '45 with just 1:28 remaining lifted Ohio State to a 16-14 triumph. Vic Janowicz's 26-yard fourth-quarter field goal provided the game's only points during a 3-0 win in '51.

Play in the first half was very even. Northwestern took an early 7-0 lead on a 40-yard touchdown pass, putting the Buckeyes behind for the first time all season. Ohio State came right back with fullback Bob Hecklinger plunging over from the 1, to complete a 65-yard march and tie the game, 7-7. But the Wildcats greater size and depth was the difference in the second half. Ohio State could advance no further than its own 47, while Northwestern drove inside the Ohio State 25 six times. The winning score came on NU's second touchdown pass, this one covering 18 yards.

Brown took the loss graciously, stating, "We were beaten today by a much better team." He was particularly impressed with the play of Northwestern's sophomore tailback who threw for both touchdowns — Otto Graham. Years later Brown remarked, "I never forgot Otto's tremendous peripheral vision and his ability to run to his left before throwing far across the field with such strength and accuracy. His fine running ability made his passing all the more effective, and he could quickly survey the field and pick out the correct receiver." Graham enrolled at Northwestern on a basketball scholarship and nearly gave up football following knee surgery his freshman season. He became an All-American in each sport.

The '41 Buckeyes finished at 6-1-1 and tied with Michigan for the second place in the conference behind Minnesota.

After two years coaching a World War II service team at Great Lakes Naval Training Center (1944-45), Brown accepted an offer to coach the All-American Conference's new franchise — the Cleveland Browns. Realizing the importance of a skilled quarterback, Brown traveled to Glenview Naval Air Station in North Carolina where Graham was completing flight training.

They soon reached an agreement and Graham became the Browns' first player. He quarterbacked the Browns during their first ten seasons through 1955, leading them to the title game each year. Cleveland won seven league championships and

The scoring pattern of the '46 game at Evanston marked the very first Ohio State game with both teams scoring in each of the four quarters. The Buckeyes won the game with the quarterly scoring as follows:

	1	2	3	4
Ohio State	7	6	12	14 — 39
Northwestern	7	6	7	7 — 27

Graham was selected All-Pro each season. The 1991 Ohio State-Northwestern game was very appropriately played in Cleveland on the 15th anniversary of their 1941 game, in the same stadium where Brown and Graham made professional football history.

BUCKS WIN IN "OVERTIME"

The 1947 contest produced one of the most bizarre and hectic finishes in college football history. The game was played at Ohio Stadium, November 8, with Ohio State winning 7-6. A series of penalties against the Wildcats enabled the Buckeyes to score the winning points four plays after time had expired.

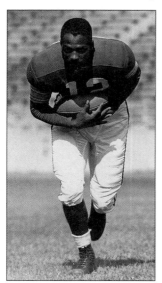

Jimmy Clark's touchdown reception after time had expired helped lift Ohio State to victory in '47

NU halfback Frank Aschenbrenner scored early in the fourth period to put the visitors on top 6-0. Jim Farrar's conversion attempt was wide — it was just his second miss of the season. Later that period, the Buckeyes drove from midfield to the Northwestern 1, where they were held on downs with just 1:47 remaining. At that point, many of the 70,203 fans headed for the exits, noticeably conceding the game to the Wildcats.

But Northwestern soon had to kick after failing to register a first down. OSU's Bob Demmel returned Tom Worthington's punt to the NU 36 with just 31 seconds remaining. On first down, quarterback Pandel Savic passed 24 yards to Demmel at the NU 12 — there were 13 seconds left. Savic's next pass was intercepted by Lawrence Day as time expired. Northwestern had apparently won 6-0. The OSU Marching Band started onto the field for its postgame show and fans were now pouring out of the stadium by the thousands.

However, Northwestern had 12 men on the field during the last play. Ohio State would have one more down. The Buckeyes tried a deep reverse with Rodney Swinehart carrying, but Swinehart was tackled at the 2. But wait — Northwestern had been offside, and Ohio State would have yet another down. This time Savic fired a lobbing pass to Jimmy Clark in the back corner of the end zone to knot the game at 6-6.

Emil Moldea's conversion attempt was blocked. But *again* Northwestern was offside. Moldea's second attempt was good, giving Ohio State the win 7-6. Three Northwestern penalties had enabled the Buckeyes to score all seven of their points after time had expired.

WEED'S FIELD GOAL HIGHLIGHTS COMEBACK

The resilient Buckeyes rallied for 17 fourth-quarter points to win at Northwestern, 24-21, in 1952. The Wildcats led 21-7 heading into the final quarter, but for the first time in history, Ohio State rallied to victory after trailing by as many as 14 points."

The Buckeyes were rebounding from an embarrassing 8-0 upset at Iowa the previous Saturday — a loss which would eventually cost them the 1952 Big Ten title. Woody Hayes had practiced his team exceptionally hard in preparation for Northwestern and as a morale builder, he also decided assistant coach Ernie Godfrey would be on the sidelines with the team for the remainder of the season, rather than scout upcoming opponents. Godfrey had been on the sidelines when the Buckeyes upset number-one ranked Wisconsin (23-14) earlier in the season, and had been given much credit for influencing the team's fine effort.

Bob Voigts was in his sixth season as Northwestern's coach. Voigts had been an All-American tackle with the Wildcats in 1938. His team entered the game with a disappointing record of 1-3-1, while the Buckeyes were 3-2.

It was a sunny afternoon in Evanston with the temperature near 70 degrees. Ohio State took the opening kickoff and moved 66 yards with ease to take an early 7-0 lead. With the ball at the Wildcat 7, freshman halfback Howard "Hopalong" Cassady took a pitchout around left end, then cut back across the middle to cross the goal line standing up.

Howard "Hopalong" Cassady's first collegiate pass was a 25-yard touchdown toss to end Tommy Hague during OSU's 27-13 Homecoming win over Northwestern on October 31, 1953.

A series of "breaks" midway through the first quarter led to Northwestern's first score. On fourth down from his own 16, Ohio State's Bill Peterson fumbled the snap from center while attempting to punt, and was smeared at the 10 by NU's Frank Hren. On second down, halfback Walter Jones knifed inside right end, but fumbled at the 2 — the ball squirted into the end zone where end Norm Kragseth picked it up for the touchdown. Kragseth's conversion tied the game at 7.

The Wildcats really took charge in the second quarter scoring twice on long passes from quarterback Dick Thomas to end Joe Collier. First, with the ball at his own 42, Thomas hit Collier with a terrific pass at the OSU 25. Collier had slipped behind the Buckeye secondary, then raced into the end zone untouched to put Northwestern on top, 14-7. Next, from the OSU 39, Collier again glided behind the defense to take another perfectly-thrown pass at the 10, before romping across the goal to give Northwestern a 21-7 halftime lead. Interestingly, Thomas and Collier had been teammates at Rock Island (Ill.) High School, where they each earned all-state honors.

While the Ohio State and Northwestern bands were putting on their halftime shows, Hayes was telling his team to "stay in there, continue to play hard and we will be OK in the second half."

The third period was scoreless but the Buckeyes had moved to a fourth-and-one at the Northwestern 1 as the quarter ended. On the first play of the final quarter, Ohio State lost a golden opportunity to score when Northwestern took over on downs after spilling Cassady for a one-yard loss. But the kicking game would be Northwestern's undoing in the game's waning minutes.

After the Wildcats were unable to move, an extremely poor Kragseth punt gave Ohio State possession at the Northwestern 18. The Buckeyes moved it in, with halfback Fred Bruney packing the pigskin the final yard around right end for the score. Tad Weed's extra point reduced the deficit to seven at 21-14.

Northwestern was again forced to punt, with Kregseth's 27-yard kick rolling dead at the NU 42. On first down, Borton passed to Bruney, who caught the ball at the 18 and sprinted into the end zone for his second touch-

Tad Weed's field goal in '52 broke a 21-21 tie

down of the quarter. End Bob Grimes threw a key block to send him on his way. Weed's third conversion tied the game at 21 with six minutes remaining.

After Northwestern was again unable to move, Kregseth's punt was blocked by tackle Irv Denker and recovered by linebacker Tony Curcillo at the Wildcat 6. Three plays and a penalty moved the ball back to a fourth down at the 11. With the ball held at the 17, Weed kicked a field goal from a very difficult angle for the three-point victory.

A left-footer out of Grandview Heights (Ohio) High School, Weed was the Big Ten's smallest player at 5'6" and 138 pounds. His fine kick was a fitting reward for the many long hours of practice he had spent preparing for just such a moment.

Late in the final period, interceptions by the Buckeyes' Marts Beekley and George Rosso ended the last two Wildcat threats, preserving one of the most thrilling Ohio State wins of all-time. Hayes was gratified beyond words by the team's fourth quarter play. Voigts also dished out high praise for Ohio State, but was visibly upset by the blocked punt which set-up Weed's winning field goal.

Mike Adamle, Northwestern All-American fullback in 1970, is the son of Tony Adamle, Ohio State center in 1946.

WILDCATS SUCCESSFUL UNDER PARSEGHIAN

Northwestern pulled off a stunning 21-0 upset of the fifth-ranked Buckeyes at Evanston in 1958. Hayes was opposed by one of his former assistants at Miami University, Ara Parseghian, who was in his third season at Northwestern. After a scoreless first half, Wildcat quarterback Dick Thornton became a one-man show, passing for two touchdowns and scoring a third to hand Ohio State its only loss that season. His first six-pointer was a perfectly executed 67-yard pass to halfback Ron Burton of Springfield, Ohio.

The upset provided an exceptionally happy Homecoming for the Dyche Stadium crowd of 51,102. It was the Buckeyes' first setback in 15 games and prevented them from repeating as Big Ten champions.

Games during the early 1960s were quite competitive. Ohio State had all it could handle before conquering Northwestern 10-0 at Evanston in 1961. Parseghian's defense held OSU to just three points in the first three quarters, a 24-yard field

goal by Dick VanRaaphorst in the second period which was his first as a collegian. In the final quarter, Bill Mrukowski went 20 yards on a roll-out inside his own left end for the game's only touchdown.

The Wildcats won both encounters at Ohio Stadium in 1962 (18-14) and '63 (17-8). Parseghian, an Akron native, had recruited well within his home state. Twenty-four members of his '62 squad were from Ohio, including two all-Americans — sopho-more quarterback Tom Myers of Troy and junior guard Jack Cvercho of Campbell. Northwestern rose to No. 1 in the 1962 weekly *Associated Press* poll before losing to Wisconsin later that season.

Since 1963, the series has been very one-sided, with Ohio State winning 21 of 22 games through 1991, outscoring the Wildcats 865-223. One of the most offensive games during this span was OSU's 52-27 win at Evanston in 1989. The Buckeyes led in total offense, 583-410, with Carlos Snow (100), Scottie Graham (102) and Dante Lee (157) each rushing for 100 or more yards.

Ohio State vs. Northwestern

DECADE	W	L	T	POINTS OSU	NU
1890	0	0	0	0	0
1900	0	0	0	0	0
1910	5	0	0	182	3
1920	1	2	0	29	37
1930	6	3	1	123	62
1940	5	4	0	123	114
1950	8	1	0	202	70
1960	5	2	0	128	64
1970	7	1	0	290	87
1980	8	0	0	397	97
1990	2	0	0	82	10
TOTAL	**47**	**13**	**1**	**1,556**	**544**

Ohio State at Home: 26-8-0
Ohio State on the Road: 21-5-1

Ohio State vs. Penn State

Highest Score in Series
Ohio State: 19 points, 31-19 loss (1980, Fiesta Bowl)
Penn State: 37-0 (1912, Columbus)

Highest Margin of Victory in Series
Ohio State: 8 points (17-9, 1975, Columbus)
Penn State: 37 points (37-0, 1912, Columbus)

Buckeyes' Most Significant Win
A 17-9 victory in 1975 was a key win during Ohio State's 11-0 regular season. It was the first encounter between Woody Hayes and Joe Paterno, as well as the school's first triumph over the Lions after four losses. Penn State finished the season at 9-3.

Buckeyes' Most Devastating Loss
Penn State scored in each quarter to upset undefeated and second-ranked Ohio State 27-0 in 1964. The Buckeyes entered the game at 6-0, Penn State at 3-4. Ohio State suffered its first shutout in 45 games. It was the widest margin of defeat (at that time) for a Hayes-coached team in Ohio Stadium.

10. The Penn State Series

NITTANY LIONS AT THEIR BEST AGAINST BUCKEYES

*P*enn State begins Big Ten play in 1993 and if past Ohio State-Penn State games are any indication of what to expect, the Buckeyes may really have their hands full.

The Lions and Buckeyes have met eight times with Penn State winning six. The two first met on November 16, 1912, at old Ohio Field, with the game producing one of the most unusual and regrettable happenings during Ohio State's early days. Penn State entered the game with a record of 6-0 having outscored their opponents 210-6. The Buckeyes were 5-1 having lost only to Michigan.

With Penn State leading 37-0 and nine minutes remaining in the fourth quarter, OSU coach John Richards abruptly ordered his team off the field — the game was over. Richards claimed PSU players had been guilty of unsportsmanlike conduct throughout the entire game and he no longer wanted to subject his players to this kind of "muckerism treatment." An OSU freshman then climbed the south goal posts and burned the Nittany Lion colors in full view of Penn State President Edwin E. Sparks, an Ohio State alumnus.

*E*arle Bruce was recruited by his namesake, Penn State assistant coach Earl Bruce, in 1949. Bruce, a star halfback at Allegheny High School in Cumberland, Md., eventually elected to play at Ohio State under coach Wes Fesler.

A group of OSU alumni and students apologized to Sparks before he left Columbus. It would be 41 years before the two schools played again.

FAVORED BUCKEYES SURPRISED IN '56

Fifth-ranked Ohio State entered its October 20, 1956, encounter with Penn State as a three-touchdown favorite. The Buckeyes were 3-0 with wins over Nebraska (34-7), Stanford (32-20) and Illinois (26-6). The Nittany Lions were 2-1 after wins over Pennsylvania (34-0) and Holy Cross (43-0) and a 14-7 loss to Army. Big Ten fans were not overly impressed with the Easterners' schedule since Michigan had overrun Army 48-14 the previous Saturday at Ann Arbor. Opposing head coaches Woody Hayes and Rip Engle were no strangers. Hayes had coached the East squad in the previous season's East-West Shrine Game, with Engle as one of his assistants.

The first quarter belonged to Penn State. The Lions put together two effective drives on their first two possessions but were unable to score. Buckeye linebacker Tom Dillman intercepted quarterback Milt Plum's pass at the OSU 10 to interrupt a drive which started from the PSU 24. Then, OSU's Don Sutherin picked off another Plum aerial at the OSU 4 after the Lions had marched from their 29.

Penn State's defense was giving the Bucks all kinds of problems. Ohio State finally secured its initial first down two minutes into the second period. The Scarlet and Gray moved to the enemy 18 where on a fourth-and-five Frank Kremblas' field goal attempt fell short. This would be the closest Ohio State would get to the Lion goal by halftime.

After a scoreless first half, Ohio State's offense appeared to be taking charge early in the third period. In machine-like fashion, the Bucks used 17 consecutive running plays (consuming nearly 12 minutes) to move 84 yards from their 13 to the Penn State 3. The big play had been Don Clark's 21-yard sprint around right end for an apparent touchdown. But the Lions' Bruce Gilmore pulled him down from behind at the 5.

Penn State's 1956 win was especially sweet for Lion captain Sam Valentine, a 5'11", 200-pound guard. Valentine had wanted to play at Ohio State, but had been told he might be too small.

With third-and-three from the 3, quarterback Frank Ellwood attempted his first pass of the drive, but Gilmore seemed to come out of nowhere to intercept in the end zone and return the ball to his own 21. This unexpected third-down call would be debated by Buckeye fans long into the night. Hayes defended his quarterback's decision, stating, "It was okay for Ellwood to pass. I was going to send Kremblas in for a field goal on fourth down if the pass was incomplete."

Tension mounted in the fourth quarter. With the Buckeyes facing a fourth and less-than-one at its own 23, it appeared Ohio State would go for the first down. But a late substitution caused a five-yard delay-of-game penalty, forcing a kick. Don Sutherin's 34-yard punt was returned by Billy Kane to the Buckeye 45, and the Lions were in business. Plum engineered a 13-play scoring drive, with Gilmore plunging over left guard for the touchdown. Plum's conversion made it 7-0 with just 3:35 showing on the clock.

But the Buckeyes came right back, moving 80 yards in five plays for a touchdown. Hayes used the halfback-option pass for the drive's two long gainers. Jim Roseboro rifled a cross-field pass to end Leo Brown for 23 yards to the Penn State 45. Next, Clark hooked up with Brown on a 42-yard option which carried to the Lion 3. From there Clark exploded over right tackle for the score.

As Kremblas readied for the conversion, Hayes (thinking he had only ten men on the field) sent Leo Brown dashing onto the field. Ohio State was penalized five yards for having 12 men in the game. Kremblas' ensuing placement attempt from the 15 was just a few inches wide to the left, and the score remained 7-6. It was Ohio State's seventh missed conversion in 15 tries that season.

On their following possession, the Lions ran out the clock to preserve the one-point win. The Buckeyes had suffered a very unexpected defeat while Penn State had registered one of the most significant wins in the school's history.

A stunned but gracious Woody Hayes told reporters, "I lost the ballgame . . . they had a better offense than we figured and their defensive line was the best we've faced this season." He personally accepted the blame for the two crucial delay-of-game penalties.

Plum was given credit for leading the Lion offense and for his excellent punting. He had a 56-yard punt which rolled dead at the Ohio State 2 in the second quarter and a 72-yard fourth quarter kick which rolled out of bounds at the Ohio State 3. Plum's coach was a young assistant who had played quarterback under Engle at Brown in the late-1940s . . . his name was Joe Paterno.

> **P**enn State's 7-6 victory in 1956 broke Ohio State's eight-game winning streak. It was Ohio State's first loss since Duke upset the Buckeyes 20-14 in the fourth game of 1955. Ironically, Duke and Penn State had been recent "fill-ins" on the Ohio State schedule after Navy cancelled a two-game series with the Buckeyes.

It was also the first OSU loss resulting from a missed conversion attempt since the Buckeyes lost to Southern California, 13-12, in 1937. The crowd of 82,584 was (at the time) the largest ever to see Penn State play.

Engle's players carried him all the way from midfield to the locker room. He told reporters, "I've never been happier," and recognized assistant coach "Tor" Toretti who had scouted Ohio State. "We beat a great team and a great coach. This has been our greatest victory. I admire Big Ten football . . I think it's tremendous," Engle related. Little did he realize his school would someday become a member of the conference he so admired.

LIONS PULL MONUMENTAL UPSET IN '64

A two-game series was played in Columbus in 1963 and '64 with Penn State again winning both games. Ohio State held a 7-0 halftime lead in '63 but the Lions' defense stiffened and did not allow the Buckeyes past the 50-yard line in the second half. PSU quarterback Pete Liske kept the Buckeye defenders off-balance with his superb ball-handling, which Hayes described as "the best I've ever seen in this stadium." The Lions scored ten second-half points to win, 10-7.

The evening before Penn State's 27-0 upset of undefeated Ohio State in 1964, Joe Paterno (then an assistant coach) predicted to SID Jim Tarman (later PSU's athletic director), "We're not only going to beat them tomorrow, we'll shut them out!" Paterno felt good about the 3-4 Lions' chances because of an excellent week of practice.

The 1964 game was the real shocker. The second-ranked Buckeyes entered the game at 6-0 while Penn State was 3-4. Ohio State had given up only 39 points in its first six games. The Nittany Lions scored in each quarter to win, 27-0, handing Ohio State its first shutout in 45 games. At the time, it was the widest margin of defeat for a Woody Hayes-coached team in Ohio Stadium. The Buckeyes

Two legends together — coaches Woody Hayes and Joe Paterno

obtained their initial first down in the third period (on a penalty), and finally crossed the midfield stripe late in the final quarter.

Penn State's rushing attack was led by fullback Tom Urbanik with 79 yards. Urbanik's younger brother, Bill, would later become a fine defensive tackle on Ohio State's national title team of 1968.

BUCKEYES FINALLY GET FIRST WINS

A two-game series in 1975 and '76 belonged to the Buckeyes but neither win was easy. The '75 match, played in Columbus, was the initial encounter between coaches Woody Hayes and Joe Paterno.

Ohio State opened the game with an 80-yard drive to lead 7-0. The key play of the series was a surprise 49-yard reverse by wingback Brian Baschnagel. Fullback Pete Johnson scored the touchdown from the 3, behind a key block by Archie Griffin.

Penn State answered with a 55-yard field goal by Chris Barr to make it 7-3. At the time, Barr's field goal was the longest in the 54-year history of Ohio Stadium. OSU's Tom Klaban then kicked his first field goal of the season, a 45-yarder to put the Bucks on top 10-3 after one quarter.

The Lions' defense stiffened to hold the Buckeyes scoreless the next 30 minutes. Meanwhile, Barr connected on a 31-yard second-quarter field goal and a 25 yarder after halftime to tighten things at 10-9 entering the final quarter.

The Buckeye then offense got rolling again with Johnson scoring his second TD on a powerful burst from the Lion 11. Klaban's conversion concluded the game's scoring at 17-9. The drive was kept alive when Archie Griffin made a breathtaking one-handed grab of a Cornelius Greene pass on a third-and-11 from the OSU 32. The play covered 23 yards for a first down to

Penn State's all-time road attendance record is 88,202 at Ohio Stadium on September 16, 1978.

the Penn State 45.

Griffin led all rushers with 128 yards — it marked his 23rd consecutive regular season game of rushing for more than 100 yards. Johnson, who gained 112 yards, was quite effective with his plunges between the tackles. Paterno admitted the Lions underestimated Johnson's strength. Punter Tom Skladany definitely was a factor, averaging 47.6 yards on five kicks.

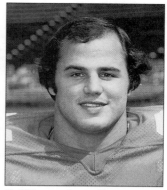

Jeff Logan's stellar performance in '76 was a key factor in the series' only game in State College

Hayes was especially proud of his young defense, which had not allowed a touchdown in its first two games of the '75 season. Tackle Nick Buonamici, playing with an injured hand, led all tacklers with 12. It was the first time Penn State had been held without a touchdown in its last 27 games.

The top-rated Buckeyes won another close one, 12-7, at Penn State in 1976. It was the first time a number-one ranked team ever appeared at State College. The winning TD was scored by halfback Bobby Hyatt on a surprise 8-yard sweep — it came on fourth-and-two with Penn State expecting fullback Johnson to carry for the first down. This was Hyatt's first and only Ohio State touchdown and his only carry of the season. The Buckeyes were led by the clever ball-handling of quarterback Rod Gerald and the running of tailback Jeff Logan, who tallied 160 yards.

SCHLICHTER AND GERALD BOTH START '78 OPENER

Penn State was OSU's opening-game opponent during Hayes' last season in 1978. Buckeye fans had speculated all summer who Hayes would go with at quarterback: senior Rod Gerald, his starter the past two seasons, or highly-touted freshman Art Schlichter. Hayes started both — Schlichter at quarterback and Gerald at split end. But Paterno's Nittany Lions (who had already played Temple and Rutgers) were ready with a tenacious pass-rush which forced Schlichter to throw five interceptions. The Lions won, 19-0. It was the first time Ohio State had been shutout in an opening game since a scoreless tie with

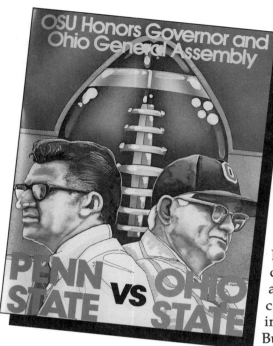

Otterbein in 1901. Ohio State and Penn State last met in the 1980 Fiesta Bowl, with the Lions winning, 31-19. This contest can best be described as two different games. Ohio State dominated play early and lead 19-10 at the half behind the fine passing of Schlichter. But the Lions made some key defensive adjustments at intermission and completely dominated in the second half. The Bucks could advance no further than their 36-yard line in the third period. Penn State's depth also played a key factor. Speaking in Columbus in 1990, Paterno stated one of his coaching goals is to take Penn State to the Rose Bowl. The series will likely become one of the Big Ten's key rivalries, with the Buckeyes hoping to fare more successfully than in the past.

Ohio State vs. Penn State

DECADE	W	L	T	POINTS OSU	PSU
1890	0	0	0	0	0
1900	0	0	0	0	0
1910	0	1	0	0	37
1920	0	0	0	0	0
1930	0	0	0	0	0
1940	0	0	0	0	0
1950	0	1	0	6	7
1960	0	2	0	7	37
1970	2	1	0	29	35
1980*	0	1	0	19	31
1990	0	0	0	0	0
TOTAL	2	6	0	61	147

Ohio State at Home: 1-5
Ohio State on the Road: 1-1
* Fiesta Bowl

Timeout

The Five Greatest OSU Games Never Played

1. 1954: Ohio State-UCLA

Undefeated and top-ranked Ohio State vs. undefeated and second-ranked UCLA would have been a dream match in the January 1, 1955, Rose Bowl. Because of the no-repeat policy, UCLA could not return. Instead, the Buckeyes defeated second-place Southern California 20-7.

2. 1935: Ohio State-Minnesota

Buckeyes and Golden Gophers shared the Big Ten title with identical 5-0 league records. A meeting between the two would have decided an outright champion. Minnesota later won the national title.

3. 1957: Ohio State-Michigan State

Buckeyes (9-1) finished first in the *United Press International* poll and second in the *Associated Press* poll. Spartans (8-1) finished third in each poll. Ohio State lost to Texas Christian while MSU was defeated by Purdue.

4. 1981: Ohio State-Iowa

The only two Big Ten teams not scheduled to meet this season. The two tied for the league title with 6-2 records. What would have been the most important conference game was instead the only one not played.

5. 1968: Ohio State-Penn State

Buckeyes (10-0) won national title with Rose Bowl win over Southern California, Nittany Lions (11-0) finished second after defeating Kansas in Orange Bowl.

Ohio State vs. Purdue

Highest Score in Series
Ohio State: 46-0 (1977, Columbus)
Purdue: 41-6 (1967, Columbus)

Highest Margin of Victory in Series
Ohio State: 46 points (46-0, 1977, Columbus)
Purdue: 35 points (41-6, 1967, Columbus)

Buckeyes' Most Significant Win
Ohio State's 13-0 triumph in 1968 ranks among the greatest victories in school history. Top-ranked Purdue entered Ohio Stadium as a 13-point favorite. This win paved the way for Woody Hayes' sophomore-dominated team to capture the national title with a record of 10-0.

Buckeyes' Most Devastating Loss
Purdue's startling 35-13 victory at Ohio Stadium in 1945 halted Ohio State's two-season winning streak at 12 and erased the Buckeyes' chances to repeat as conference champions. It was the first loss for coach Carroll Widdoes who succeeded Paul Brown as head coach in 1944.

11. The Purdue Series

'68 TRIUMPH
ONE OF
BUCKEYES'
FINEST

*T*he Buckeyes and Boilermakers have battled 39 times through 1991 with Ohio State leading the series at 27-10-2. Twenty-six of the games have been played in Columbus. The two first met at old Ohio Field in 1919 with Chic Harley leading the Buckeyes to a 20-0 triumph. Ohio State shutout Purdue the first six games in the series, outscoring the Boilermakers 117-0. Purdue's first win came at Ohio Stadium in 1938, 12-0.

Halfback Stu Holcomb, Ohio State's 1931 captain, served as Purdue's head coach from 1947-55. Holcomb was later president of the Chicago White Sox Baseball Club.

Ohio State's first season-opening game against a conference opponent was a 7-0 win over Purdue at Ohio Stadium in 1924. It also was the first opener against an opponent from outside the state of Ohio. The game's lone touchdown came on a 56-yard pass from halfback Bill Hunt to fullback Marty Karow on the first play of the second quarter. This was Ohio State's first league victory in Ohio Stadium, which was dedicated in 1922. The Buckeyes had lost all five of their home conference contests during the '22 and '23 seasons.

PURDUE DECLINES CHANCE TO ERASE LOSS

The outcome of the October 5, 1940, game at Ohio Stadium was seriously questioned the following week. Ohio State started strongly and led 14-0 at the half on touchdowns by Dick Fisher and captain Jim Langhurst. But the Boilermakers dominated the second half and tied the game at 14-14 with scores by John Petty and Bill Buffington.

Late in the fourth quarter, Ohio State advanced to a fourth-and-nine at the Purdue 12 with just 19 seconds remaining. Coach Francis Schmidt elected to send tackle Charlie Maag into the game to attempt a field goal. Maag's 29-yard kick was perfect and Ohio State had won a real thriller 17-14.

Charlie Magg's 29-yard kick was the game winner in 1940

The following Tuesday, Columbus sportswriter Lew Byrer became aware that Maag had been an "illegal substitution" late in the fourth quarter and brought this to the attention of the Ohio State athletic department. College football rules in 1940 prohibited a player from returning to play in any quarter once he had seen action in that quarter and Maag had played the very first down of the final quarter. Both coaching staffs had been unaware of Maag's status and Maag admitted "he simply forgot he had been in on the first play of the fourth quarter." Ohio State reportedly contacted Purdue and offered to forfeit the game but Purdue cordially declined and the final score remained.

The 1943 game was played at Cleveland Municipal Stadium with Purdue winning big over Ohio State's "Baby Bucks,"

Alliance (Ohio) High School produced two excellent quarterbacks in the early 1950s — John Borton, who was an Ohio State co-captain in 1954 and Len Dawson, who co-captained Purdue in '56.

30-7. The Boilermakers, who captured the '43 league title with a 9-0 record, benefitted from the transfer of All-American guard Alex Agase from Illinois as part of the wartime naval training program. Purdue fullback Tony Bukovich scored 13 touchdowns that season before being assigned to active naval duty after just four games.

Underdog Purdue erased Ohio State's hopes to repeat as Big Ten champions with a startling 35-13 victory at Ohio Stadium in 1945. It broke the Buckeyes' two-season winning streak at 12 and handed Carroll Widdoes his first loss since succeeding Paul Brown as head coach at the beginning of the 1944 season.

The Boilermakers were paced by the excellent passing of quarterback Bob DeMoss, who threw for two touchdowns, and the running of fullback Ed Cody, who tallied the other three. Purdue built a 28-0 lead before Doc Daugherty passed to Bud Kessler for 36 yards and Ohio State's first touchdown. The Buckeyes drove 64 yards for their final score with Alex Verdova taking it across from the five after catching a lateral from Chuck Gandee. Ohio State finished the 1945 campaign at 7-2, Purdue at 7-3.

"I DESPISE TURNOVERS" — WOODY HAYES

Woody Hayes' strong distaste for turnovers was partly created by the Buckeyes' 21-14 setback at Ohio Stadium in 1952. Purdue's three touchdowns resulted from a fumble recovery, a blocked punt and an interception. Less than four minutes into the game, the Boilermakers needed just five plays to lead 7-0 after recovering fullback John Hlay's fumble at the OSU 26. End Johnny Kerr went through untouched and blocked Bill Peterson's second quarter punt and guard Tom Bettis picked the ball up on the bounce at the nine and rambled across the goal to increase Purdue's lead to 14-0. In the third period, safety Phil Mateja intercepted one of John Borton's throws and returned it to the Ohio State 30, setting up fullback Max Schmeling's scoring smash from the three five plays later.

Ironically, Purdue fumbled five times and Ohio State recovered *all* five. But the Buckeyes could transform only two into touchdowns. A win over Purdue would have ultimately earned Ohio State the '52 conference championship. Purdue and Wisconsin shared the crown with 4-1-1 league records, followed by the Buckeyes at 5-2.

Ohio State relied on its second-half defense to secure a 20-7 triumph on a very sunny but cold afternoon in Ohio Stadium on November 9, 1957. The Buckeyes built a 20-0 halftime lead on touchdowns by Don Clark, Dick LeBeau and Frank Kremblas, but the second half was an entirely different game. The Boilermakers scored quickly on a 24-yard pass play from Ross Fichtner to Tom Fletcher. Ohio State's fine defense then held the visitors twice on the Ohio State 3 and again at the Ohio State 16 to preserve the win.

The following year's contest was very similar — Ohio State dominated the first half while Purdue controlled the second. Unfortunately, the game ended in a 14-14 tie which eliminated both teams from the 1958 conference title race.

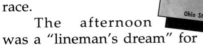

The afternoon was a "lineman's dream" for Ohio State offensive tackle Jim Marshall, who scored both of the Buckeyes' touchdowns. In the first period, he scooped up a blocked punt and rambled 22 yards for his first six-pointer. Marshall returned an interception 25 yards for his second score late in the second quarter to give the Buckeyes a 14-0 lead at the half. End Jim Houston assisted with both of the scoring plays by blocking the punt and deflecting the pass into Marshall's arms. In the second half, Ohio State could muster only one first down and 37 yards of offense.

The Buckeyes scored by almost every possible means to deal sixth-ranked Purdue a stunning 15-0 upset in 1959. It was a delightful change for Ohio State's 83,391 homecoming fans since their team's offense had been shutout the two prior Saturdays by Southern California and Illinois. Placekicker Dave Kilgore booted field goals of 36 and 35 yards and kicked the extra point after quarterback Tom Matte scored the game's only touchdown on a 32-yard scamper in the second quarter. The Buckeyes also recorded a safety when Pur-

> The Buckeyes' 35-point loss to Purdue in 1967 (41-6) was the largest margin of defeat during Woody Hayes' 276 games at Ohio State.

due's Jim Tiller was tackled in the end zone, after fielding a punt on the 16 and racing backwards in an attempt to avoid being tackled.

LOWEST LOW TO HIGHEST HIGH

There could hardly have been a sharper contrast between the games of 1967 and '68. Ohio State suffered one of its most humiliating setbacks, 41-6, in '67, and pulled off one of the top victories in school history the following season, 13-0.

The 1967 score could have been much worse. Hayes thanked Purdue coach Jack Mollenkopf for "holding down the score" by pulling most of his starters in the third quarter after leading 35-0 at halftime. Ohio State's touchdown came on a pass from Kevin Rusnak to Billy Anders with just 28 seconds remaining. Hayes was receiving some intense fan criticism — it was the Buckeyes' second defeat in just the season's third game and their seventh in their last 11 over two seasons.

Ohio State opened its 1968 conference schedule October 12 against powerful Purdue, the preseason pick for a second consecutive league title. Remembering the embarrassing 41-6 loss exactly 52 weeks earlier, the Buckeyes were ready for the nation's number-one ranked team. OSU was rated fourth in the weekly *Associated Press* poll. Purdue, with highly-talented halfback Leroy Keyes and quarterback Mike Phipps, was a solid 13-point favorite. A then-record Ohio Stadium crowd of 84,834 saw Hayes start nine sophomores on offense and defense with five others seeing considerable action.

Although Ohio State advanced deep into Purdue territory three times, the first half was scoreless. Early in the third period, with Phipps throwing under heavy pressure, cornerback Ted Provost intercepted and scampered 35 yards for one of Ohio Stadium's most celebrated touchdowns. Later that quarter, Jim Stillwagon intercepted another Phipps aerial, returning it to the Purdue 25. Four plays later, Kern was shaken up and replaced

Jack Tatum may be best remembered at Ohio State for his dominance of Leroy Keyes in '68

by senior Bill Long. On his first play, Long faded back to pass, then raced 14 yards up the middle for the Buckeyes' second score. Jim Roman's conversion finished the scoring at 13-0, for one of the biggest wins in Ohio State history.

Woody Hayes called it "our greatest victory" and "the greatest defensive effort I have ever seen." The Buckeyes led in total offensive yardage 411-186 and in first downs 22-16. Hayes gave substantial credit to his defensive coaches Lou McCullough, Lou Holtz and Bill Mallory — their unit had held Purdue to just 186 yards in total offense. Jack Tatum was magnificent, especially with his defense of Keyes who was held to just 19 yards rushing. Phipps completed just ten of 28 passes for 106 yards and was sacked four times. Fullback Jim Otis led the Buckeye attack with 144 yards in 29 carries. The Boilermakers, who were averaging 41 points in three winning starts this season, had been held scoreless for the first time in 24 games.

Ohio State was equally impressive against Purdue the following season winning 42-14 to tie its own Big Ten record with 17 consecutive conference victories. The triumph assured the nation's number-one ranked team at least a share of the 1969 league title and also stretched Ohio State's overall winning streak to 22, longest in school history. Tenth-ranked Purdue entered the game at 7-1, losing only to Michigan (31-20) five weeks earlier. The 25-degree temperature in snow-covered Ohio

Stadium had little effect as Hayes substituted liberally when the score reached 42-7 after three quarters.

Halfback Leo Hayden led the Buckeyes' rushing attack with 130 yards including a 59-yarder for the day's longest gain. One of the most spectacular plays was a 57-yard punt return by Larry Zelina for the Buckeyes' final score. Ohio State's defense intercepted five of Phipps' passes and recovered three fumbles.

The undefeated Buckeyes may have been looking ahead one week to their showdown with undefeated Michigan and nearly let one get away in 1970. Ohio State escaped West Lafayette with a 10-7 verdict after Fred Schram's 30-yard field goal into a strong wind broke a 7-7 tie with just 2:04 remaining. Fullback John Brockington's powerful 26-yard scoring burst gave the Buckeyes an early 7-0 first quarter lead. But Stan Brown returned the ensuing kickoff 96 yards to tie, setting the stage for Schram's winning kick.

The Buckeyes' defense saved the day, holding Purdue to three first downs and 131 yards in total offense. The Boilermakers were in great position to take the lead after recovering a blocked punt at the Ohio State 17 early in the final period, but the effort failed when linebacker Doug Adams stopped Brown in mid-air on a fourth-and-one at the eight. Quarterback Ron Maciejowski's timely fourth quarter running and passing put the ball in position for the tie-breaker.

ARCHIE SETS ULTIMATE RECORD

Archie Griffin became major college football's all-time rushing leader while leading the Buckeyes to a 35-6 triumph over Purdue in 1975. The game was played October 25 before a crowd of 69,405, at the time the third largest in Ross-Ade Stadium history. The talented tailback rushed for 130 yards that afternoon to increase his career total to 4,730 yards, 15 more than the previous mark held by Cornell's Ed Marinaro.

The Buckeyes entered the contest as the nation's top-ranked team with a record of 6-0 against very rugged competition. Ohio State's first four victims had been Michigan State (21-0), Penn State (17-9), North Carolina (32-7) and UCLA (41-20). Going into this weekend, the combined record of these four teams was 16-3-1, excluding their losses to Ohio State — and the three setbacks had been by only 18 points.

It was Ohio State's first meeting with Purdue since 1970

and its first on Ross-Ade Stadium's "Prescription Athletic Turf (PAT)." The surface is a system which utilizes natural grass planted over a layer of sand and topsoil on top of a plastic liner. Coach Alex Agase's hard- luck Boilermakers entered the contest at 1-5.

After Purdue was unable to move on its first possession, Ohio State took over at its own 40. On the Buckeyes' first play from scrimmage, fullback Pete Johnson shot through the middle for 60 yards and his 17th touchdown of the season. The big hole was opened when tackle Scott Dannelley neutralized Purdue's tackle, center Rick Applegate took out the middle guard and guard Ted Smith blocked the inside linebacker. Pur-  due's safety went for a fake pitch to Griffin and Johnson was on his way. Tom Klaban's conversion made it 7-0 just 1:37 into the game. Interestingly, Griffin had kidded Johnson the previous evening about scoring on his very first carry of the game.

The Boilermakers came back with a 22-yard field goal by Steve Schmidt to make it 7-3. It was the first score against Ohio State that season by a Big Ten opponent.

Griffin returned the ensuing kickoff 53 yards to the Purdue 37. Seven plays later, Johnson scored his second touchdown of the quarter on a burst from the three to make it 14-3. The drive's biggest gainer was a 16-yard toss from quarterback Cornelius Greene to split end Lenny Willis.

Schmidt kicked his second field goal, a 27-yarder, midway through the second quarter to cut the Buckeye margin to 14-6.

Ohio State opened some breathing room on its next possession driving 80 yards in 12 plays to make it 21-6 at the half. The touchdown came on a perfectly thrown ball from Greene to wingback Brian Baschnagel, who then waltzed untouched into the right corner of the end zone.

At this point it appeared that Griffin might not break Marinaro's record until the following Saturday at home against Indiana. At halftime, he had only 36 of the needed 116 yards.

The Buckeyes received the second-half kickoff and quickly increased their lead to 28-6. Greene passed for his second touchdown, a 41-yarder to Lenny Willis to conclude an 80-yard, ten-play drive.

Later in the third period, Ohio State put together one of Hayes' patented ball-control drives, moving 90 yards in 11 plays for their fifth and final touchdown of the afternoon. On the first play of the fourth quarter, Greene scampered 28 yards around end for the score. Klaban's placement finalized the scoring at 35-6, but the best was yet to happen.

Fred Schram, whose fourth-quarter field goal won the 1970 game, never played high school football. Schram was selected MVP of the Massillon High School baseball team his senior year and decided to walk-on as a placekicker at Ohio State in the fall of 1968. He credits much of his success to the fine instruction he received from placekicking coach Ernie Godfrey.

After an exchange of punts, Ohio State's defense held Purdue on downs at the Boilermaker 38. The Buckeye offense returned to the field with just 8:26 remaining. Griffin had run for 107 yards, needing just nine more for the record. On first down, he carried for 23 yards to become college football's most prolific ground gainer. It was an off-tackle slant behind Dannelley, who he cut inside of for the record. Griffin received a standing ovation from the entire crowd as Ohio State's offensive unit was replaced by the second team. It also was his 28th consecutive regular-season game of rushing for more than 100 yards.

Griffin gave much of the credit to his offensive line. "Yards were tough to get today," he said, "but our offensive line was grinding it out all the way. I've always played with great lines ever since I've been at Ohio State." Hayes was especially elated over his back's latest milestone and the squad regarded it as a team accomplishment.

The game's statistics were somewhat peculiar — Purdue led in first downs 22-21 and in total offensive plays 81-60. The Boilermakers had possession of the ball 33 1/2 minutes. Johnson led all rushers with 131 yards and Griffin had 130. Ohio State led in total offensive yards 458-358.

Griffin finished his career rushing for 5,177 yards in 845 carries. He is currently fourth in all-time career rushing behind

Tony Dorsett of Pitt (6,082 yards, 1,074 carries), Charles White of Southern California (5,598 in 1,023 carries), and Herschel Walker of Georgia (5,259 yards in 994 carries). Griffin's average gain of 6.13 yards per carry still stands as a major college record.

The seventh game of '76 against Purdue produced both bad news and good news. First, fleet-footed sophomore quarterback Rod Gerald injured his lower back and was lost for the remainder of the season. With Gerald sidelined, Hayes went with Jim Pacenta, an inexperienced senior who rallied the Buckeyes for three second-half touchdowns and a 24-3 win over the Boilermakers. Pacenta's pin-point passing and fine leadership guided Ohio State to three more wins in their next four games and a share of the Big Ten title with Michigan.

Freshman fullback Joel Payton scored four touchdowns

> **F**ullback Joel Payton's 26 points in 1977 are the most scored against Purdue by one player in a single game.

and a two-point conversion to lead Ohio State's surprisingly easy 46-0 victory in 1977. Coach Jim Young's Boilermakers came to Columbus with a record of 2-2, the Buckeyes were 3-1. Young, who was in his first of five years as Purdue's head coach, had been a reserve fullback on Hayes' first national title team in 1954. The Boilermakers were quarterbacked by freshman Mark Hermann, who finished the season leading the Big Ten in both passing and total offense.

SCHLICHTER VS. CAMPBELL

Can you imagine a team losing a game by 12 points after its quarterback connected on 31 of 52 passes for 516 yards and three touchdowns? It happened to Purdue and quarterback Scott Campbell at West Lafayette in 1981. Art Schlichter also hit for three scores on 19 of 33 passing for 336 yards as Ohio State outscored the Boilermakers 45-33. Schlichter was especially effective calling audibles at the line of scrimmage.

Earle Bruce called it "one of the great victories since I've been at Ohio State." The teams combined for 48 first downs, 1,007 yards in total offense, ten touchdowns and three field goals. Thirty-four of the game's 78 points were scored in the final quarter. It was just Purdue's second loss at Ross-Ade Stadium in its last 23 games.

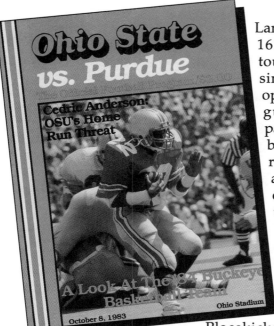

Cornerback Garcia Lane returned punts for 161 yards and two touchdowns in 1983 to single-handedly break open a tight game and guide the Buckeyes past Purdue 33-22. Tailback Keith Byars rushed for 135 yards and caught four passes totaling 120 yards to become the first Buckeye to top the century mark in both rushing and receiving in the same game since Ray Hamilton in 1949. Placekicker Paul Allen kicked first quarter field goals of 21 and 41 yards while Thomas "Pepper" Johnson led the defense with 11 tackles.

				POINTS	
DECADE	**W**	**L**	**T**	**OSU**	**PU**
1890	0	0	0	0	0
1900	0	0	0	0	0
1910	1	0	0	20	0
1920	4	0	0	84	0
1930	1	1	0	13	12
1940	3	3	1	113	131
1950	4	1	1	112	54
1960	2	2	0	82	79
1970	4	1	0	131	43
1980	7	2	0	286	178
1990	1	0	0	42	2
TOTAL	**27**	**10**	**2**	**883**	**499**

Ohio State-Purdue Summary

Ohio State at Home: 19-5-2
Ohio State on the Road: 8-5-0

Ohio State vs. Wisconsin

Highest Score in Series
Ohio State: 62-7 (1969, Columbus)
Wisconsin: 34 points, 46-34 loss (1941, Columbus)

Highest Margin of Victory in Series
Ohio State: 59 points (59-0, 1979, Columbus)
Wisconsin: 21 points (21-0, 1915, Madison)

Buckeyes' Most Significant Win
Ohio State's 31-14 come-from-behind win over second-ranked Wisconsin in 1954 was a monumental victory during the Buckeyes' successful drive for the national title. The game featured a remarkable 88-yard interception return by Howard "Hopalong" Cassady and excellent defensive play by end Dean Dugger.

Buckeyes' Most Devastating Loss
Wisconsin's 17-7 win in 1942 nearly cost Ohio State its first national championship. It was the Buckeyes' only loss that season. Fortunately for Ohio State, undefeated Georgia Tech and Boston College were both upset in their last regular season games, paving the way for the Buckeyes to capture the crown.

12. The Wisconsin Series

'80s Kind To Badgers

Ohio State and Wisconsin first met in 1913, the same season the Buckeyes joined the Big Ten Conference. The two played sporadically through the mid-'40s and have met each season since 1948, the third longest continuous series in Buckeye football (Ohio State-Illinois continuous since 1914, Ohio State-Michigan since 1918). Ohio State holds a commanding edge in the overall series at 45-12-4 through 1991. But five of the 12 Badger wins came from 1981-87 with Wisconsin victories in '81 and '82 preventing Ohio State from being Rose Bowl-bound.

HARLEY SPARKS INITIAL VICTORY

Sophomore halfback Chic Harley led Ohio State to an electrifying 14-13 come-from-behind triumph over powerful Wisconsin in 1916. This thriller was Ohio State's first win against the Badgers and was one of the most significant victories during the Buckeyes' earlier seasons. It brought national attention to the college football program which was emerging in Columbus.

The game was played November 4 at old Ohio Field along North High Street. It was a beautiful Homecoming afternoon and the crowd of 12,500 was (at the time) the largest ever to see a football game in the state of Ohio. Numerous mail requests for tickets had been returned unfilled and scalpers were getting between $5 and $7 for their $2 seats.

Wisconsin was one of seven charter members of the Western Conference in 1896 and had already captured four league titles before Ohio State joined the conference. Both teams entered this '16 encounter undefeated—the Buckeyes at 3-0 and Wisconsin, 4-0. The Badgers had outscored their four opponents 91-10. Ohio State had recorded a major milestone two weeks earlier with a 7-6 win at Illinois for the school's very first victory over the Illini.

Ohio State coach John Wilce had religiously drilled his squad until dark each evening in preparation for the Badgers. At a wild Friday evening pep rally attended by more than 2,000 students and fans, Wilce seemed extremely confident about the Buckeyes' chances. Wisconsin refused to wear numbered jerseys so Wilce likewise had his team dressed in uniforms without numbers.

It was the Badgers' first road game of the season and Coach Paul Withington apparently underestimated the strength of Wilce's Buckeyes. Instead of accompanying his squad to Columbus, Withington put assistant E. E. Soucy in command while he traveled to Minneapolis to scout the Minnesota-Illinois game, two strong teams the Badgers would face in late November. Withington's absence may have had a psychological effect upon his players who appeared to be overconfident. The contest obviously concluded much differently than Withington anticipated.

The visitors dominated play in the first quarter but were unable to score. Known for its crushing ground attack, Wisconsin also effectively passed much more than expected. Early in the second period, the Badgers drove 47 yards for the game's first touchdown which came on a pass from Paulie Meyers to Glenn Taylor. Ebenezar Simpson's conversion gave Wisconsin the lead, 7-0.

The Buckeyes came right back on their next possession to tie the game with Harley scoring on the type of run which would soon make him a legend. With the ball at the Badger 27, Harley darted around right end and found a small hole after barely getting past the line of scrimmage. He then made a sharp turn to his left and headed for the far corner of the end zone. With only Taylor to beat, he veered back to his right and crossed the goal line directly under the goal post. Harley kicked the extra point to make it 7-7 at the half.

Emotions ran high between the coaches during games in 1917 and 1919-22. Ohio State coach John Wilce had played at Wisconsin and captained the Badgers' 1909 squad while Wisconsin coach John Richards had been head coach at Ohio State in 1912.

The Buckeyes dominated play in a scoreless third period leading in first downs 5-1. In the decisive fourth quarter, Harley made one of his most celebrated runs. Fielding a Taylor punt at his own 20, he headed diagonally toward the east sideline and, after picking up a key block from end Charles "Shifty" Bolen, sped 80 yards for the all-important go-ahead touchdown. Harley's conversion was his 14th point of the afternoon as Ohio State had taken the lead for the first time with only eight minutes remaining.

But the Badgers came right back. Taking over at the OSU 47, they moved to a fourth-and-goal at the one. The ball was given to Louis Kreutz who butted across to reduce the margin to one. Two key factors in the drive were a ten-yard pass from Simpson to W. M. Kelley and a 15-yard penalty against the Buckeyes. Wisconsin's all-important conversion attempt, however, was unsuccessful, leaving the score at 14-13. Time expired after Ohio State ran two plays and the Buckeyes had just accomplished their biggest victory in the first 27 years of Ohio State football.

Harley was carried off the field on the shoulders of exuberant students who had swarmed onto the playing field by the thousands. Wilce couldn't have been more elated as his Buckeyes had defeated Wisconsin for the very first time after losses the three previous seasons. Wilce especially praised the sterling defensive play of guard Charlie Seddon, a 5'7", 150-pounder who had started his very first game. Seddon went on to become an excellent lineman and was affectionately known as the "watch charm" guard.

The Buckeyes finished the season with wins over Indiana, Case and Northwestern to capture their first Big Ten championship and complete the first undefeated-untied season in school history (7-0). The Badgers lost to Minnesota and tied Illinois to finish at 4-2-1.

Harley also led Ohio State to an important 16-3 triumph at Madison in 1917. He passed 38 yards to Bolen for the first touchdown and kicked a 38-yard field goal for the game's final score. At Madison in 1919, Harley's 15-yard field goal made the difference as Ohio State edged the Badgers 3-0.

The Buckeyes won another thriller at Ohio Field in 1920 in a game which decided the conference championship. The Badgers took a 7-0 halftime lead after driving 75 yards late in the

All-American Pete Stinchcomb, star of the 1920 contest

second period. Ohio State finally scored midway through the final quarter on a 36-yard pass from quarterback Hoge Workman to halfback Pete Stinchcomb. But Stinchcomb's conversion attempt hit the upright and bounced back onto the field, leaving Wisconsin with a 7-6 lead.

After the Badgers were unable to move, Ohio State took over at its own 10 with just three minutes remaining. Operating against the clock, Workman directed his squad 90 yards for the winning score. With third-and-nine at the Badger 48, Stinchcomb caught another of Workman's passes on the dead run for the touchdown and a 13-7 victory. Ohio State finished the regular season at 7-0, Wisconsin's record was 6-1. In the book *On Wisconsin*, Oliver Kuechle and Jim Mott describe the loss as "one of the biggest heartbreaks in Wisconsin history."

"MASSILLON DAY" AT OHIO STADIUM

Interestingly, the Badgers' highest score in the series was in a losing effort in 1941, 46-34. It was one of the wildest games between the two schools with the Buckeyes outscoring Wisconsin seven touchdowns to five. The game was publicized as "Massillon Day" at Ohio Stadium with the Massillon High School band spelling out "PAUL" and "HARRY" in honor of the two head coaches, OSU's Paul Brown and Wisconsin's Harry Studldreher. Both had grown up in Massillon.

Ohio State threw only four passes that afternoon and all went for touchdowns. After Wisconsin tied the game 20-20 in the third period, fullback Jack Graf put the Buckeyes ahead to stay on a perfectly executed 64-yard spinner play. It was an extremely difficult loss for the Badgers, who were paced by the running of fullback Pat Harder and passing of quarterback Bud

Seelinger.

Wisconsin defeated Ohio State 17-7 in Madison for the Buckeyes' only setback in 1942. The sixth-ranked Badgers, who entered the game at 5-0-1, had been pointing for Ohio State all season. The game was broadcast to what was believed to have been (at the time) the largest audience ever to hear a football game. Over 200 stations carried NBC announcer Bill Stern's broadcast throughout the United States and to the many servicemen around the world.

The contest has been nicknamed the "Bad Water Game."

> **D**uring Ohio State's 46-34 win in 1941, the Badgers' second touchdown came on a "fifth down" six-yard pass from Bud Seelinger to Tom Farris. After Farris failed to score from scrimmage on fourth down, the Badgers called timeout. Referee Jim Masker became confused and awarded Wisconsin an extra down. Coach Paul Brown protested vehemently to no avail following Masker's miscount.

Many Ohio State players became ill from the drinking water on the train to Madison on Friday. By Saturday afternoon, nearly half the squad was unable to play at full strength. Wisconsin, however, was extremely strong and would have been a very worthy opponent under any condition.

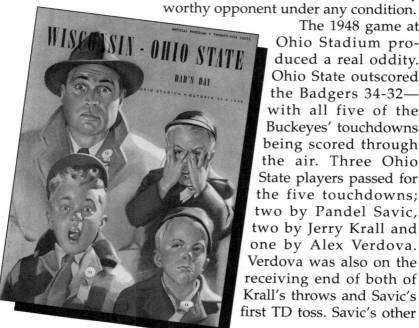

The 1948 game at Ohio Stadium produced a real oddity. Ohio State outscored the Badgers 34-32—with all five of the Buckeyes' touchdowns being scored through the air. Three Ohio State players passed for the five touchdowns; two by Pandel Savic, two by Jerry Krall and one by Alex Verdova. Verdova was also on the receiving end of both of Krall's throws and Savic's first TD toss. Savic's other scoring pass went to Joe Cannavino, while Verdova's was caught by Sonny Gandee. The lead changed hands four times. Ohio State's winning score came on Krall's second TD pass to Verdova with just 1:06 remaining.

HAYES' SQUADS DOMINATE BADGERS

Woody Hayes had great success against Wisconsin going 25-1-2 during his 28 seasons. His single setback came at Madison, 12-3, in 1959. The Buckeyes' 23-14 victory at Ohio Stadium in 1952 was Hayes' first "big win" at Ohio State. The Badgers entered the October 11 contest as the nation's top-ranked team. Led by the passing of quarterback John Borton and the running of "Hopalong" Cassady and Fred Bruney, Ohio State scored its three touchdowns on drives of 88, 64 and 55 yards. Linebacker Tony Curcillo spearheaded the defense which held the Badgers' very potent offense inside the Ohio State 20 five times without scoring.

The following season in Madison, the Buckeyes bounced back from a two-touchdown fourth quarter deficit to defeat Wisconsin 20-19. The sensational comeback was completed when quarterback Dave Leggett connected with Cassady on a perfectly thrown 60-yard touchdown pass play with just 2:31 left.

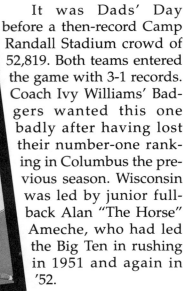

It was Dads' Day before a then-record Camp Randall Stadium crowd of 52,819. Both teams entered the game with 3-1 records. Coach Ivy Williams' Badgers wanted this one badly after having lost their number-one ranking in Columbus the previous season. Wisconsin was led by junior fullback Alan "The Horse" Ameche, who had led the Big Ten in rushing in 1951 and again in '52.

Ohio State scored first midway through the first quarter with Cassady powering himself into the end zone from the three. Tommy Hague's all-important conversion made it 7-0. Wisconsin then took charge of the game, scoring in each of the first three quarters to lead 19-7 heading into the final period. Quarterback Jim Miller scored the first and third touchdowns on end sweeps from the OSU 12 and 10 and passed four yards to end Norbert Esser for the other. But the Badgers missed their first two conversion attempts which became quite costly in the end.

Ohio State and Wisconsin each had outstanding running backs who wore jersey No. 40. The number was retired at Wisconsin after Elroy "Crazylegs" Hirsch wore it in 1942, and No. 40 has not been issued at Ohio State since Howard "Hopalong" Cassady wore it from 1952-55.

The Buckeyes nearly scored in the second quarter but Cassady was knocked out-of-bounds at the one-yard line after catching a fourth-down pass from Leggett. Finally, on the first play of the fourth quarter, OSU's Bobby Watkins bulled into the end zone from the three to cap a 59-yard drive and narrow the Badger lead to 19-14.

Late in the final stanza, Ohio State held Wisconsin on downs at the Wisconsin 40. With a fourth-and-two, linebacker Mike Takacs nailed Ameche for no gain at the line of scrimmage. On first down, Leggett connected with Cassady for the 60-yarder. The fleet halfback never broke stride after hauling in the strike on the dead run at the 36. Hayes' never-say-die warriors had taken the lead 20-19 with just 2:30 remaining.

But the Badgers bounced back driving to the OSU 17. With just 22 seconds remaining, Bill Miller's 23-yard field goal attempt was wide to the right by inches and the Buckeyes had won a real thriller. Hayes couldn't have been prouder as he heaped praise upon the efforts of both squads. His team had just captured one of the most thrilling Buckeye-Badger encounters of all-time.

CASSADY'S 88-YARD RETURN A STADIUM CLASSIC

The 1954 contest is one of the best-remembered games in Ohio Stadium history. It was Homecoming as number-two-ranked Wisconsin invaded Columbus to take on fourth-ranked

"Hop" Cassady seemingly played his best against the Badgers, especially in the 1954 contest

Ohio State. Both teams were 4-0. The Buckeyes were rated the Big Ten's top offensive team while the Badgers were the league's best defensively. A record 400 press passes were issued to sportswriters and broadcasters from all over the country, who were covering one of the season's top intercollegiate games.

Williams, realizing the Badgers had not won in Columbus since 1918, tried to change their luck by having his squad stay Friday evening in Springfield, Ohio, rather than a Columbus hotel. Winning this game was also a personal goal for Williamson, who had compiled a fine 34-12-4 record during his six seasons as the Badger boss. Ohio State was the only Big Ten opponent his teams had not defeated.

The Buckeyes had their chances during a very bruising first half but trailed 7-3 at intermission. Late in the third period, Wisconsin seriously threatened to increase its four-point lead. With second-and-four at the OSU 20, quarterback Jim Miller took to the air but Cassady intercepted at the 12 and, behind several key blocks, electrified the crowd with a spectacular 88-yard touchdown return which soundly shifted the game's momentum. It was Miller's first interception of the '54 season and the first time all year the Badgers had been scored upon in the second half.

Cassady's memorable run completely fractured Wisconsin's poise and Dean Dugger staged a one-man campaign against any Badger comeback. Dugger participated in every tackle as Ohio State held Wisconsin on downs during a crucial series early in the fourth quarter. On fourth down, he nailed halfback Billy Lowe for a 12-yard loss, and Ohio State took over at the Wisconsin 27. Ohio State scored three times in the final quarter to win 31-14 in a game much closer than indicated by the final score.

The Buckeyes limited Ameche to just 42 yards in 16 carries. Ameche, who that season would win the Heisman Trophy, had been unable to score against Ohio State for the fourth consecutive season. Wisconsin finished

Dean Dugger helped keep Alan Ameche from scoring against the Buckeyes during his career

the year at 7-2, good for ninth place in the season's final *Associated Press* poll. Ohio State went on to complete one of the most successful seasons in school history with a record of 10-0 and a 20-7 Rose Bowl victory over Southern California. It was the first of three national championship seasons for fourth-year coach Woody Hayes.

Wisconsin played in the Rose Bowl following the 1952 and 1962 seasons after suffering a single conference loss each of these years. Ohio State had defeated the Badgers 23-14 in 1952 and 14-7 in '62.

A 16-13 win over Wisconsin was also a very pivotal game during Hayes' second national title season in 1957. Each team entered the October 26 encounter in Madison with 3-1 records. The Badgers were pointing for this one and quickly jumped to a 13-0 lead on two first quarter touchdown sprints by halfback Danny Lewis.

Halfback Don Clark finally put the Buckeyes on the board with a sensational 71-yard scamper around right end. Following his blockers to perfection, Clark scored standing up to make it 13-7. Fullback Galen Cisco scored Ohio State's second touchdown on a three-yard plunge to tie the game 13-13 after one quarter. Don Sutherin booted a 20-yard field goal early in the

With starting quarterback Rex Kern injured, Ron Maciejowski went the distance and led the Buckeyes to a 43-8 triumph at Madison in 1968. "Super Sub" had a superb afternoon, passing for 153 yards and a touchdown, and rushing for 124 yards and three touchdowns.

third quarter to put the Buckeyes on top to stay, 16-13. Wisconsin moved to the Ohio State seven late in the final period but a key fumble recovery by the Bucks' Bob White ended the threat.

Hayes' team won another big encounter at Camp Randall Stadium in 1961. Wisconsin was sky high for its October 28 homecoming battle and Badger quarterback Ron Miller played an exceptional game, completing 13 of 23 passes for 219 yards and two touchdowns. Six of Miller's strikes were caught by All-American end Pat Richter for 104 yards and a touchdown.

But Hayes' mighty ground attack proved to be superior as Ohio State ground out a hard-earned 30-21 victory. Ferguson and his understudy, Dave Katterhenrich, led an awesome rushing effort which netted 357 yards. Ferguson rushed for 120 yards in 20 attempts and Katterhenrich added 91 in 17 carries including the game's first touchdown on a 17-yard burst up the middle. Ohio State completed the 1961 season at 8-0-1, Wisconsin finished at 6-3.

The Buckeyes really dominated play in the 1970s, winning all ten games and outscoring the Badgers 395-74. All-American defender Tim Fox excited Ohio State's 1975 homecoming crowd by turning a complete flip in the end zone after returning a Badger punt 75 yards for his team's third touchdown as Ohio State scored in each quarter to win 56-0.

BADGERS' FIRST WIN
IN HORSESHOE

Wisconsin really had the Buckeyes' number in the 1980s, winning five of the seven games from 1981-87. Ohio State had won 21 consecutive games over the Badgers before losing 24-21 at Madison in 1981. Wiscon-

Former Woody Hayes assistants Earle Bruce and Dave McClain were the opposing head coaches for the 1979-85 Ohio State-Wisconsin games. Both had been members of Hayes' Big Ten championship staffs in 1969 and '70.

sin's 6-0 conquest in 1982 was the Badgers' very *first* win in Ohio Stadium. The Badgers had made 25 previous trips to Columbus since Ohio Stadium was dedicated in 1922, losing 22 and tying three. Their last win in Columbus had come 64 years earlier at old Ohio Field in 1918 (14-3).

Ohio State returned to the winning trail in 1983, outscoring Wisconsin 45-27. The Ohio Stadium homecoming crowd of 89,203 was highly entertained as the Buckeye offense scored in each quarter and accounted for 525 total yards. Tailback Keith Byars ran for 174 yards and quarterback Mike Tomczak completed 12 of 14 passes (including 11 straight) for 162 yards. Badger quarterback Randy Wright hit on 23 of 39 for 319 yards and three touchdowns. Ohio State's defense helped immensely by intercepting four of Wright's passes.

Ohio State vs. Wisconsin

				POINTS	
DECADE	W	L	T	OSU	UW
1890	0	0	0	0	0
1900	0	0	0	0	0
1910	3	4	0	42	70
1920	1	0	0	13	7
1930	2	0	2	19	7
1940	5	2	0	147	110
1950	7	1	2	172	115
1960	10	0	0	285	101
1970	10	0	0	395	74
1980	5	5	0	238	162
1990	2	0	0	66	26
TOTAL	**45**	**12**	**4**	**1,377**	**672**

Ohio State at Home: 24-4-3
Ohio State on the Road: 21-8-1

13. Non-Conference Games

PROMINENT NON-LEAGUE ENCOUNTERS

*T*he majority of Ohio State's greatest moments have been in Big Ten Conference play or post-season bowl competition, but the Buckeyes have also experienced some celebrated non-conference games. This includes two early games against near-by Ohio opponents and an interesting afternoon in 1935 against the University of Chicago, a charter member of the Big Ten, and who was led by the Heisman Trophy's inaugural winner, Jay Berwanger.

CAPTAINS DEBATE LENGTH OF HALVES

Ohio State ended with a 2-0 win over Denison in 1905 without running a single play from scrimmage. Relations between the two schools became strained when Ohio State charged Denison with using two ineligible players on the grounds of professionalism. In an effort to save the game this dispute was dropped, but another developed just prior to kick-off over the length of the halves.

Ohio State insisted upon playing 35-minute halves while Denison wanted the halves to be shorter. When no agreement could be reached following a heated debate between the opposing coaches and captains, the referee ruled in favor of the Buckeyes and the longer halves. Denison refused to take the field! After a warning and a two-minute wait, the game was forfeited to Ohio State.

The Buckeye varsity stayed on the field and scrimmaged the second-teamers but few of the 2,000-plus spectators stayed to watch. Most fans strongly criticized the handling of the entire affair, and stood in line to receive a refund on their tickets. While Ohio State may have won the game, it lost at the gate. Ticket sales totaled $1,078 while the refunds amounted to $1,206 — a loss of $128. Apparently, several children sneaked in to old Ohio Field that afternoon, then stood in line to receive their "refunds."

COLUMBUS "TOO FAR" FOR OHIO WESLEYAN CO-EDS

One of Ohio State's early rivalries was with Ohio Wesleyan. The two played a total of 29 times beginning with OSU's very first game on May 3, 1890. Ohio Wesleyan was also the opponent for the very first game played in Ohio Stadium on October 7, 1922. The last contest between the two was played in 1932 and the Buckeyes held a decided edge in the series at 26-2-1.

One of the series' biggest games was played on October 31, 1908, at old U-Field along North High Street before a crowd of 3,300. Tickets sold for fifty cents each. In 1908, touchdowns counted five points; conversions, one point; and field goals, four points. Since it was customary during this era for opposing captains to mutually determine the length of the game, the Ohio State and Ohio Wesleyan captains decided on a 30-minute first half and a 25-minute second half.

The Methodists (nickname changed to Battling Bishops in 1925) were coached by Branch Rickey, a former star athlete at Ohio Wesleyan who later distinguished himself as a major league baseball executive. Rickey broke baseball's color barrier with the Brooklyn Dodgers' signing of Jackie Robinson in 1947. The Buckeyes were coached by the very popular and successful Al Herrnstein, a Michigan graduate who scored six touchdowns during the Wolverines' 86-0 trouncing of Ohio State in 1902.

The Methodists held a spirited pep rally Friday evening with Rickey openly predicting victory. A large cheering section accompanied the visitors to Columbus including most of the male student body. Co-eds were not permitted to attend since the faculty felt "it would not be proper" for them to leave the Ohio Wesleyan campus. The co-eds' petition to have this decision reversed was not accepted because of the "relentless position of the faculty."

The Buckeyes won the game 20-9 but it was anything but easy. Rickey was visably disappointed with the outcome but praised Ohio State for its superior second-half play.

COLUMBIA INVADES COLUMBUS

Columbia University's football team may be best known today for its inability to win. The Lions piled up an NCAA record 44-game losing streak in the 1980s. During the 1920s, however, Columbia was one of the nation's top powers. At that time, it was also the nation's largest university with a student enrollment of 15,000.

When the Lions came to Columbus in 1925 to meet Ohio State for the first time, they featured a powerful running attack and were rated by most analysts as the strongest team in the East, if not the country. They were coached by Charlie Crowley, who in 1911-12 had paired with Knute Rockne as the starting ends at Notre Dame.

The Buckeyes started strongly and outplayed the stunned visitors at almost every phase of the game. Using a complex and balanced rushing and passing attack, Ohio State scored in the second quarter to take a 6-0 lead at halftime. The touchdown was scored by fullback Marty Karow, who in this game also called the offensive signals.

Fullback Marty Karow called the offensive plays in the '25 Columbia contest

Early in the third period, tackle Leo Uridil kicked a 28-yard field goal to give Ohio State a 9-0 advantage and that's how it ended. The victory was particularly noteworthy because it was the Buckeyes' first major win at home since the dedication of Ohio Stadium in 1922. Proving the 1925 game was no fluke, the two met the following season in a return engagement at New York's Polo Grounds, with the Buckeyes winning again 32-7.

GETTING NAVY'S GOAT

It would seem to be a perfect marriage: the Navy and a lot of water. But from the beginning of Ohio State's soggy homecoming game on November 7, 1931, nothing went well for the Midshipmen. It was the nation's top intersectional contest that weekend but the Middies should have known it would be a long afternoon at Ohio Stadium — all signs pointed to it.

Navy's mascot goat, which was a somewhat dirty gray from all its travels, accompanied the Midshipmen from Annapolis to Columbus. The night before the game, a group of mischievous Ohio State students sneaked into the barn where the goat was kept and dyed a portion of the animal with Mercurochrome. Needless to say, on Saturday morning the Navy plebes were stunned when they first saw their mascot — in the scarlet-and-gray colors of Ohio State.

The game proved to be worse for the Middies. Ohio State won 20-0 and used the "unconventional play" to score all three touchdowns. In the second period, with the ball on the Navy 35, OSU quarterback Carl Cramer's pass was deflected by Navy end Larry Smith, but the ball fell squarely in the hands of end Sid Gillman. Gillman, later a legendary college and professional coach, raced into the end zone for the first touchdown.

Near halftime, guard Martin Varner blocked a Navy punt which was returned 32 yards by end Junius Ferrall for OSU's second score. Ferrall also scored the final touchdown on a 20-yard interception return in the third period.

It would be 50 years before Ohio State and Navy would meet again, in the 1981 Liberty Bowl. Quarterback Art Schlichter, playing his final game for Ohio State, threw for the 49th and 50th touchdown passes of his career as the Buckeyes held on for a 31-28 victory.

COLLEGE FOOTBALL'S MOST EXCITING GAME

The Ohio State-Notre Dame encounter of November 2, 1935, is a game which will live in infamy in the annals of Ohio State football. Both teams were undefeated and aiming for the national championship. The Irish were 5-0 with wins over Kansas, Carnegie Tech, Wisconsin, Pittsburgh and Navy. Notre Dame's captain, Joe Sullivan, had died of pneumonia prior to the season, so instead of electing another captain the team was dedicating each game to Sullivan.

The game attracted record media coverage including writers Grantland Rice, Paul Gallico and Damon Runyon. Mild-mannered Elmer Layden, who had been one of Rockne's Four Horsemen in 1924, guided Notre Dame. Taking a page from Rockne's manual, Layden waged psychological warfare by telling reporters his team would be lucky to hold Ohio State to five or six touchdowns. The Buckeyes were coached by Francis Schmidt, master of the razzle-dazzle offense.

The student manager of Notre Dame's 1935 team was Woody Stillwagon, father of Ohio State's Jim Stillwagon, who captured both the Outland Trophy and Lombardi Award in 1970.

Demand for tickets was at an all-time high. Even during the depths of the Great Depression, Ohio State officials estimated 200,000 tickets could have been sold. The actual attendance was 81,018.

The Buckeyes struck early when fullback Frank Antenucci intercepted a Notre Dame pass at the OSU 25, advanced it ten yards then lateralled to halfback Frank Boucher who raced 65 yards for the game's first touchdown. Dick Beltz's conversion made it 7-0. The errant Irish pass had been thrown by halfback Mike Layden, younger brother of the coach.

Early in the second quarter, OSU quarterback Stan Pincura picked off another pass and returned it to midfield. From there, the Buckeyes marched in for their second score with Joe

Quarterback Tippy Dye scrcambles for yardage against the Irish in 1935.

Williams taking it across from the three. Ohio State held a 13-0 halftime lead but had dominated action much more than the score indicated. The Buckeye defense had been tenacious, applying great pressure to the Irish passing attack and completely smothering running plays at their inception.

Layden surprised everyone by announcing his second team "shock troops" would start the second half. The third ·quarter was scoreless but the visitors were gaining momentum. The tide really turned on the third quarter's last play when Irish halfback Andy Pilney returned one of John Kabealo's booming punts 53 yards to the Ohio State 12.

The game's final 15 minutes were truly unbelievable. First, Notre Dame moved it in from the 12, with Steve Miller bolting over from the one. The kick was missed and the Buckeyes led 13-6.

Ohio State was unable to move on its ensuing possession and again punted. Notre Dame quickly marched for what appeared to be another score, only to have Miller fumble into the end zone from the OSU one. Ohio State's Jim Karcher recovered for a touchback and the Buckeyes' lead appeared to be secure.

After Ohio State was again forced to punt, the Irish took over at their 20 with three minutes remaining. Behind beautiful protection, Pilney promptly moved his team 80 yards on four completions, with the touchdown coming on a 15-yard toss to

Layden. Again the all-important conversion was missed and the Buckeyes appeared to be in position to hold on at 13-12 with 1:30 remaining.

Schmidt had committed a serious tactical error in the final quarter, pulling his starting backfield and replacing them with his shorter reserves. Under 1935 college rules, a player could not return in any quarter after being taken out in that same quarter.

As expected, Notre Dame tried an onside kick but the Buckeyes recovered at their own 46. While trying to run out the clock, Ohio State fumbled out-of-bounds on second down. Again the rules of '35 became a significant factor — possession was awarded to the team that last *touched* the ball before it went out, rather than the last to have possession. Irish center Henry Pojman had brushed the ball on its way out and Notre Dame was awarded the ball on its own 49 with 55 seconds remaining.

A stout-hearted Pilney again went to work. Finding his receivers covered, he masterfully weaved his way 32 yards to the Ohio State 19 before sustaining a wrenched left knee on a very hard tackle. Pilney was carried off the field on a stretcher, and was replaced by Bill Shakespeare.

Shakespeare's first pass went in and out of the hands of a Buckeye defender for an incompletion . . . with 30 seconds remaining. Behind great protection, Shakespeare calmly hit big Wayne Millner in the end zone for what proved to be the winning touchdown. The extra point attempt was again missed but it didn't matter — the Irish had just staged one of the most memorable finishes in college history to win the game 18-13.

Ohio State's second-half collapse is vividly explained by the game's statistics. The Buckeyes made nine first downs before halftime but only one in the last two quarters. Nine of Notre Dame's 11 first downs came after intermission. The goal posts were uprooted and taken to the Deshler Wallack Hotel at Broad and High streets, where Irish fans celebrated long into the night.

BUCKEYES SURVIVE BERWANGER

Ohio State and Notre Dame were still emotionally drained the following Saturday. The Irish lost at home 14-7 to Northwestern, a team Ohio State had defeated 28-7 just three weeks earlier. The Buckeyes had to come from behind to defeat Chicago 20-13. The Maroons, who were three-to-four touchdown underdogs, led 13-0 midway through the third quarter. Ohio State finally put together three scoring drives to come away with a very hard-earned victory.

The contest was played at Stagg Field on the Chicago campus and the Buckeyes left for Chicago by train following Thursday's practice. Two pep rallies that evening, one on campus and a second at Union Station, helped erase some of the squad's down-hearted feelings.

The Buckeyes quartered at the Windemere Hotel near the Chicago campus. The University of Michigan football team, en route to a game against Illinois at Champaign, was also staying at the same hotel. OSU coach Francis Schmidt had scheduled a Friday workout for his team at Stagg Field. Interestingly, Michigan had also planned a Friday practice for Stagg Field. When Schmidt learned about this arrangement, he had his team work out at a public park rather than share Stagg Field with the Wolverines.

Early in the second half, Chicago's Jay Berwanger swept OSU's left end, reversed his field and raced 85 yards for the Maroon's second touchdown. Berwanger's run rates with the greatest of all time. In his book, *Football: College History* author Tom Perrin describes it as "the run which won the Heisman for Berwanger. He sliced through tackle at the 20-yard line, headed for the outside, then turned back toward center. At midfield, he was sandwiched between two defensive backs. He juked each one and ran between them. Once in the clear, he outran his pursuers for the touchdown."

Lew Byrer, veteran sports editor for The Columbus Citizen, called it "as pretty a run as I have ever seen." Writer Russ Needham characterized Berwanger as "the best back I have seen in college football in the last ten years."

GLORY OUT WEST

Ohio State scored a major upset with a 33-0 trouncing of the Southern California at the Los Angeles Coliseum in 1941. It was just the second game for first-year coach Paul Brown; the Buckeyes had defeated Missouri 12-7 in the opener at Ohio Stadium the previous week.

This victory over Southern Cal was Ohio State's first triumph over a Pacific Coast team. It also was the first time the Trojans had been shutout in 11 seasons dating back to 1930 when Rockne's Notre Dame team defeated them 27-0.

The Buckeyes used 11 ball carriers to outgain USC, 469-67 yards in total offense. In typical Brown fashion, the Buckeyes were better conditioned and simply beat the Trojans at almost every aspect of the game. A return match was held in Columbus the following fall, with Ohio State winning 28-12.

Jack Graf: Big Ten MVP in 1941

PAUL BROWN LEADS THE ENEMY

Brown returned to Ohio Stadium for the 1944 season's fourth game, only this time he operated along the east sidelines, directing the visiting Great Lakes Naval Training Center Bluejackets. Brown became coach at Great Lakes upon entering the Navy following the '43 season. His service team included two former Buckeyes: Ernie Plank, an end in '43 and Jim Rees, a tackle from '42. Also on his squad was George Spencer, a quarterback fresh out of Bexley High School who would later play for the Buckeyes in '46 and '47.

Both teams were 3-0 with Ohio State ranked fourth and Great Lakes sixth. This meeting between Widdoes and Brown drew considerable attention and was broadcast nationally by NBC's Bill Stern and CBS's Ted Husing. The attendance of 73,477 was (at the time) the fifth-largest crowd in stadium history and another 10,000 were turned away the day of the game.

After dominating the early play, Ohio State finally made it 6-0 on Dick Flanagan's one-yard plunge with just 19 seconds remaining in the first quarter. Great Lakes came to life in the second half and made it 6-6 going into the final period. One Buckeye third-quarter drive was stopped when Tom Keane tried a short pass but was intercepted by his brother, Jim, a defender for Great Lakes.

The superior strength of Ohio State's line began to show and the fourth period belonged to the Buckeyes. Ohio State scored three times, twice by Les Horvath, to win 26-6 in a game somewhat closer than indicated by the final score. Brown was disappointed with his team's loss but praised Widdoes and the Buckeyes for their outstanding play. Tackle Russ Thomas, who played the entire 60 minutes, drew special attention for his efforts from both Widdoes and Brown.

WASHINGTON STATE SERIES EXPLOSIVE

Ohio State has won all seven of its games with the Washington State Cougars, yet this series has provided more than its share of excitement. The games have been high scoring affairs establishing many Ohio State offensive records.

The two first met at Ohio Stadium on October 18, 1952.

Washington State had great difficulty getting to the game. After flying to Milwaukee, the team traveled to Columbus by train. From Union Station in downtown Columbus, the Cougars boarded a bus and mistakingly traveled to Delaware, Ohio, then returned to stay at the Deshler-Wallick hotel near Broad and High streets.

Quarterback John Borton completed 15 of 17 passes for 312 yards and all five touchdowns to lead Ohio State past the Cougars 35-7. His touchdown tosses covered 12, 54, 15, 70 and 26 yards. Four of Borton's scoring passes were caught by senior end Bob Grimes, who had ten receptions for 187 yards.

Ironically, Washington State was expected to have the better passing attack. In 1951, quarterback Bob Burkhart established a Pacific Coast Conference record with 15 touchdown passes while end Ed Barker set an NCAA receiving record with 847 yards.

The Buckeyes and Cougars did not meet again until October 6, 1973. Ohio State had moved to number-one in the weekly *Associated Press* poll following impressive wins over Minnesota and Texas Christian, but the TCU victory was costly as fullback Champ Henson was lost for the season with a leg injury. The following Monday, coach Woody Hayes moved junior linebacker Bruce Elia to full-back, a position he had played the previous year. With just five days practice at his old position, Elia rushed for 57 yards and two touch-downs to help Ohio State defeat Washington State 27-3 at Ohio Stadium.

Quarterback John Borton's five touchdown passes and end Bob Grimes' four touchdown catches against Washington State in 1952 are Ohio State single-game records which stand yet today.

The two teams met the following season on the west coast, with Ohio State winning easily 42-7. The game was played at the University of Washington campus in Seattle. Washington's stadium seated 58,000, compared with 23,000 on the Washington State campus in Pullman.

After building a 35-7 halftime lead, Hayes used his reserves most of the second half. He was especially pleased with no Buckeye fumbles or interceptions. Archie Griffin had one of his finest games rushing for 196 yards on 21 carries. His 75-yard run for the Buckeyes' fourth touchdown was the longest of his OSU career and fifth longest in school history.

The series resumed at Ohio Stadium in 1979, Earle Bruce's first season as head coach. The Buckeyes used the big play to outscore the Cougars 45-29, but the win wasn't easy. Washington State led in first downs 28-16 and in total plays from scrimmage 82-56. The Bucks managed a slim margin in total offensive yardage, 419-408.

Ohio State built a 24-3 halftime lead but was outscored 26-21 in the second half. After Washington State put ten points on the board early in the third quarter, quarterback Art Schlichter teamed with tailback Calvin Murray on an 86-yard touchdown pass play, longest in Ohio State football (breaking the record of 80 yards from Joe Sparma to Bob Klein against Michigan in 1961). Linebacker Jim Laughlin led the defense with nine solo tackles, a fumble recovery and a blocked punt.

When the two next met in 1984, the Buckeyes played a near perfect game, winning 44-0. The day's biggest applause came midway through the second quarter when the Buckeyes, leading 10-0, took possession at their own 47. Senior quarterback Mike Tomczak, who was making his first appearance of the

1984 season, had been recuperating from a leg injury suffered in the spring game and was held out of OSU's opening win over Oregon the previous Saturday.

The 1985 encounter was the most explosive with the two teams combining for 80 points. Each team scored in each of the four quarters, as follows:

	1	2	3	4		
Washington State	14	3	3	12	—	32
Ohio State	7	28	3	10	—	48

Offense again dominated during Ohio State's 33-19 win at Ohio Stadium in 1991. Coach John Cooper went with Kirk Herbstreit at quarterback in place of an injured Kent Graham. The Buckeyes amassed 24 first downs and 479 yards in total offense, compared with 28 and 449, respectively, for the Cougars. Thirty-eight of the game's 52 points were scored in the second half. Buckeye linebacker Steve Tovar scored the game's final points on a safety, racing 96 yards after intercepting a pass on a two-point conversion attempt following Washington State's last touchdown.

ARCHIE'S SENSATIONAL DEBUT

It was the second game of 1972 against North Carolina. Just a freshman, Griffin was listed as the fifth-team tailback, and "just hoped to get into the game." In the season-opening win over Iowa, the 18-year-old Columbus Eastmoor graduate had been in for one play which resulted in a fumble.

Backfield coach Rudy Hubbard had been telling Hayes that Griffin was ready and earned a second chance at contributing. After the Buckeyes had gained only 13 yards on their first two possessions, Hayes decided to give the rookie a shot. Griffin was so startled he started onto the field without his helmet. Hayes' decision produced one of the most spectacular performances in Ohio Stadium history as Griffin set an OSU single-game rushing record with 239 yards while leading the Buckeyes past North Carolina 29-14. The old record of 229 yards had been established by fullback Ollie Cline during a 14-0 win at Pittsburgh in 1945.

The Tar Heels led 7-0 early in the first quarter after blocking a Gary Lego punt and recovering it in the end zone. Griffin then ran for 116 first-half yards to help Ohio State lead 9-7 at halftime. Ohio State's scoring came on a 22-yard first quarter field goal by Blair Conway and quarterback Greg Hare's 17-yard option early in the second period.

The Buckeyes scored twice in the third period on touchdowns by fullbacks Randy Keith and Champ Henson. Henson's one-yard plunge was set-up by Griffin's longest run of the day, a 55-yard dash down the east sideline to the North Carolina 14. Midway through the fourth quarter, Griffin scored his first collegiate touchdown on his final carry of the afternoon, a nine-yard slash outside left tackle.

Tailback Elmer Lippert also helped the cause, rushing

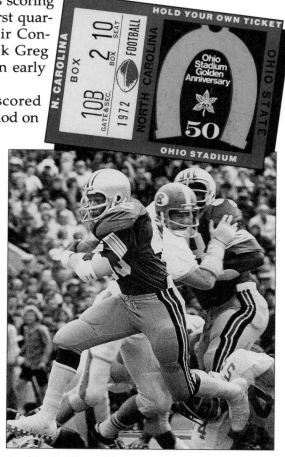

Archie Griffin adds to his '72 exploits in a 32-7 victory over North Carolina three years later

for 116 yards including a 68-yard sprint for the game's longest run. An elated Hayes was complimentary of the blocking of Keith, tackles John Hicks and Doug France and guard Chuck Bonica. Linebacker Vic Koegel led the defense with 17 tackles.

VON SCHAMANN PROVIDES MAJOR DISAPPOINTMENT

Oklahoma's dramatic 29-28 victory in 1977 is one of the most memorable and thrilling games in Ohio Stadium history. It also was one of the most hard-hitting contests in recent years. Relying on their great speed, the Sooners took control early and

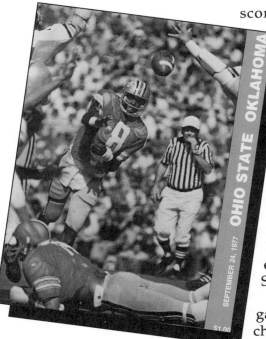

scored on their first four possessions to take a 20-0 lead. Ohio State was yet to register a single first down and a rout seemed entirely possible. At this point, ABC-TV, who was airing the game regionally, decided to shift some of its affiliates to the Penn State-Maryland game because of the one-sidedness of the Buckeye-Sooner battle.

But the tone of the game in Columbus soon changed drastically. In a complete turnabout, the Buckeyes scored 28 consecutive points during the second and third quarters to grab the lead 28-20. First, Ron Springs scored from 30 yards on a pitchout to finish an 80-yard march. Linebacker Dave Adkins then recovered a Sooner fumble at the Ohio State 19, setting up a beautiful scoring dash by Rod Gerald on first down to bring Ohio State within six at halftime, 20-14.

On the Buckeyes' second drive of the third period, freshman fullback Joel Payton plunged across from the one to complete a 52-yard drive. The crowd went totally bananas as Vlade Janakievski's extra point put Ohio State ahead 21-20. Two minutes later, OSU's Kelton Dansler intercepted a Sooner pass at the Oklahoma 33, setting up a short scoring march which finished with a 16-yard pass to tight end Jimmy Moore, and suddenly it was 28-20. By this time, ABC-TV had gone back to Columbus to pick up the remainder of the game.

Oklahoma then got a big break, recovering an Ohio State fumble at at the Oklahoma 43 with 6:24 remaining in the game. Elvis Peacock's one-yard touchdown dive at 1:29 finished a 13-play, 57-yard drive which tightened things up at 28-26. The march was sustained when Ohio State was offside when the

Sooners failed to convert a fourth-and-four situation at the 12. Oklahoma went to Peacock on an option pitch for an attempted two point conversion but Paul Ross, Mike Guess, and Tom Blinco dropped him short of the goal line and the two-point margin appeared to be safe.

The Sooners then did the obvious — an onside kick — which they recovered at midfield with 1:21 remaining. Four plays moved the ball to the OSU 23. Enter Uwe von Schamann, a German-born kick specialist who moved with his family to Fort Worth, Texas, from West Berlin when he was 14 years old. Hayes called time out to let the soccer-sytle kicker ponder his challenge, but it didn't matter. Von Schamann calmly booted a 41-yard field goal with just three seconds on the clock to earn Oklahoma the thrilling triumph.

Many of Ohio State's disheartened defenders dropped to the turf, too shocked to move. After coming back from a 20-point deficit, the defeat was doubly difficult to digest. However, a return match at Norman in 1983 produced a much better finish. The Buckeyes totaled 412 yards of offense including 234 passing from Mike Tomczak to defeat the second-ranked Sooners 24-14. Tight end John Frank had one of the top games of his career catching seven passes for 108 yards and scoring the game's first two touchdowns.

SCHLICHTER LEADS COLISEUM COMEBACK

Trailing 13-10 with just 2:21 remaining in the game, sophomore quarterback Art Schlichter guided his team 80 yards to lift Ohio State past UCLA 17-13 at the Los Angeles Coliseum in 1979. Schlichter was outstanding, completing six consecutive passes for 62 of the 80 yards. The drive's key play was a 22-yard strike to Gary Williams at the UCLA 3 with just one minute left.

The winning touchdown was scored on a two-yard toss to tight end Paul Campbell near the back line of the end zone with just 46 seconds remaining. It was just his second reception as a tight end. Campbell, normally the starting fullback, had moved to the line the previous week after Earle Bruce's tight end corps had become depleted by injuries.

Ohio State dominated the first half statistics but trailed 10-7 at halftime. UCLA recovered a blocked punt at the Ohio State 13 in the first quarter to set up the game's first touchdown. The Buckeyes received a huge lift when tailback Calvin Murray broke a play to the outside and raced 34 yards for their first touchdown right before the half.

Bruce was overjoyed with the outcome and hailed it as a great team victory. He lauded Schlichter's efforts during the winning drive and heaped praise on the Ohio State defense, particularly linebackers Jim Laughlin and Al Washington and tackle Luther Henson. It was the season's fourth game and the comeback gave Bruce's young team a lot of confidence. Ohio State went on to seize the outright Big Ten title with an overall record of 11-1.

Timeout

Ohio State's All-Time Team

(One Person's Opinion)

*I*t would be very difficult to select Ohio State's finest season. Would it be 1916, '42, '54, '68, '73 or '79?

It is even more perplexing to select the Buckeyes' all-time team. Ohio State has had more than its share of outstanding players. Comparing these players from different eras makes the selection of an all-time squad even more difficult. Each fan has his or her own opinion, and (just for the fun of it) this is mine.

Offense

Quarterback	Rex Kern	
Running Backs	Keith Byars	Chic Harley
	Archie Griffin	
Offensive Line	John Hicks	Jim Parker
	Gomer Jones	Bill Willis
	Jim Lachey	
End	Wes Fesler	
Wide Receiver	Gary Williams	

Defense

Defensive Line	Bob Brudzinski	Jim Stillwagon
	Jim Houston	
Linebackers	Tom Cousineau	Chris Spielman
	Randy Gradishar	Jack Tatum
Defensive Backs	Arnold Chonko	Vic Janowicz
	Tim Fox	Mike Sensibaugh

Specialists

Punter	Tom Skladany
Punt Returner	Neal Colzie
Place Kicker	Vlade Janakievski
Kickoff Returner	Hopalong Cassady

Buckeye Bowl Record

SEASON	YEAR	BOWL	BUCKEYES	OPPONENT
1920	1921	Rose	Ohio State 0	California 28
1949	1950	Rose	Ohio State 17	California 14
1954	1955	Rose	Ohio State 20	So. California 7
1957	1958	Rose	Ohio State 10	Oregon 7
1968	1969	Rose	Ohio State 27	So. California 16
1970	1971	Rose	Ohio State 17	Stanford 27
1972	1973	Rose	Ohio State 17	So. California 42
1973	1974	Rose	Ohio State 42	So. California 21
1974	1975	Rose	Ohio State 17	So. California 18
1975	1976	Rose	Ohio State 10	UCLA 23
1976	1977	Orange	Ohio State 27	Colorado 10
1977	1978	Sugar	Ohio State 6	Alabama 35
1978	1978	Gator	Ohio State 15	Clemson 17
1979	1980	Rose	Ohio State 16	So. California 17
1980	1980	Fiesta	Ohio State 19	Penn State 31
1981	1981	Liberty	Ohio State 31	Navy 28
1982	1982	Holiday	Ohio State 47	Brigham Young 17
1983	1984	Fiesta	Ohio State 28	Pittsburgh 23
1984	1985	Rose	Ohio State 17	So. California 20
1985	1985	Citrus	Ohio State 10	Brigham Young 7
1986	1987	Cotton	Ohio State 28	Texas A & M 12
1989	1990	Hall of Fame	Ohio State 14	Auburn 31
1990	1990	Liberty	Ohio State 11	Air Force 23
1991	1992	Hall of Fame	Ohio State 17	Syracuse 24

Overall: 11-13
Rose Bowl: 5-7

Highest Bowl Score
Ohio State: OSU 47, BYU 17 (1982 Holiday)
Opponent: OSU 17, Southern California 42 (1973 Rose)

Highest Margin of Victory in Bowl
Ohio State: 30 points (BYU, 47-17, 1982 Holiday)
Opponent: 29 points (Alabama, 35-6, 1978 Sugar)

14. The Bowl Games

BOWLING WITH
THE BUCKEYES

*P*ost-season bowl games have brought the Buckeyes both enormous delight and bitter disappointment. Rose Bowl triumphs over Southern California concluded two of Ohio State's finest seasons in 1954 and '68, while setbacks in the Pasadena classic spoiled what otherwise would have been undefeated-untied seasons in 1920, '70, '75, and '79.

Ohio State's first ten bowl appearances were in the Rose Bowl, primarily because the Big Ten Conference prohibited its members from playing in other bowls prior to 1975. In all, the Buckeyes have appeared in 12 Rose Bowls, seven times against Southern California. Through the 1991 season, Ohio State also made 12 appearances in nine other bowls. The first was a 27-10 triumph over Big Eight Conference champion Colorado in the January 1, 1976, Orange Bowl, during which Woody Hayes opposed one of his former assistants, Bill Mallory, now head coach of the Indiana Hoosiers.

Eight of the Buckeyes' 24 bowl games have been decided by three points or less. The only shutout has been a 28-0 loss to California during Ohio State's very first bowl appearance in the January 1, 1921, Rose Bowl. The Buckeyes participated in post-season play 15 consecutive seasons from 1972-86. Woody Hayes was 5-6 in bowl games and Earle Bruce was 5-3.

California's "Wonder Team" of legendary coach Andy Smith completed an undefeated season with a 28-0 lacing of favored Ohio State in the Rose Bowl of January 1, 1921. The Golden Bears' second touchdown resulted from a play which has grown into a legend. California's great end, "Brick" Muller, was on the passing end of a touchdown that netted 37 yards from scrimmage. But, with Muller fading far behind the line of scrimmage before he threw, the actual distance in flight of his pass to Brodie Stephens has remained a controversy. Today, 53 yards is recognized as the official distance. The setback was Ohio State's only loss that season and it would be 29 years before the two would again clash.

COME-FROM-BEHIND WINS BECOME HABIT FORMING

The Rose Bowl agreement committing the Big Ten and (what is now) the Pacific-Ten Conference champions began with the 1946 season — Illinois defeated UCLA 45-14. Ohio State made its first appearance against the California Golden Bears after sharing the 1949 conference title with Michigan. It had been a season of courage and determination on the part of a senior-dominated squad which entered the game with an overall record of 6-1-2. Coach Wes Fesler's Buckeyes had

come from behind for three of their six victories. California entered the contest unbeaten since losing the previous season's Rose Bowl to Northwestern 21-14.

After a scoreless opening quarter, fullback Fred "Curly" Morrison appeared to have scored the game's first touchdown with a powerful ten-yard burst over left guard, but the Buckeyes were penalized back to the California 23 for illegal use of hands. Morrison fumbled on the next down and the Golden Bears recovered on their 26. California then marched 74 yards to take a 7-0 lead with halfback Jim Monachino scoring from four yards on a pitch-out around the Buckeyes' right end.

The Golden Bears moved the ball freely after receiving the third quarter kickoff, and threatened to increase their lead to

Coach Wes Fesler and the Buckeyes celebrate their victory in the 1950 Rose Bowl

14-0. But halfback Vic Janowicz ended the drive with a jumping interception of Bob Celeri's pass at the Ohio State 25 and returned it 54 yards to the California 31. From there, the Buckeyes tied it up 7-7 with Morrison going over the middle on a fourth down call from the two. Another key play during the drive was a seven-yard jump pass from Jerry Krall to Ralph Armstrong on a fourth-and-five from the Golden Bears' 14. Years later when discussing the game, quarterback Pandel Savic recalled, "Vic's interception and return turned things around for us and it really took the spirit out of California's attack."

California started its next drive from its own 26. After three plays netted only two yards, Buckeye tackle Bill Trautwein blocked Celeri's punt attempt and center Jack Lininger carried the pigskin to the six. It again required four downs for Ohio State to score with Krall taking it over left tackle from inside the two. Jimmy Hague's conversion made it 14-7 and the Buckeyes had tallied twice within a span of 3:46.

The Golden Bears retaliated to tie the game on their next possession. Aided by a key block from fullback Pete Schabarum, Monachino scored his second touchdown, this time on a picture-perfect, 44-yard run around end with just 31 seconds remaining in a very frenzied third quarter.

With the game still tied 14-14 and just over three minutes remaining, Celeri was forced to punt on fourth down with the ball resting at the California 16. Celeri fumbled a low pass from

With thanks to Jimmy Hague, Ohio State's 17-14 win over California on January 2, 1950, was the first Rose Bowl to be decided by a kick.

center then kicked the ball off his wrong foot (left) on the run. It rolled out of bounds at the 13, giving the Buckeyes one of the game's biggest breaks. Three running plays netted just over eight yards so Fesler sent Dick Widdoes and Tom Watson in with instructions for Hague to attempt a field goal on fourth down. Ohio State, wanting to go for the first down, signaled them off the field so Widdoes and Watson returned to the sideline. Fesler, however, sent them back onto the field, but by this time the Buckeyes were penalized five yards for delay of game. With Widdoes spotting the ball at the 18-yard line, Hague responded beautifully under tremendous pressure and booted the ball through the uprights for one of the biggest field goals in Ohio State history. The Buckeyes led 17-14 with 1:55 remaining.

The Golden Bears made a courageous effort in the closing seconds but Widdoes intercepted "Boots" Erb's pass at the Ohio State 11, and the Buckeyes ran out the clock to preserve their first Rose Bowl victory. Erb was the son of Charlie Erb, who quarterbacked California to its victory over Ohio State in the 1921 Rose Bowl, while Widdoes was the son of coach Carroll Widdoes, who guided the Buckeyes to the National Civilian Championship with a 9-0 record in 1944.

Senior Curly Morrison, who gained 127 on 24 carries, had played the finest game of his career and was selected the game's most valuable player. Fesler, who was carried off the field by his team, claimed, "This is the biggest thrill I've ever had in football. Every boy dreams of playing in the Rose Bowl and winning . . . and we coaches do, too. It was a great football game." For California coach Lynn "Pappy" Waldorf, losing to Ohio State on a late-fourth-quarter field goal was nothing new. Waldorf had been Northwestern's coach when Ohio State's Max Schnittker's 32-yard field goal, with just 1:28 remaining, lifted the Buckeyes to a 16-14 win in 1945.

WOODY'S FIRST OF EIGHT TRIPS TO PASADENA

Ohio State's 20-7 conquest of Southern California in the January 1, 1955, Rose Bowl completed one of the most successful seasons in school history. The Buckeyes of fourth-year coach Woody Hayes captured the Big Ten and national titles with a 10-0 record. Southern California was coached by Jess Hill and entered the game with a record of 8-3.

The game was played in an all-day downpour — players

were slipping and slither-
ing in a quagmire that
extended from end zone
to end zone. More than
100,000 tickets had been
sold but only 89,191
attended. Ticket scalpers
were forced to sell tick-
ets for little more than
fifty cents. Serious
problems developed in
the open press box
when the rain dam-
aged Western Union
circuit wires, prevent-
ing many writers
from filing their pre-
game stories.

Ohio State entered the
game a 13-point favorite. On the eve of the
game, a "Good Luck Telegram" was received from Columbus
carrying the signatures of approximately 4,200 Buckeye fans.
The document measured more than 40 yards in length.

The Buckeyes took the opening kickoff and drove to the
USC 19 but Tad Weed's 27-yard field goal attempt fell short.
Later in the period, Ohio State put together an 11-play, 69-yard
drive which produced the game's first touchdown. Quarterback
Dave Leggett sneaked three yards over right guard on the second play of the second quarter and Weed converted to make it
7-0. The key play of the series was a 26-yard sweep around left
end by halfback Jerry Harkrader.

The Trojans fumbled on their next possession and Leggett

Faye Lloyd of the *United Press* became the first female sportswriter to cover a Rose Bowl when she reported on the Ohio State-Southern California clash of January 1, 1955.

recovered on the USC 35. Bobby
Watkins carried 14 yards
through right tackle on first
down and Leggett then combined with Watkins on a 21-yard
scoring pass for the Buckeyes'
second touchdown. Watkins
conversion made it 14-0 with
almost 13 minutes of the second

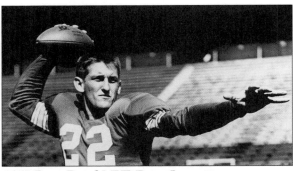

1955 Rose Bowl MVP Dave Leggett

period remaining. The fine senior halfback from New Bedford, Mass., had just realized a lifetime dream — scoring a touchdown in the Rose Bowl.

Near the half, the Buckeyes' Hubert Bobo dropped back to punt from the OSU 32. Trojan end Leon Clark rushed Bobo, forcing him to step aside as Clark went rushing past. Bobo took a few steps forward, then stopped and punted 54 yards to the USC 14. It was a masterful kick, especially on the muddy surface and against Clark's tremendous pressure.

Southern Cal's Aramis Dandoy picked up Bobo's punt and started up the east sideline. Picking up two key blocks, Dandoy headed back toward midfield. Ohio State's fleet Jimmy Roseboro was gaining ground in pursuit but a tremendous block cut him down, springing Dandoy to the end zone. Dandoy's 86-yard scamper still stands as the longest punt return in Rose Bowl history.

The third quarter was scoreless but Southern Cal really caused some anxious moments. First, the Trojans held Ohio State on downs at the USC 4. Then, on first down, Jon Arnett circled his own right end and dashed 70 yards to the Ohio State 26 as the third period ended. But the Buckeye defense stiffened as Southern Cal was able to gain only three yards on its next four tries.

Starting from the OSU 23, Leggett guided his team 77 yards for the game's clincher. Harkrader took it across from the eight on a pitchout around USC's right end to conclude the scoring at 20-7. By this time, the Buckeyes were mud-soaked to the skin, but it didn't matter — they had concluded a perfect season.

Meeting with reporters, a jubilant Hayes said he felt his team's "overall strength" and the "turnover margin" were keys to Ohio State's success. "It was a great team victory," he related, also praising halfback Hopalong Cassady and end Dick Brubaker for their excellent play.

The Buckeyes led in first downs 22-6 and in total offensive yardage 360-206, while Southern Cal lost the ball three times on fumbles. Quarterback Dave Leggett was selected the game's most valuable player after handling the ball 80 times in the mud and rain without a single fumble.

SUTHERIN'S FIELD GOAL SAVES THE DAY

Even though heavily favored over Oregon in the Rose Bowl of January 1, 1958, Ohio State struggled to win 10-7. The Buckeyes drove 79 yards on their first possession to lead 7-0 with quarterback Frank Kremblas scoring the touchdown from the one and kicking the extra point. The drive's two longest gainers were a 27-yard run by halfback Don Clark and a Kremblas-to-Jim Houston pass play which covered 31 yards. In the second period, Oregon halfback Jim Stanley's five-yard scoring slash around left end capped an 80-yard drive and tied the game.

After a scoreless third period, halfback Don Sutherin provided the winning margin — a 34-yard three-pointer with 14:02 remaining. Interestingly, Oregon's Jack Morris had missed from nearly the same spot in the third quarter. The game was a moral victory for the Ducks whose inspired play kept

Longtime Buckeye fan Jerry Pausch, a 1961 graduate of Ohio State, helped tear down the goalposts following Ohio State's 10-7 Rose Bowl win over Oregon. Pausch brought back to Columbus a piece of the upright through which Don Sutherin kicked the winning field goal. Twenty-five years later in 1982, Sutherin autographed the upright while the two met in Canada where Sutherin was a coach with the Ottawa Roughriders. Pausch proudly displays his relic at a recent home game.

them much closer than expected. Oregon quarterback Jack Crabtree was selected the game's MVP and Ohio State's Joe Cannavino was the defensive standout with two interceptions and a key fumble recovery at the Ohio State 24 late in the final period.

The Buckeyes, with a record of 9-1, were awarded the *United Press International* national championship and finished second to Auburn (10-0) in the final *Associated Press* rankings.

#1 MEETS #2

There have been 25 games between the No. 1 and No. 2 nationally ranked teams since the weekly *Associated Press* poll was initiated in 1936. Ohio State has played in one of these games — the 1969 Rose Bowl against second-ranked Southern California. The Buckeyes entered the game at 9-0, the Trojans at 9-0-1. It was the first Rose Bowl between unbeaten teams since the Big Ten-Pac Eight contract was initiated in 1947.

After a scoreless first period, Southern Cal built its lead to 10-0 when Heisman Trophy winner O. J. Simpson took a pitchout to his left, reversed his direction and raced 80 yards for the game's first touchdown. It was the second longest scoring run in Rose Bowl history. The Buckeyes used a 69-yard drive to finally get things untracked with Jim Otis plunging over from the one for Ohio State's first touchdown. Jim Roman's 26-yard field goal three seconds before the half tied it up at 10-10.

Ohio State broke it wide open in the second half. First,

Roman kicked a 25-yard field goal to make it 13-10 after three quarters. In the final period, Rex Kern threw scoring passes of four and 16 yards to halfbacks Leo Hayden and Ray Gillian. The Trojans scored a controversial touchdown with 45 seconds remaining to make the final score 27-16.

The Buckeye defense had been superb with two interceptions and three fumble recoveries while Ohio State's offense did not commit a turnover. Hayes offered special credit to reserve quarterback Bill Long, whose play on the scout team helped prepare the Buckeye defense. Kern was selected the game's MVP while Otis and Hayden combined for 191 yards rushing. Simpson, who closed his college career rushing for 171 yards, greatly impressed the Buckeyes with a visit to their locker room after the game to offer his congratulations.

Ohio State had captured the national title after completing the fourth undefeated-untied season in school history. But Hayes didn't stay long to enjoy the win — he left in just two days for one of his many visits with U. S. troops in Vietnam.

ATHLETIC DIRECTORS' CHOICE JUSTIFIED

Ohio State and Michigan shared the 1973 Big Ten title with identical 7-0-1 records after the two battled to a 10-10 tie in the regular-season finale at Ann Arbor. The selection of Ohio State as the Rose Bowl representative by a reported 6-4 vote of the conference athletic directors touched off one of the most heated controversies in league history. But the Buckeyes really made the most of the opportunity, defeating a fine Southern California team 42-21. Trailing 21-14 early in the third quarter, Ohio State scored the game's last 28 points to give the Big Ten its first Rose Bowl triumph in five years.

OSU's offense accounted for 449 yards, 320 of them on the ground. Archie Griffin led all rushers with 149 yards in 22 carries including an excellent 47-yard run for the game's final touchdown. Fullback Bruce Elia bulled across for another touchdown from the one and big Pete Johnson, a freshman, scored three times on power plunges of 1, 1, and 4 yards.

Quarterback Cornelius Greene was named the game's MVP in view of his slick ball-handling and pin-point passing. His throwing was decisive on several drives as he completed six of eight tosses for 129 yards. Tight end Fred Pagac, now OSU's linebackers coach, was Greene's prime receiver with four catches for 89 yards. Greene also scored from the two following a spectacular 56-yard punt return by Neal Colzie.

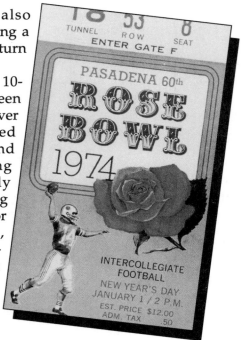

The 1973 Buckeyes, at 10-0-1, may very well have been the finest Ohio State team ever assembled. They outscored their opposition 413-64 and led the nation in scoring defense, surrendering only 4.3 points-per-game during the regular season. Except for the 10-10 tie at Michigan, their closest call was the 21-point Rose Bowl triumph over Southern California. They averaged 37.5 points-per-game, highest of any team in school history.

Ohio State was a solid favorite over UCLA in the 1976 Rose Bowl, especially after having defeated the Bruins by 21 points in the season's fourth game. The Buckeyes dominated play in the first half, holding UCLA without a first down until late in the second quarter. But Ohio State squandered several scoring opportunities and led only 3-0 at halftime after gaining 174 yards and 11 first downs.

The dam really broke in the second half. Behind the passing of quarterback John Sciarra and the running of Wendell Tyler, the Bruins outscored Ohio State 16-0 in the third period and went on to win 23-10. The defeat, one of the most difficult in all of Ohio State football, cost the Buckeyes the national title. Ohio State (11-1) finished fourth behind Oklahoma, Arizona State and Alabama. UCLA (9-2-1) finished fifth, and Michigan (8-2-2) came in eighth after losing to Oklahoma 14-6 in the Orange Bowl.

HEISMAN WINNER DENIES BUCKEYES '79 TITLE

Ohio State had advanced to number one in the weekly *Associated Press* poll following the close of the 1979 regular season. Rose Bowl opponent Southern California, at 10-0-1, was

Ohio State All-American tackle John Hicks became the first college player to appear in three Rose Bowls (1971, '73, '74).Two-time Heisman winner Archie Griffin is the only player in college history to have started four Rose Bowls.

third behind second-place Alabama (11-0). The Trojans took a 10-0 lead, but the Buckeyes came back to tie at halftime on a 35-yard field goal by Vlade Janakievski and a 67-yard scoring pass from Art Schlichter to Gary Williams. Janakievski connected on two additional field goals in the third and fourth periods to put the Bucks on top 16-10 with just 5:21 remaining.

But Southern Cal wasn't finished. With Heisman Trophy winner Charles White leading the charge, the Trojans drove 83 yards in eight plays with White getting the touchdown from the one. Eric Hipp's conversion put the Trojans ahead 17-16 and that's how it ended. Ohio State had come within a single point of the national title during coach Earle Bruce's first season.

Offense was the name of the game in the January 1, 1984, Fiesta Bowl as the Buckeyes and Pitt Panthers combined for 897 yards in total offense. With Ohio State trailing 23-21 and only 39 seconds remaining, quarterback Mike Tomczak passed to split end Thad Jemison for a 39-yard touchdown to win 28-23. Jemison, who was selected the game's MVP, tied a Fiesta Bowl record with

Placekicker Rich Spangler's 52-yard field goal during Ohio State's 20-17 loss to Southern California on January 1, 1985, is the longest in Rose Bowl history.

eight catches. Keith Byars scored an earlier touchdown on a 99-yard kickoff return.

The Buckeyes' most recent bowl victory was a convincing 28-12 win over Southwest Conference champion Texas A&M in the January 1, 1987, Cotton Bowl. Ohio State's defense played extremely well, establishing a Cotton Bowl record with five interceptions, two of which were returned for touchdowns by Chris Spielman and Michael Key. It marked the first and only time a Big Ten team has played in the Dallas classic.

ACKNOWLEDGEMENTS

*T*o learn more about the long and glorious history of Buckeye football, the author interviewed more than 200 former players, coaches, sportswriters, sportscasters, band members, cheerleaders, fans and others connected with the Ohio State football program. Without the generous time and assistance provided by the following, much of this book's information could not have been developed.

Don Alexandre
Ron Althoff
Bill Anders
Ron Anderson
Paul Ballinger
Marty Bannister
Red Barber
Brian Baschnagel
Rick Bay
Frank Beckman
Jay Berwanger
Tim Brooks
Bill Booth
John Borton
John Bozick
Jim Browder
Paul Brown
Earle Bruce
Jack Buck
Frank Buffington
Norman Burns
Tom Burris
Paul Butterfield
J. C. Caroline
Joe Carr
Bill Carroll
Roy Case
Bert Charles
Ollie Cline
Tim Clodjeaux
Bill Conley
Dale Conquest
Beano Cook
Lee Corso
Linda Crossley
Jimmy Crum

Walter Davis
Roger Deerhake
Dave Diles
Doug Donley
Ed Douglas
Dean Dugger
Merv Durea
Tippy Dye
Seana Elam
Bump Elliott
Frank Ellwood
Gene Fekete
Bob Ferguson
Sue Ferguson
Earl Flora
Randy Ford
Nate Fraher
Steve French
Greg Frey
Bo Gallo
Bob Gates
Mike Gleason
Al Goebel
Bob Goldring
John Gordon
Carl Graf
Jack Graf
Otto Graham
Bob Greene
Archie Griffin
Bob Grimes
Laurie Gundlach
Dick Guy
Martin Haffey
Jimmy Hague
Gary Hahn

George Hall
Ray Hamilton
Tom Hamilton
Tom Hamlin
Pat Harmon
John Havlicek
Mike Hawkins
Anne Hayes
Tom Hayes
Dick Heekin
Dick Heine
Dan Heinlen
Chalmer Hixson
Gary Hoffman
Dale Hollandsworth
Marv Homan
Denny Hoobler
Joe Hotchkiss
Paul Hornung
Herb Howenstein
John Hummel
Jimmy Hull
Bertha Ihnat
Clancy Isaac
Vlade Janakievski
Vic Janowicz
Bill Jobko
Jim Jones
Ruth Jones
Ed Johnson
Bob Joslin
John Kabealo
Mike Kabealo
Dave Kaylor
Dave Kelch
Ike Kelley

Rex Kern
Deve Kesling
Kaye Kessler
Vic Ketcham
Bob Kidwell
Orlas King
Lee Kirk
Vic Koegel
Denny Koehl
Frank Kremblas
Paul Krebs
Jude LaCava
Mike Lawler
Greg Lashutka
Fred Legg
Dave Leggett
George Lehner
Ted Lilley
Jerry Lima
Ed Littler
Jeff Logan
Frank Machinsky
Bruce Madej
Dan Magnuson
Jerry Marlow
Bob Masys
Tom Matte
Eric Mayers
Will McClure
Jim McDonald
Bill Mentor
John Metzger
Carole Miller
Mike Miller
Rusty Miller
Bob Momsen
Tony Momsen
Fred Morrison
Skip Mosic
Frank Moskowitz
Bernie Mudrock
Nancy Muldoon
John Mummey
Dick Murray
Bill Myles
Jim Nein
Phil Neuman

Dave Nicolls
Ed Orazen
Jim Parker
Dave Parr
Joe Paterno
Jerry Pausch
Tom Perdue
Tom Pierce
Warren Pierce
Andy Pilney
Jeff Rapp
Brian Rapp
Gary Rasor
Sharon Rich
Bob Ries
Rick Rizzs
Marty Rozenman
Mark Rudner
Ed Rupp
Phil Samp
Esco Sarkkinen
Pandel Savic
Bob Scanlon
Dick Schafrath
Bo Schembechler
Bob Schlegel
Art Schlichter
Sandy Schwartz
Gary Schottenstein
Paul Shimp
Dick Slager
Gene Slaughter
Dick Smith
Inwood Smith
Terry Smith
Steve Snapp
Matt Snell
Mike Snyder
Pam Stanton
Roger Stanton
Sue Stanton
Don Steinberg
Dave Stephenson
Tom Stewart
Mark Stier
Jim Stillwagon
George Strode

Don Sutherin
Danny Swain
Paul Sweeney
Oris Tabner
Hiram Tanner
Bob Taylor
Fred Taylor
Jimmy Thompson
Tony Thompson
Dave Tingley
Kenny Tinkler
Jim Toms
Don Unverferth
Rick VanBrimmer
Dick VanRaaphorst
Nick Vista
Lee Vlisides
Bill Wahl
Paul Warfield
Gene Warman
Howard Warner
Nick Wasylik
Bobby Watkins
Bill Watts
Dick Weber
Jim Wharton
J. T. White
Dick Widdoes
Roger Williams
Bill Willis
Dan Wilson
Howard Yerges, Jr.
Jim Zabel
Larry Zelina
Fred Zimmerman
John Zimmerman

Photographs used with permission of:
The Ohio State University Archives, Department of Photography and Sports Information Department: Pages vi, 1, 2, 3, 5, 6, 7, 8, 9, 16, 17, 20, 21, 34, 49, 58, 61, 62, 70, 81, 83, 85, 103, 117(2), 157, 159, 166, 171, 172, 178, 181, 191, 196, 210, 214, 215, 221, 224, 227, 239, 242. Chance and Sonny Brockway, Brockway Sports Photos: Pages 15, 18, 19, 23, 25, 37, 52, 75, 88, 98, 102, 106, 130, 136, 189, 200, 231. University of Illinois Athletic Department: Page 46. The Detroit News: Page 91. The Michigan Daily/George N. Hall: Page 112. Northwestern University Athletic Department: Page 176.
Heisman Trophy: Courtesy Vic Janowicz
Lombardi Award: Courtesy Jim Stillwagon
Ohio State Football Equipment: Courtesy Bill Conley and Danny Swain